Forewords by BENNY J. SIMPSON *and* DAVID K. NORTHINGTON

Drawings by PHILLIS UNBEHAGEN

University of Nebraska Press ❧ Lincoln and London

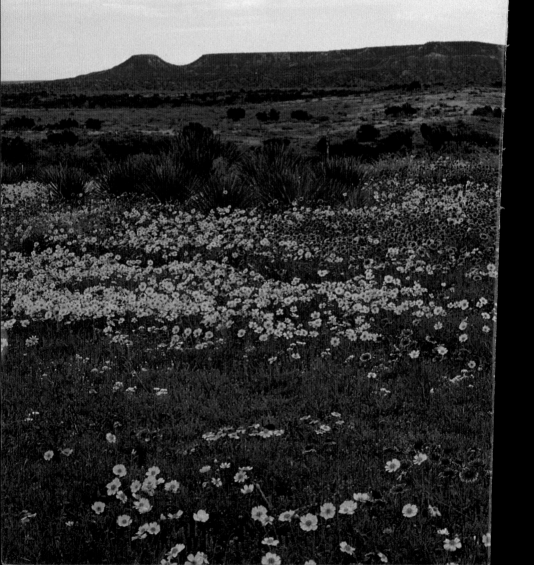

Wildflowers
of the Western Plains

A FIELD GUIDE   BY ZOE MERRIMAN KIRKPATRICK

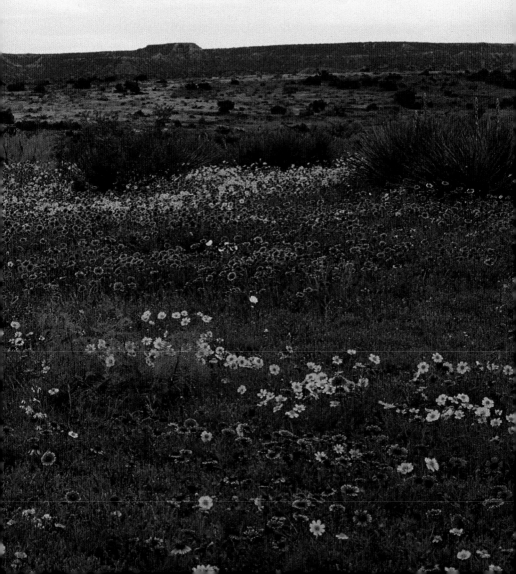

First Nebraska paperback printing: 2008

Library of Congress Cataloging-in-Publication
Data
Kirkpatrick, Zoe Merriman, 1935–
Wildflowers of the western plains: a field
guide / Zoe Merriman Kirkpatrick. —
1. Nebraska paperback printing
p. cm.
Includes bibliographical references and index.
ISBN 978-0-8032-1905-2 (pbk.: alk. paper)
1. Wild flowers—Great Plains—Identification.
2. Wild flowers—Great Plains—Pictorial works.
I. Title.
QK135.K57 1992b
582.130978—dc22 2008010504

Printed in China by Regent Publishing
Services, Ltd.

Dedicated to
the special men in my life:

JACK,

my loving, patient husband, and

KENT, CLIFF, WILL,
JOEL, AND BEN,
our sons,

who learned more about wildflowers,
by "osmosis,"
than they ever thought possible.

And in memory of my late parents,
EDWIN AND ELSIE MERRIMAN.

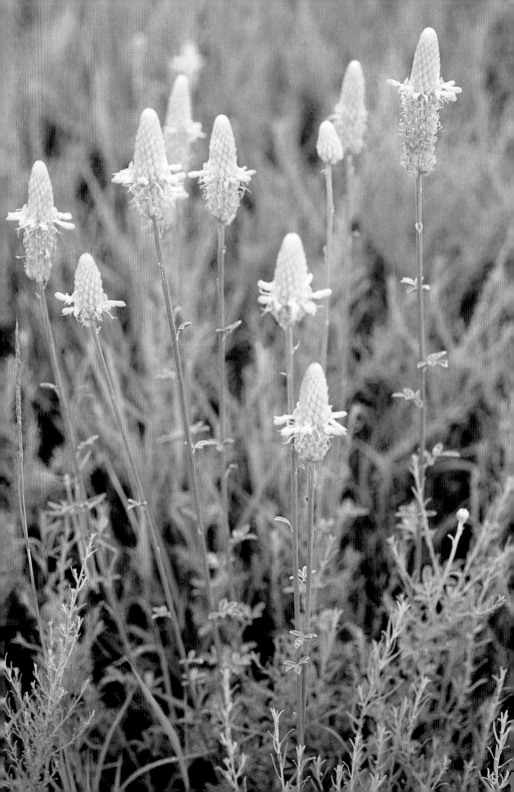

ACKNOWLEDGMENTS

Rarely does a book become a reality through the efforts of just one person, and this is no exception. With the help and encouragement of many people over a long period of time, a dream is finally accomplished.

This book would still be in my "long-range plans" (and my slide collection boxes) if it weren't for the encouragement and expert technical advice of my friend David Northington, who edited each species account that I wrote. His faith in me and belief in this project kept me bolstered up during the creative process. Pat, his wife, was always there with her positive words. I thank them both.

Benny Simpson was kind to write the Foreword, and he also reviewed pages of manuscript, offering useful advice. He has supported me with his enthusiasm from the time he learned of my plans to write this book.

Allan D. Zimmerman examined all the cactus slides and species accounts that I wrote. His information was invaluable to me. Likewise, Marshall C. Johnston reviewed the balance of the slides, checking the species as to accuracy. I am honored by their sharing their knowledge with me and giving their time so willingly.

A special thanks goes to B. L. Turner and Guy Nesom, who identified plant specimens and reviewed slides for me. They made some seemingly difficult species fall nicely into place.

To Phillis Unbehagen, my talented friend who lent her artwork to this endeavor, I extend profound thanks. She very patiently worked with me many Sunday afternoons and then on her own time, in between, to render the line drawings I wanted. Her husband, Ted, was our biggest fan and constant source of support.

To Richard Sanders, I owe a debt of gratitude not only for educating me along the way in the intricacies of my word processor but also for helping with important details pertaining to my manuscript.

My heartfelt thanks go, also, to the capable staff at the University of Nebraska Press.

For accompanying me on my many photographic expeditions and helping gain access to other ranches all these years, I thank Lil Conner, Mary Miller, Polly Cravy, Frank and Alylene Runkles, and Doris Giddens. They shared their time and friendship as we searched the plains, canyons, pastures, hillsides, and roadsides for old familiar and newly discovered (for us) wildflowers.

My most ardent supporters and best "public relations people" have always been my parents, Edwin and Elsie Merriman.

Jim Smith and John W. Phillips shared much information. There are those kind friends and neighbors who thoughtfully brought to my attention some beautiful, currently blooming wildflower they felt I might need to see and photograph. Also there have been many delightful people who, following my slide presentations, came to me asking when the information and photographs were going to be in a book. They all had a part in coaxing *Wildflowers of the Western Plains* out of my head and on to the printed page.

Z.M.K.

Opposite: *Dalea aurea* Golden Dalea

CONTENTS

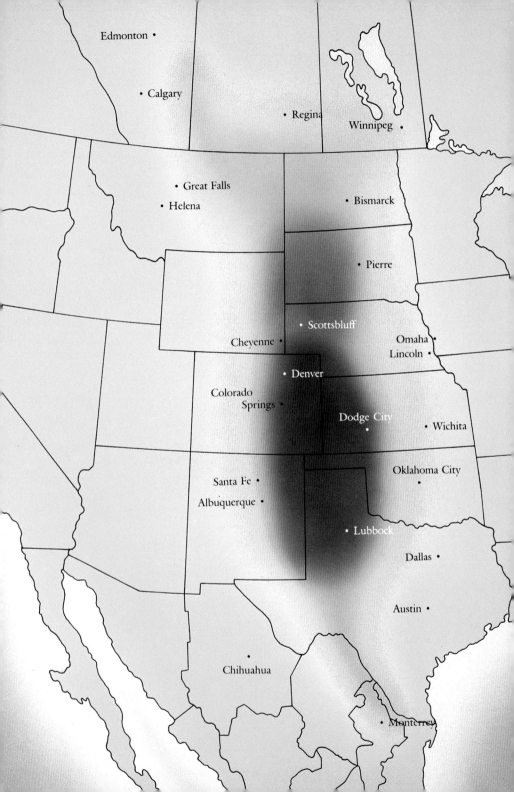

FOREWORD

by Benny J. Simpson
Research Scientist
Texas Agricultural Experiment Station

I once saw a shortgrass prairie consumed by fire. It was finally controlled within half a mile of our ranch on the Rolling Plains in northwestern Texas. Literally dozens of square miles of grassland of the historic Matador Ranch were consumed in this fierce fire. Firefighters (ranchers, farmers, and business owners) from four counties fought this blaze with wet gunnysacks and shovels and hoes.

It was a sight that I'll never forget, but even more unforgettable was the wildflower show that occupied this land the next year. As far as the eye could see was an unbroken carpet of bright red and yellow Indian Blanket (*Gaillardia pulchella*). Not one blade of grass broke this multihued carpet of bright red and yellow. It was the last prairie wildfire I have witnessed and the last explosion of colorful wildflowers in such awesome numbers over such a vast acreage.

But on a somewhat lesser scale, this wildflower extravaganza can be witnessed almost every year on Zoe Kirkpatrick's Western Plains—at least when moisture is adequate. For the Western Plains, with their almost unlimited horizons and their lack of forests and woods, seem to have been created for spring and sometimes fall displays of a riotous palette of colorful wildflowers. In mountains and forests, wildflowers occur in small bunches or perhaps sizable drifts but never in the almost unlimited tapestry seen from horizon to horizon on the Western Plains.

The Great Plains are generally thought of as starting at the 98th Meridian, which is also roughly the 30-inch rainfall line. For our purposes the Western Plains vaguely follow the 99th Meridian at about the 26-inch rainfall line north through central Texas, Oklahoma, Kansas, Nebraska, the Dakotas, and into Manitoba. On their western edge, the plains are bounded by the Rocky Mountains but reach southward to the Rio Grande, and species of western-plains wildflowers occur as far south as Coahuila, Mexico.

On the Western Plains is the fabled Staked Plains of Llano Estacado of Texas and New Mexico. This area of almost 37,000 square miles (22 million acres) is where Zoe Kirkpatrick learned about and studied the wildflowers of the Western Plains. Here, the spirit of frontier and native America remains and can be heard in the names of flowers such as Woolly Loco, Tahoka Daisy, Beard-tongue, Snakeweed, Scurf Pea, and Bear Grass. And here, in this book, Zoe Kirkpatrick writes about them all with vast knowledge and great love.

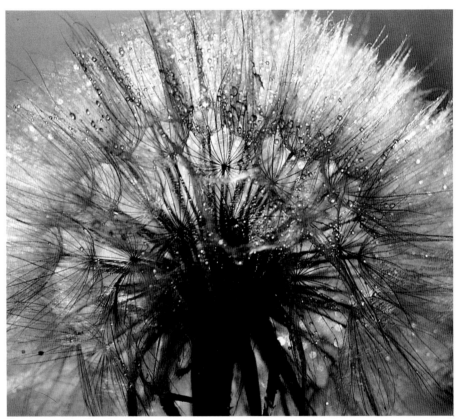

Tragopogon major Goatsbeard

FOREWORD

by David K. Northington

Executive Director
National Wildflower Research Center

Our world is rapidly changing. Our appreciation of the role that wild native flora plays in the world's ecological balance is the responsibility of all of us, not just the scientists.

In the twenty-first century, we will be practicing what the environmental awareness of the end of the twentieth century has revealed. Recognizing and knowing our wildflowers and native plants is one of the most fun and fulfilling environmental activities.

In *Wildflowers of the Western Plains,* Zoe Kirkpatrick has provided what might be considered the ultimate tool in learning about our native flora. The balance of accurate and useful botanical descriptions, high-quality photographs, and interesting remarks about each of these plants gives something for everyone and everything for all of us.

Accurately identifying native plants requires current and technically accurate descriptions and associated botanical information. Such information is important, but is hard to make lively and exciting. The user of this guide will discover that the author has succeeded in finding the right balance between accuracy and readability, between technical thoroughness and clarity.

No photographer can do full justice to the true beauty of a wildflower responding to the movement of a gentle breeze or reflecting the nuances of natural light. It is also difficult to keep a small flower in scale with a closeup, or reflect delicate details in a wide shot of a group of plants. The author has kept such difficulties in mind when capturing these native beauties on film. Additionally, she has tried to balance her written descriptions with what we can see in the photographs, so that they complement each other. She has even gone out "one last time" for many of the species included in this work, trying to capture an even better visual example to correspond with the written descriptions—literally up to press time.

Finally, what makes this book truly unique is the balance provided by the author's remarks following the descriptive information. A collection of legends, descriptions of historical uses by early settlers and Native Americans, observations, and humorous and useful personal accounts and experiences with many of the wildflowers complete the coverage provided in *Wildflowers of the Western Plains.* Learning the native flora of one's region is a delightful undertaking in itself; however, even if it were an assigned and dreaded task, Zoe Kirkpatrick's enthusiasm, knowledge, and style would make it fun. Enjoy.

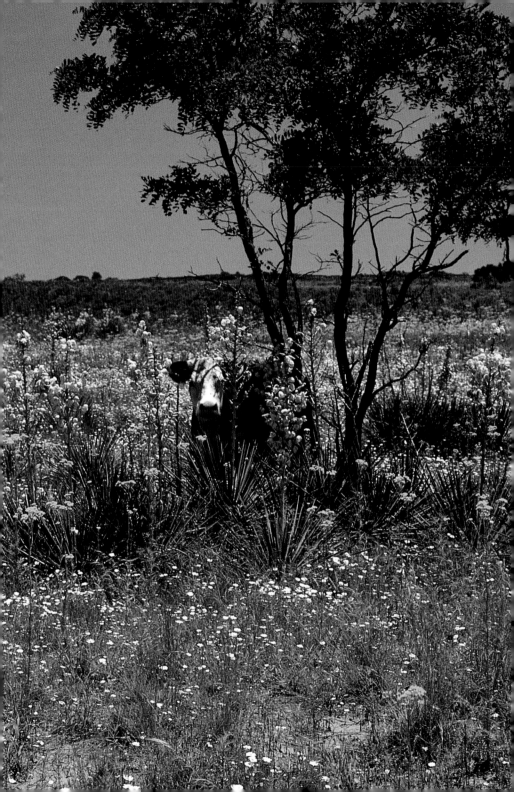

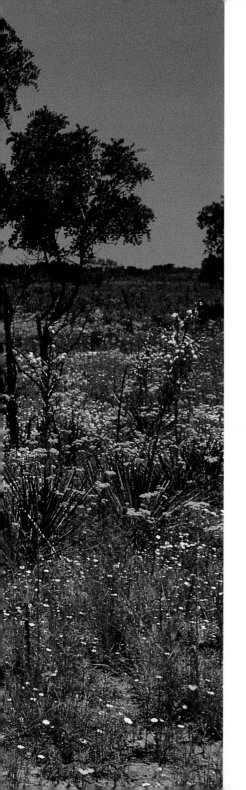

GUIDE TO PLANT NAMES AND PLANT FAMILIES
by David K. Northington

Taxonomists are botanists who classify and name the biological organisms on Earth, and although the lay public (and even other botanists) bemoan the seemingly never-ending changes in scientific names, there are reasons for those changes. Understanding the basis for those changes is important to all who enjoy learning the native wild-flowers of our region. The rules governing the naming of organisms establish that the earliest validly published scientific binomial (genus and species) for a species is the name that is to be used.

Periodic realignments and changes in scientific names occur when earlier published names are discovered. Names can also change as our ability to better evaluate and categorize organisms improves. Since each recognized species has only one valid scientific name, it is important to make these changes when necessary. It is also useful, even to the non-botanist, to learn the scientific names, especially for plants. Common names often are lacking or only minimally useful because the same common name is used for different species, or because a given species has several regionally recognized common names.

Varietal and/or subspecies names are sometimes added when taxonomists feel a given species has recognizable subunits that are genetically different but not so distinct as to deserve recognition at the species level. The author of *Wildflowers of the Western Plains* has made every effort to use a single reference for scientific names by using as the standard the *Manual of the Vascular Plants of Texas* by Donovan Stewart Correll and Marshall Conring Johnston, as updated by Johnston in *The Vascular Plants of Texas*, 2d ed. (1990). Exceptions have been made only in a few instances in the Cactaceae, which were reviewed by cactus expert Allan D. Zimmerman, as noted in the author's acknowledgments. When known, the most recognizable of the common names are also included.

A given genus can include from one to many different species. For example, there is only one species of human, *Homo sapiens*, and only one species of *Ginkgo*, *Ginkgo biloba*. There are many species of the sunflower genus *Helianthus*, four of which are found in this guide: *Helianthus annus*, *H. ciliaris*, *H. Maximiliani*, and *H. petiolaris*. There are also many other plants that share a suite of common characters with *Helianthus*, and all are grouped together in the Sunflower Family, Compositae. As with a genus, a plant family can contain one or more genera.

All plant families have names ending in the letters *-aceae;* however, there are a small number of families that were originally given a name not ending in *-aceae*, and those older names are also valid—in fact they are found more commonly in popular literature than the *-aceae* names. For example, the following families have both names:

Compositae   = Asteraceae (sunflowers)
Cruciferae   = Brassicaceae (mustards)
Labiatae   = Lamiaceae (mints)
Leguminosae = Fabaceae (beans)
Gramineae   = Poaceae (grasses)

Because plant families contain genera that are genetically and morphologically similar, grouping the wildflowers included in this guide by family is done to help users become more familiar with the local flora. Although grouping wildflowers by flower color seems easy and useful, it results in confusion and possible inaccuracies. Flower color is often one of the most variable of plant characters, and many species exist in nature with two, three, or even four different-colored flower forms.

A brief guide to families is provided to help users of this guide learn some of the largest and most common plant families. When used in combination, these diagnostic characteristics will take you quickly to the correct family, or rule out all but two or three closely related families.

FAMILY DIAGNOSTIC FEATURES

CACTACEAE (Cactus Family)	Succulent stems (pads or barrels) with spines; flowers having numerous petals and stamens.
COMPOSITAE (ASTERACEAE) (Daisy, Sunflower, or Aster Family)	Small flowers grouped together in compact heads usually displaying outer "ray" and inner "disk" flowers with the entire head often appearing to be the "flower."
CRUCIFERAE (BRASSICACEAE) (Mustard Family)	Flowers typically small, having only four petals, arranged in pairs across from each other; fruit having various shapes but always with two chambers and arranged scattered down the flowering stalk below the flowers. Flowering in early spring.

GERANIACEAE (Geranium Family)	Regular (radially symmetrical) flowers with five non-fused petals, fruit with an elongated, beak-like projection with the seed around its base (thus the "stork's-bill" common name).
LABIATAE (LAMIACEAE) (Mint Family)	Plants with square (quadrangular) stems, opposite leaves, and highly irregular (bilaterally symmetrical) flowers; crushed leaves often have a minty smell.
LEGUMINOSAE (FABACEAE) (Bean or Legume Family)	Plants with compound leaves and fruit (legumes) that are pea-pod-shaped. Flowers of one subgroup are highly irregular (bilaterally symmetrical) as in sweet peas; another subgroup has mimosa-like flowers with inconspicuous petals and many stamens, forming spherical clusters.
MALVACEAE (Mallow Family)	Regular flowers with five petals and numerous stamens fused by the filaments into a "stamen tree."
ONAGRACEAE (Evening Primrose Family)	Regular flowers with four sepals, four petals, and, usually, eight stamens. The petals arise from a tube that comes off the top of the (inferior) ovary; fruit four-chambered.
SCROPHULARIACEAE (Snapdragon Family)	Broadly irregular flowers with five fused petals (two upper and three lower petals) and an open throat with four stamens together on the upper surface of the flower throat, which is often hairy or "bearded"; leaves commonly opposite.
SOLANACEAE (Potato or Nightshade Family)	Regular flowers with five fused petals whose lobes flair at right angles from the floral tube; fruit tomato-like with two chambers.
VERBENACEAE (Vervain Family)	Closely related to the Labiatae; square stems and opposite leaves, but with only slightly irregular flowers clustered together in a tight inflorescence (each flower looks similar to a gingerbread man in outline).

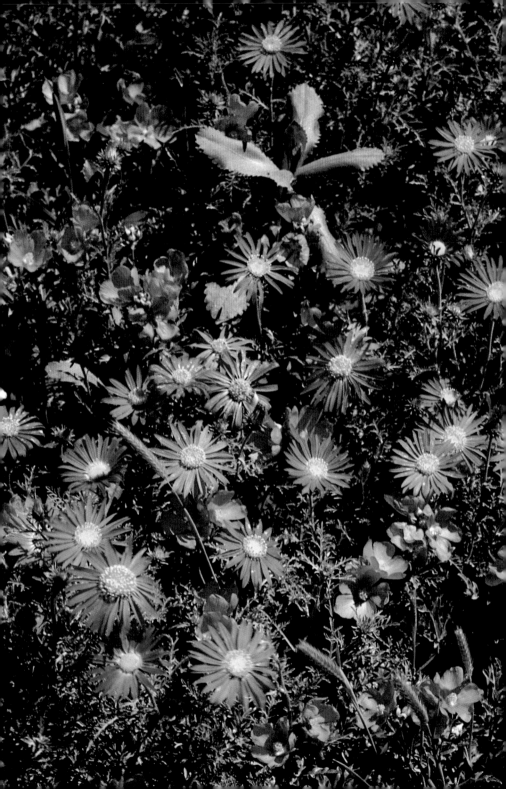

INTRODUCTION

Twenty-five years ago this started out to be merely a personal collection, "just for fun," of all the different wildflowers that grew on our ranch. Since then, I have reared five sons, traveled innumerable miles, taken countless photographs, and devoted many years to research and study, in the course of which this book has evolved.

A new book on wildflowers? Do we need yet another? Has the field (pun intended) not been covered? The answers? Yes. Yes. No. There are many books in the market-place today on the subject of wildflowers. There are books that cover selected areas such as the Big Bend, the Hill Country, and the Rio Grande Valley of Texas. There are books on wildflowers of Oklahoma, New Mexico, Kansas, and the Mountainous West to name a few more. But I have noticed that wildflowers have never recognized state lines. They spill over those boundaries and cross the rivers that divide and separate states, growing wherever nature provides suitable conditions. There is not yet one book that adequately addresses the beautiful array of hardy wildflowers that bloom in that huge expanse called the Western Plains; an area which includes the Rolling Plains, Southern High Plains and Panhandle High Plains of Texas as well as the panhandle and western portions of Oklahoma, western Kansas, the plains of southeastern Colorado, and the plains of eastern New Mexico.

The purpose of this book, then, is to provide information on and photographs of the majority of the more common wildflowers that thrive in the relatively high elevations (with severe winters) and the semiarid climate of these Western Plains. I have included mostly herbaceous plants along with a few shrubs and small trees. Some rare specimens are included, even though they may never be seen in their native environment by the layperson. This seems a satisfactory way to share their beauty and existence.

Over the years a wildflower slide program developed which I have presented to thousands of people. The continual requests for a book of these wildflowers prove that there is genuine interest in and a need for a semitechnical, illustrated, informative field-guide publication of this type. With the layperson in mind; as well as the student, I have used technical terms translated into everyday language for easier reading and understanding. This book would be suitable for use by serious students of botany and plant taxonomy along with their more technical textbooks.

Wildflowers of the Western Plains is arranged alphabetically by families and then alphabetically, by genus, within each family. The scientific names are from *The Vascular Plants of Texas: A List, Up-dating the Manual of the Vascular Plants of Texas,* 2d ed., by Marshall C. Johnston (1990). Some names in the Cactaceae were provided by Allan D. Zimmerman.

Modern taxonomists are striving to unify the family names of the Plant Kingdom so that each family ends in -aceae. There are several (eight or nine) families that now have two valid names, the older one being better known and the newer one conforming to the rule for all other plant families by ending in -aceae and having a common genus as the root of the family name. Leguminosae (Fabaceae), Compositae (Asteraceae), Cruciferae (Brassicaceae), and Labiatae (Lamiaceae) are four examples. In this text, the older, more familiar family name is

Opposite: Mixed wildflowers. *Photo by John Lott.*

used along with the newer one in the short introduction to each family included in the book.

Common names of wildflowers are an enjoyable and easy way to attempt to remember the hundreds of different species, but these names can change from region to region, being misspelled, mispronounced, and misunderstood. Sometimes a flower has several common names. The only accurate method of identification is to use the Latin name that each species has been given by taxonomists. In this text, I have used both the Latin names and the common names to add flavor and interest.

Occasionally the introduction to a plant family is accompanied by an illustration to aid in visually recognizing some characteristic of that particular family. Phillis Unbehagen, talented artist, teacher, and friend, contributed the artwork. Her knowledge and training in the field of botany is clearly evident in her sketches.

The information on each individual flower is written following a format that includes a description of the plant, the flower, the fruit, the approximate range of distribution, and finally a remarks section, in which personal thoughts, observations, recipes, legends, folklore, and medicinal uses are shared. An illustrated glossary, a glossary, a bibliography, and an index conclude the book.

Because of my lifelong interest in Native Americans and their folklore, all manner of legends pertaining to wildflowers, and medicinal uses of native plants, this book contains bits and pieces of all of these plus personal comments and observations, as well as an occasional recipe I have found and/or tried.

While working on this book, I must confess that if the plant was in season, I often stopped, went out, and gathered some specimens. With recipe in hand, I cooked them and offered a new "treat" to my family from time to time—enough times, I admit, that when any of the boys would pass the stove and lift the lid to the pot, I would be asked, "What kind of a 'weed' are we eating tonight?" To date, we have survived each new "weed." There are other comments offered in this book, however, that are not firsthand. I state if we have eaten or otherwise tried the plants in any way. Some of the medicinal uses are merely hearsay and are included more for interesting reading than to take the place of the local pharmacy. *I do not encourage the eating or medicinal use of any plant unless one is absolutely, beyond a doubt, positive of its identity.*

For those of us who live on the Western Plains, the diversity and loveliness of our part of this country's native flora are real and unmistakable. Although the wildflowers that grow here may not all "shout their presence from afar," their grace and colors are inspiring and the plants are worth searching for and finding. Their tenacity and hardiness are worthy of our admiration, and descriptions and interesting information about them are worth studying and learning. It is my hope that my love of the colorful flora of the area will be apparent in this book and because of it others will benefit and, likewise, appreciate the beauty that abounds here.

Z.M.K.

Wildflowers of the Western Plains

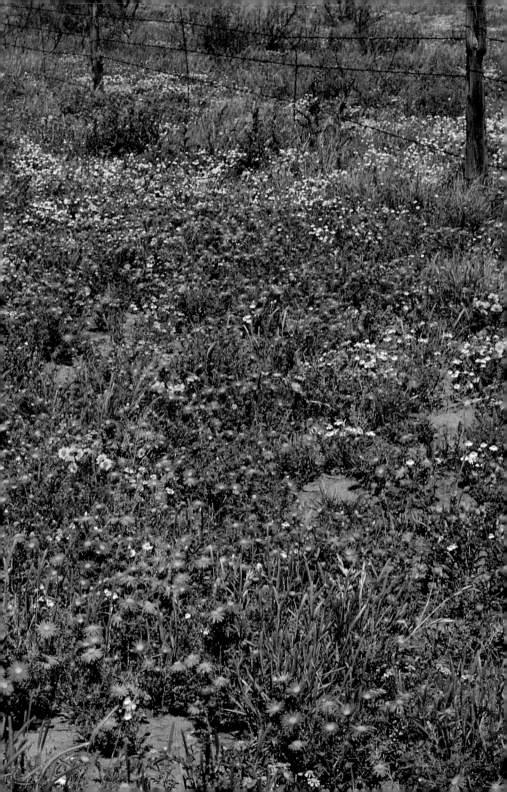

ACANTHACEAE
Acanthus Family

The Acanthus Family includes not only herbs (flowers), but also trees and shrubs. The leaves generally have no teeth or lobes. The stems are square, and the blue, purple, or lavender flowers are either obviously 2-lipped or radially symmetric. There are usually 5 petals and 2 to 4 stamens. On the Western Plains, Snake Herb (*Dyschoriste linearis*) is the most common member of this family.

Dyschoriste linearis
Snake Herb, Narrowleaf Dyschoriste

Plant: Snake Herb is an herbaceous perennial, meaning that its aboveground parts are not woody and die back annually, but its underground parts overwinter and the plant grows again each spring, for 3 or more years. The several stems are erect and square, and are 6–12 inches tall. The leaves are simple, opposite, and mostly linear, ¾–2½ inches long. They are without teeth or lobes, but have fringed edges.

Flower: Purple and obviously 2-lipped, meaning the corolla is divided into upper and lower segments, resembling lips. The flowers are borne singly in the axils. Each flower has 5 sepals, united at the base, that end in long bristle-like tips or "tails," and 5 petals united to form a flaring, tubelike corolla, usually not more than 1 inch long. The surface of the corolla is covered with soft hairs. There are purple stripes or sometimes spots in the throat of the flower. It blooms April–August if there is enough rain; otherwise it stops blooming by late June.

Fruit: An oblong capsule, ⅜–½ inch long, containing several lens-shaped or flat seeds.

Range: Sandy or silty flats and rocky places on the dry prairies of Oklahoma, over most of Texas, west to New Mexico, and south into northern Mexico.

Remarks: Snake Herb is a lovely, low, branched plant, one of about 50 species included in the predominantly tropical genus *Dyschoriste*. How unusual that this one is so prolific on the semiarid Western Plains.

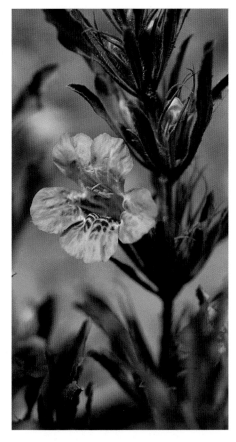

Dyschoriste linearis Snake Herb

ALISMATACEAE
Water Plantain Family

Members of the Water Plantain Family are not overly abundant on the Western Plains. They grow in water, on muddy banks, and sometimes even in wet sand. On the Western Plains, they are most commonly found around the muddy edges of playa lakes. Because these plants grow in water or muddy places, they have long-stalked leaves and an even longer flowering stem. A typical flower has 3 green sepals, 3 white petals, numerous stamens, and many pistils.

Sagittaria longiloba
(Arrowhead Plant)

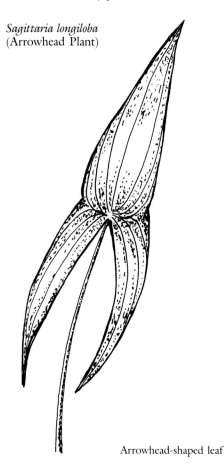

Arrowhead-shaped leaf

Sagittaria longiloba
Arrowhead Plant, Arrowhead, Water Plantain, Flecha de Agua

Plant: Perennial marsh or aquatic plant, 1–3 feet tall. Under the surface of the mud, it forms rhizomes (long, creeping underground stems), the ends of which are starchy tubers. The leaves are emersed and grow erect or slightly spreading. This species has leaves that are long, narrow, and shaped like arrowheads. The portion above the basal lobes can be up to 6 inches long and 3½ inches wide. The long, linear to lanceolate basal lobes are backward-pointing (like barbs on an arrowhead), always longer than and usually twice as long as the body or upper portion of the leaf blade.
Flower: The flowers are usually unisexual, but male and female flowers grow on the same stem. The naked flowering stems, or scapes, are taller than the leaves. Each flower has 3 green sepals and 3 white petals. In most species, the upper flowers on each scape have 6 or more stamens. The lower flowers have pistils only. The plant blooms from June to September.
Fruit: The pistils change into flat, thin-margined seeds with a laterally inserted triangular beak, in a tight round ball.
Range: Preferring the shallow water of ditches, ponds, roadsides, and the edges of playa lakes on the Western Plains, this water-loving plant ranges from Mexico to Arizona, Texas, Oklahoma, Kansas, Nebraska, and Colorado.
Remarks: This genus gets its name from the arrowhead shape of its leaves. It grows in shallow playa lakes, ponds, mud, or sometimes damp sand. The crisp white flowers are easy to see silhouetted against the muddy water of these wet places.

The Native Americans used the tubers as a staple food, and the early European settlers did the same, calling them "duck potatoes" or "swan potatoes." I have never found enough specimens to feel free to pull them up and sample their table-worthiness.

AMARYLLIDACEAE
Amaryllis or Daffodil Family

The Amaryllidaceae closely resemble the Liliaceae, or Lily Family. Both families have flowers with 6 perianth parts, united into a tube, and 6 stamens. The leaves are thinly linear and grow from a bulb or corm. The main difference is that in Amaryllidaceae, the ovary is inferior. It is embedded in the flower stalk below the flower, where a slight bulge can be seen. In Liliaceae, the ovary is superior and easy to locate.

On the Western Plains, the White Rain Lily, *Cooperia drummondii*, is fairly common, appearing 2 or 3 days after a rain. The Yellow Rain Lily, *Zephyranthes longifolia*, is less common and is seen only rarely, again after a spring rain.

Some authors are now grouping certain members of Liliaceae and Amaryllidaceae into a new family, Agavaceae. Publications in the future will probably include this new family. In this book, the older classifications are used for the relatively few species involved.

Cooperia drummondii
White Rain Lily, Cebolleta

Plant: A mostly perennial herb, with leaves and stem rising from a bulb about the size of a small onion, which is sometimes found as deep as 1 foot underground. It has several coats, or layers, like the skins on an onion bulb, which are black or brown in color. The fleshy leaves are linear and very narrow, only about ¼ inch wide. There are 2–5 erect, gray-green leaves 6–12 inches long.

Flower: The hollow leafless stem is 4–9 inches tall with a solitary flower on the tip. Three white petals and 3 white sepals together form a tube, 2–3 inches long, that flares out into broader lobes that are blunt at the tips. Where the white tube broadens,

the throat may become pink-tinted on the outer surface. Below the flower is a pair of bracts, which look like a papery tube (spathe). Blooms appear after rains from June into September.

Fruit: The stigma has 3 parts; therefore the capsule that forms after the blossom is gone is 3-celled and matures to be about ½ inch in diameter. The seeds are flat, black, and D-shaped.

Range: This is the most widely distributed *Cooperia* known and grows well in open fields and woods from northern Mexico through parts of New Mexico and most of Texas and Louisiana into Kansas.

Remarks: The ability to spring up in small to large patches after a rain, gives this plant its common name. The lightly scented flower opens in the late afternoon or evening. The lobes gradually spread open during the night and appear fully open the next morning. Ordinarily, a flower lasts only 1–2 days, but in cloudy weather one may last up to 4 days.

Zephyranthes longifolia
Yellow Rain Lily, Atamasco Lily

Plant: Growing from a bulb, the leaves of this lily are very narrow (1/16 inch wide or less) and 6–10 inches long. Usually 2 or 3 narrow, linear leaves accompany a solitary flower. The plant grows 4–8 inches tall.

Flower: Each bulb produces 1 bright yellow blossom subtended by a bract-like spathe. There are 3 petals and 3 sepals that look alike. They are ¾–1 inch long and ¼ inch wide. The stamen filaments join the throat of the floral tube. The stigma is 3-cleft at the tip. The plant blooms after rains in May, June, and July.

Fruit: The ovary is 3-celled and grows above the spathe. After the blossom dries up, the capsule bearing the seeds becomes larger, rounder, and definitely 3-lobed. Each lobe contains flat, black, D-shaped seeds that are distributed on the ground when the mature capsule dries and splits open.

Range: Preferring alkaline soils, this lily can be found on the Western Plains, in Arizona, and in the highlands of central Mexico.

Remarks: Yellow Rain Lily is not a common flower that can be counted on to appear every summer after a rain. Typical of rain lilies, the flowers open for a day and then are gone. If the day is cloudy, they may not open, but wait for the sun another day.

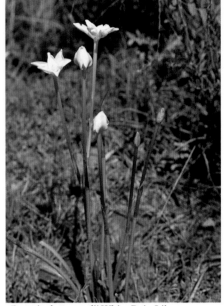

Cooperia drummondii White Rain Lily
Opposite: *Zephyranthes longifolia* Yellow Rain Lily
S. longiloba flower

Sagittaria longiloba Arrowhead Plant

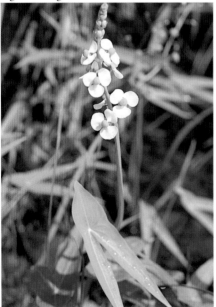

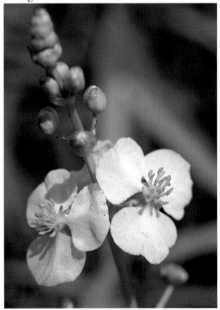

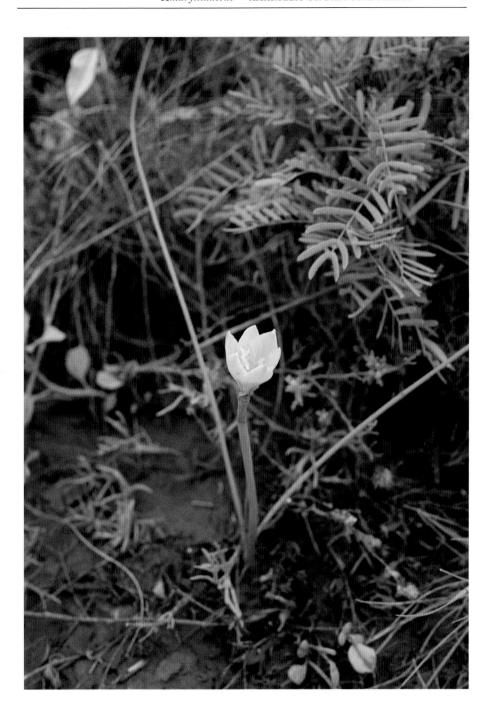

ASCLEPIADACEAE
Milkweed Family

Members of the Milkweed Family are perennial herbs, vines, or shrubs, deriving their names from the milky sap that is a characteristic of most of them. (Milky sap is found in only a few other families.) The leaves are usually paired opposite one another on the stem but can be alternate or whorled. They are simple, entire, and linear to inverted egg-shaped.

The unusual structure of the 5-merous, bisexual, usually umbellate flower sets this family apart from all others, along with the milky sap. The calyx consists of 5 separate or basally united, deeply lobed sepals that abruptly bend down (reflexed). The corolla consists of 5 petals, usually basally united. In addition to the sepals and petals, a corona, or circle of parts of variable structure, may or may not be present. When it is, it usually consists of 5 erect, cupped elements, often curving toward the center of the flower and mistaken for petals. Each individual element is called a "hood," a most conspicuous part of the flower. In some species, each hood may have a beaklike structure, called a "beak," also pointing toward the center of the flower. Within the corona, the 5 stamens are fused to a large stigmatic surface. The superior ovary produces a pair of follicles (dry fruit that opens along a single suture) in which many seeds are packed tightly together, usually bearing long silky comas, or "tails."

For the adventuresome, who might like to dissect this unusual flower, one will find more complexities inside the corona, where the stigma is fused to the anther sacs, on the tips of the stamens. The adjacent anther sacs are connected to each other by slender arms (translators). Pollination occurs when an insect pulls the translators up, carrying with them the pollen mass from the individual anther sacs. This pollen mass is then deposited on the stigmatic surface of a different flower to complete pollination. To explore even more, use the tip of a pin and pull the translators, with their pollen mass, loose from a flower.

A milkweed flower is clearly an unusual-looking creation, with a center full of fusion and confusion, but once learned, never forgotten.

All milkweeds have asclepain in their plant parts and in their sap. Asclepain is a proteolytic enzyme that gives credence to the old pioneer remedy of applying the white milkweed juice daily to get rid of warts.

Asclepias asperula
Antelope Horns, Green-flowered Milkweed, Silkweed

Plant: A perennial milkweed 1–2 feet tall, Antelope Horns has spreading stems and often forms large clumps. The irregularly grouped leaves have lanceolate blades 4–8 inches long. The plant is thickly covered with minute hairs.

Flower: The many flowers, having both stamens and pistils, are crowded into a ball, which can measure 3–4 inches across, on the end of each stem. The inner perianth of the flower is a pale creamy-green, with lobes up to ½ inch long. The 5 petals are partially divided, and in the center is a corona, out of which grow 5 white stamens with knobs for anthers. The hoods curve up in a semicircle and are colored a dark purple. Plants can be found blooming from April to August.

Fruit: The seeds are oval-shaped and about ⅜ inch long. Each is tipped with a tuft of hairs about 1¼ inches long and is a soft tawny color.

Range: This milkweed prefers dry, sandy, and rocky places. It can be found from Texas to Kansas, Utah, Colorado, southern California, and Mexico.

Remarks: Antelope Horns has unusual flowers that do not look typically flowerlike because of the modified petals, the fusion of the anthers to the stigma, and all of these being the same creamy-green color. Each individual flower is interesting in its own right. The anthers, which curve up and have knobs on their tips, are most unusual. From a distance, the ball-shaped heads look like popcorn balls stuck on stems. All parts of this plant ooze a milky sap when broken.

The common name Antelope Horns comes from the shape of the green seedpods. As they grow in length and begin to curve, they resemble antelope horns.

Asclepias engelmanniana
Narrow-leaved Milkweed

Plant: Perennial 2–4½ feet in height. The stems are stout with from 1 to 4 branching from the ground. The leaves are close together on the lower third of the stem. As they grow up the stem, the leaves become grouped in 3's at the nodes, and toward the upper third of the stem, they are paired at the nodes. Very narrow in shape, they measure only ¹⁄₁₆–⅛ inch wide, but can grow up to 9 inches long.
Flower: Several to many flower clusters grow from the upper nodes. Each cluster has 20–28 small, pale-green flowers that look very crowded. The corolla is abruptly bent downward and wheel-shaped. Each petal turns up at the tip and is a somewhat darker brownish or purplish color on its underside. The corona rises up about ¼ inch tall and is squared off at the top. It has no horns. One can find this plant blooming during June and July.
Fruit: The oval seeds are about ⅜ inch long and have a pale tawny, silklike tail about 1¼ inches long.
Range: Highway right-of-ways, prairies, washes and draws, hillsides, Caprock ledges, and canyon breaks in Texas, Nebraska, Arizona, and Mexico.
Remarks: A very tall and slender plant, this one is not easy to see by the side of the road, while traveling at a fast speed. If one

does notice it, however, it is swaying, ever so gracefully, with the other grasses and flowers. The flower clusters look like rubber balls growing at the tops of the tall plants. Closer inspection reveals the many tightly-wadded-together flowers in each cluster.

Asclepias latifolia
Broad-leaved Milkweed

Plant: Perennial with strong, straight stems up to 2 feet tall. Numerous, opposite, broad leaves, up to 5 inches long and about 4–6 inches wide, grow from very short stalks directly on 1 tall stem. The leaves are indented at the base and rounded on the end; they are coarse and have prominent veins.
Flower: The pale green to yellowish flowers are arranged in umbels (convex or flat-topped clusters of blossoms). Each flower has both stamens and pistils. The large leaves almost hide the flower clusters, which are on short stalks. There are 5 sepals and 5 pale green petals, which are united below. The lobes are about ½ inch long. The short, broad (somewhat square) hoods are cup-shaped with a longer horn that curves in. The plant blooms from May to September.
Fruit: The fruit is a follicle, a dry fruit that splits open with a single split at maturity. The oval seeds are about ¼–⅜ inch long and each has tawny-colored silklike hairs or appendages.
Range: Short grasslands and disturbed areas, spreading to roadsides and railroad rights-of-way in Texas, Nebraska, Utah, New Mexico, southeastern California, and Mexico.
Remarks: Broad-leaved Milkweed stands tall and erect. It has the largest and broadest leaves of all the milkweeds that grow on the Western Plains. It seems to grow in almost every prairie dog town still in existence. Broad-leaved Milkweed, prairie dogs, and burrowing owls appear to coexist quite well.

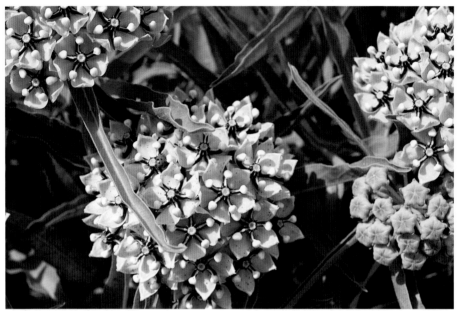

Asclepias asperula Antelope Horns

Opposite: *A. latifolia* Broad-leaved Milkweed

A. engelmanniana Narrow-leaved Milkweed   *A. engelmanniana* close-up

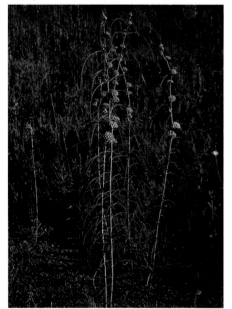

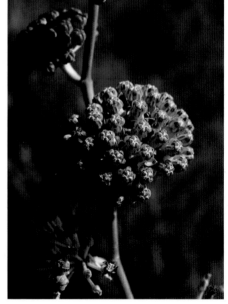

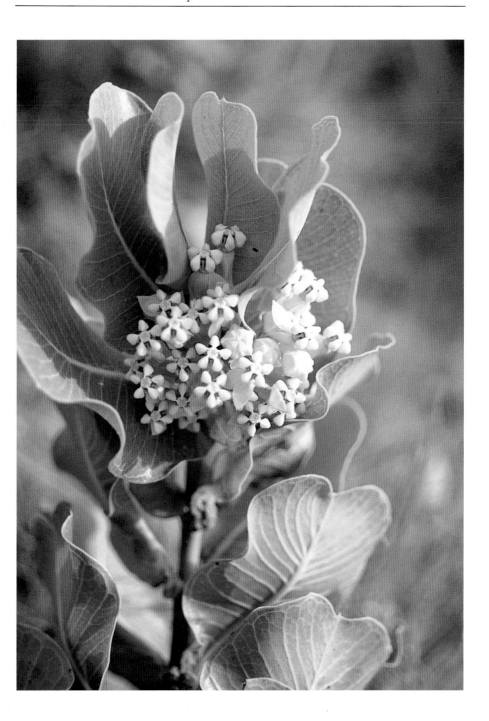

Asclepias oenotheroides
Milkweed, Hierba de Zizotes

Plant: A low herbaceous perennial milkweed with a cluster of stems that spreads outward. The stems can be from 2 to 16 inches long depending on the amount of rainfall received during the growing season. The leaves have a long diamond shape, with smooth blades on long stalks, arranged opposite one another across the stem. As with most members of this family, the stems and leaves contain a milky white, sticky sap.
Flower: The flowers are greenish-white (sometimes yellow) and arranged in umbels. There are 5 sepals, and 5 petals ($\frac{1}{3}$–$\frac{1}{2}$ inch long), united below. The corolla is bent down. The hoods are narrow, spreading at the tips, with beaks that adhere to the hoods except at their tips, where each beak is longer and incurved. Milkweed blooms from March or April until frost on the Western Plains.
Fruit: The seedpods grow erect on stalks that bend downward. The seeds are oval, $\frac{1}{4}$–$\frac{5}{8}$ inch long, each bearing a tannish silklike coma, or appendage (tail).
Range: This hardy plant can grow in rocky places, clay soils, salt marshes, fields and roadsides, hills and plains in Texas and New Mexico, spreading southward into Central America.
Remarks: This is a rather ordinary-looking plant, yet the flowers are anything but ordinary. They are complex, intricate, and amazing. It is, however, a member of a family that includes many toxic species and is considered a "noxious weed" by many.

Asclepias speciosa
Showy Milkweed

Plant: An herbaceous perennial with strong unbranched stems, Showy Milkweed grows 2–4 feet tall. A dense wool covers the plant except for the top side of the

leaves. The opposite leaves have short stalks, are oval to thin lance-shaped and grow up to 8 inches long, $1\frac{1}{2}$–5 inches wide with rounded or blunt tips. Very visible veins extend from the midrib to the edges.
Flower: The large flower clusters grow laterally in the axils of the leaves. Each individual flower in the cluster is large ($\frac{3}{4}$ inch across) with the 5 corolla lobes about $\frac{1}{2}$ inch long and rosy-purple in color. These 5 pointed lobes are bent backward. The 5 hoods are pointed at their tips and spreading. The plant blooms from May to September.
Fruit: An erect follicle, $3\frac{1}{2}$–$4\frac{1}{2}$ inches long, covered with white woolly hairs. The follicle is full of oval seeds $\frac{1}{4}$–$\frac{3}{8}$ inch long; each bearing a tuft of white hairs (coma) on its tip.
Range: Showy Milkweed grows quite well in the panhandle of Texas, eastern New Mexico, northern Arizona, and northern California. It also grows in Canada. Adapting well to different habitats, it thrives on roadsides and railroad rights-of-way as well as in cultivated fields and pastures.
Remarks: Showy Milkweed is the largest of the milkweeds. The color is a delicate pinky-rose making it worthy of its common name. The flowers emit a faintly sweet fragrance.

Native Americans reportedly boiled the flowers and fruit and ate them. They used the dried pods as utensils.

Asclepias tuberosa
Butterfly Weed, Orange Milkweed, Pleurisy Root

Plant: This herbaceous perennial grows from woody roots on stout strong stems. The plant usually forms clumps of several stems rising from the thick roots. If it branches at all, it is only in the upper or flower-bearing portion of the plant. It is a tall, hairy wildflower growing to heights of

36 inches. The alternate leaves are lance-shaped, 1–4½ inches long and 1¼ inches wide, bearing rough hairs on their surfaces. They appear crowded around the stems.
Flower: The numerous flowers grow in single up to several umbellike cymes on the tips of the stems. Each flower is bright orange, red-orange, or rarely yellow, 5-lobed, small (½ inch across) with the deeply cleft lobes turned abruptly backward, hiding the calyx. These lobes are ¼–⅜ inch long. The hoods are lance-shaped, about ¼ inch long with basal, needlelike, inward-curving beaks that are slightly longer than the hoods. Butterfly Weed blooms from June to September.
Fruit: Typical of milkweeds, this plant develops smooth, erect follicles, 3–6 inches long and ½–¾ inch wide. They are filled with oval seeds ¼ inch long tipped with a white tuft of hairs (coma).
Range: Butterfly Weed grows by the roadsides and in prairies, dry fields, and canyons from Ohio to Utah, New Hampshire to Minnesota and Colorado, Arizona, New Mexico, and Texas.
Remarks: My most memorable sighting of this plant was in the panhandle of Texas one gray, cloudy day in June. When I spotted it in a dry creek bed, my first thought was that I had seen a "burning bush." The fiery-orange, in the damp atmosphere and gray light, was astounding and vivid beyond belief. The plant was almost 3 feet tall, thick and rounded, probably 3 feet wide, and entirely covered with blossoms. Bees and butterflies were frantically flitting from flower to flower. It is a much-preferred nectar source for bees, butterflies, and flies. Unlike other milkweeds, it does not have the milky-white sticky sap. Instead it contains a watery sap.

Without a doubt, this colorful plant wins the prize among milkweeds for showiness.

As one of its common names indicates, it has been used for relief of pleurisy by using the chopped root in a tea. Reportedly, too much can quickly cause nausea. I think I'll just enjoy it visually.

Sarcostemma cynanchoides var. *cynanchoides*
Vine Milkweed

Plant: Vine Milkweed has trailing or twining stems that grow to 3 feet and are many-branched. The leaves, which grow in pairs, are broad, triangular-lanceolate in shape, indented at the base (somewhat like an elongated heart shape), and can be up to 3 inches long.
Flower: The whitish-green flowers grow in a ball-shaped cluster with up to 20 flowers in a single cluster. The corolla, or inner perianth of the flower, is somewhat bell-shaped, cleft into 5 lobes, ¼–½ inch long. The crown, or corona, is composed of 5 stamens close enough together to form a column that looks like a disk-shaped, crown ring in the center of the corona. The corona also includes 5 small round saclike bladders or air cavities, corresponding to the hoods or cups of *Asclepias* flowers. These air cavities are below the 5 anthers. This milkweed blooms in July and August.
Fruit: The fruit of each flower is a pair of follicles with a spindle shape. The seeds are flat with tufts of hair at their ends.
Range: Vine Milkweed is found in sandy soils, sand hills, and canyon breaks, usually climbing on shrubs or fences, in Texas, Oklahoma, Utah, California, and Mexico.
Remarks: Vine Milkweed is one of the showier of the several species of milkweeds found on the Western Plains.

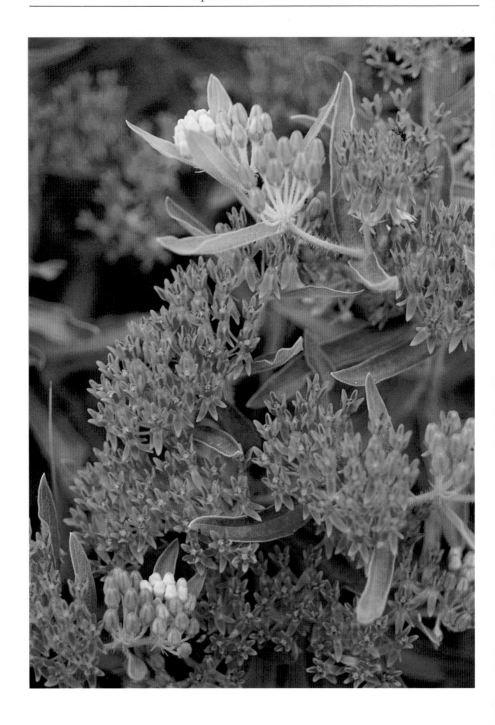

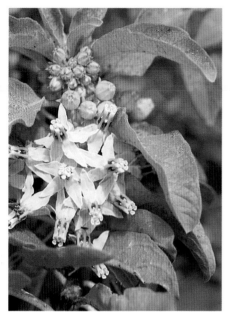
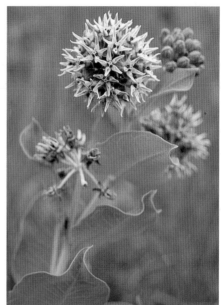

Asclepias oenotheroides Milkweed
Opposite: *A. tuberosa* Butterfly Weed
Sarcostemma cynanchoides close-up

A. speciosa Showy Milkweed

S. cynanchoides Vine Milkweed

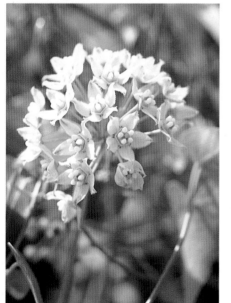
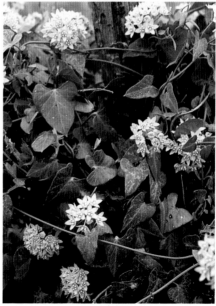

BERBERIDACEAE
Barberry Family

The Barberry Family consists of shrubs and herbs. The leaves are arranged alternately on the stems. Sepals and petals overlap each other in the bud and grow in 2 rows of 3 each. Stamens grow below the single pistil. The anthers open by 2 hinged valves to quickly splatter pollen over insects as they crawl by.

This is a family of only 9 genera worldwide, having a natural distribution limited mostly to the northern temperate regions. Many of its members have been introduced into cultivation as landscaping plants.

Berberis trifoliolata
Algerita, Agarita, Agarito, Currant-of-Texas, Desert Holly

Plant: An evergreen shrub 3–6 feet tall, with rigid spreading branches that often form thickets. Leaves are alternate, trifoliolate (compound with 3 leaflets), stiff, leathery, and toothed, with needle-sharp tips. The branches bear no thorns. The prickly leaves are blue-green or gray-green on top and greener underneath. The wood is bright yellow.
Flower: The flowers, which smell of saffron, are yellow, 3/8–1/2 inch across, blooming in umbellike clusters. Each flower has 6 petallike sepals, 6 petals, 6 stamens, and 1 pistil. Algerita usually blooms in March.
Fruit: Ripening in June, the fruit is a red berry about the size of a pea. The seeds are reddish-brown to brownish-black. When sampled, the berries are acid, or tart, to the taste.
Range: Algerita prefers hills, overhanging cliffs, and rocky slopes. It can be found in Arizona, New Mexico, central, south, and west Texas, and Mexico. On the plains of Texas, it hugs the Caprock Escarpment of

the Llano Estacado as it meanders northward.
Remarks: This is a most unusual shrub in that it has such yellow wood inside its gray stems. Early settlers prized the roots and wood as a yellow dye source. Craftworkers today use it in interesting wood carvings and for small yellow wooden beads as well as for other jewelry.

The plant is useful to wildlife, as quail and small animals find cover in it. Birds relish the ripe fruit, later depositing the seeds in their droppings to become new plants.

Algerita is considered a good honey source. It has an unusual pollination mechanism that is found in all barberries. The 6 stamens in each flower are extremely sensitive to the touch. When any nectar-seeking insect flies into the flower and touches the stamens, they spring out and throw pollen over the insect's head. When the next flower is visited, this pollen may be placed on the pistil.

On the Western Plains, where fresh fruit was difficult to find, our forefathers and mothers happily gathered Algerita berries for use in cobblers, since it was the first fresh fruit of the season.
Recipe: When the fruit is ripe, Algerita berries are excellent for jelly or wine as well as pies and cobblers. Though difficult to pick because of the sharp leaves, the results of gathering are worth the pain and effort. My recipe is not a clear jelly, nor is it a true preserve. We call it Algerita Butter.

Put about 3½ quarts of ripe berries in a large vessel. Add water to cover, and boil until they begin to burst open. Pour the juice and berries through a colander. Mash all the pulp you can through the colander with a wooden pestle, throwing away the seeds and skins. To 6½ cups of juice and pulp (add a little water if necessary to make 6½ cups), add one package of Sure-Jell or other pectin. Bring to a boil and add 7 cups of sugar. Allow it to come to a second hard boil, then let boil for 3 minutes more, and remove from heat. Quickly pour into jars, seal, and set aside to cool. Enjoy!

BORAGINACEAE
Borage or Forget-me-not Family

Plants in the Borage Family differ from each other very much. While some are small and bristly or hairy with tiny white or blue flowers, others grow to 3 feet and have showy yellow flowers. Usually they are characterized by their inflorescences, 1-sided cymes that are coiled in bud and then uncoil as the flowers open. In some species, the flowers are borne singly, having petals which form a funnel or tube. A 4-lobed ovary forms 1–4 small, prickly seeds.

Lithospermum incisum
Puccoon, Golden Puccoon, Gromwell

Plant: A perennial herb whose stems grow from a dye-filled dark root forming basal rosettes of hairy leaves. These leaves are lanceolate but broadest at the outer half and are 1¾–2½ inches long. The basal leaves usually dry up before the plant blooms. The stems rise up to 12 inches tall, branching at the top and bearing longer, more linear leaves, becoming smaller near the flowers. The upper stem leaves are commonly 1¼–2½ inches long and ¼–½ inch wide.

Flower: The bright yellow flowers have 5 united sepals and 5 petals, united to form a 5-lobed tube, ½–⅔ inch across at the flaring end and ¾–1¼ inches long. The lobes look as if they are torn on the edges, giving the golden yellow blossom a fringed effect. The 5 stamens rise from the trumpet-shaped corolla tube with one 4-lobed pistil. These spring-blooming flowers are more or less infertile but bloom from March to May with each flower lasting several days or even weeks.

Later in the summer and into the fall, the plant produces smaller, almost invisible flowers. Hidden in the upper parts of the leaf nodes, they fertilize themselves without opening. Technically, these flowers are "cleistogamous," which means "having closed pollination."

Fruit: From the late, hard-to-see flowers come very fertile seeds. There are 4 oblong oval-shaped nutlets about ⅛ inch long. Inside each one is a bony, white seed.

Range: Puccoon grows throughout most of Texas, in Arizona, and into Mexico. It prefers prairies, fields, open woods, and roadsides.

Remarks: The Native Americans used several plants for dye sources, calling all of them "puccoon." The long red taproot of this *Lithospermum* was used for purple dye.

The early golden blossoms are bright and cheerful after a long winter, and their "crinkly" edges set them apart from other yellow spring flowers.

It is interesting that this particular plant blooms twice in a season, the first time with a pretty yellow "all-show-but-won't-grow" sterile blossom, then much later with a tiny "no-show-but-will-grow" blossom that produces fertile seeds.

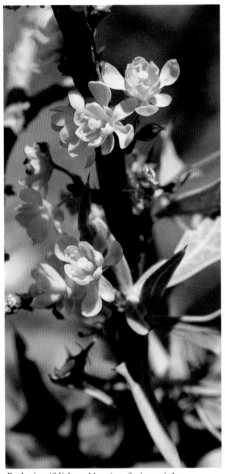 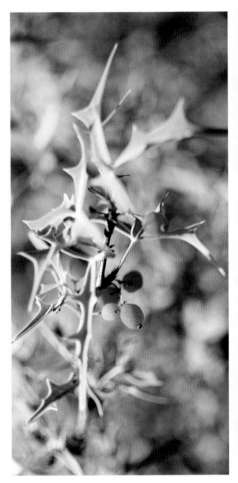

Berberis trifoliolata Algerita; fruit at right

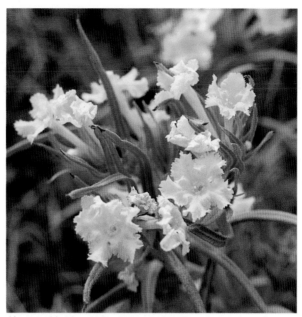

Above and below: *Lithospermum incisum* Puccoon

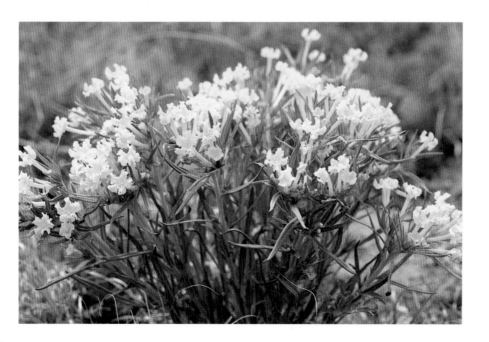

Parts of a Cactus

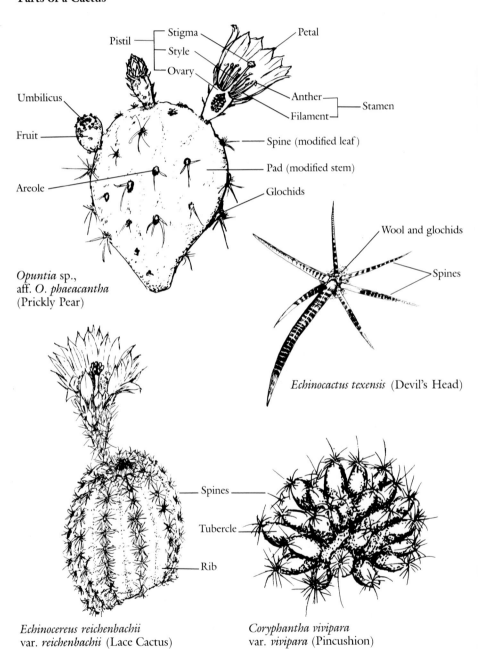

Pistil
Stigma
Style
Ovary
Petal

Umbilicus

Anther
Filament
Stamen

Fruit

Spine (modified leaf)

Pad (modified stem)

Areole

Glochids

Wool and glochids

Spines

Opuntia sp.,
aff. *O. phaeacantha*
(Prickly Pear)

Echinocactus texensis (Devil's Head)

Spines

Tubercle

Rib

Echinocereus reichenbachii
var. *reichenbachii* (Lace Cactus)

Coryphantha vivipara
var. *vivipara* (Pincushion)

CACTACEAE
Cactus Family

The Cactus Family, one of the few that grow naturally only in the Western Hemisphere, is one of the most remarkable families in the Plant Kingdom.

There are some characteristics that cacti share with other plants, such as fleshy stems, few to no leaves, and sharp spines. Other features are found only in cacti; these include areoles (those spots or openings, round or elongated, either raised or pitted, that are usually arranged in rows or spirals over the surface of the plant). A cactus areole is an area of the epidermis, or outer skin, from which the spines grow. It is a "short shoot," an axillary bud that never grows out into a normal green "long shoot." The spines coming out of these areoles are modified leaves; they are always arranged in clusters and can be either rigid or flexible. The combination of numerous intergrading petals and sepals (perianth segments), an inferior ovary (one that grows sunken down in the stem making the flower parts appear to come from above the ovary), with only one seed chamber, and a single style with several stigma lobes, is unique to Cactaceae. Other families have one or two of these features, but only Cactaceae have this particular combination. One other most insidious feature is the presence of glochids, those minute, almost invisible barbed hairs that grow in clusters in the areoles, in *Opuntia* (prickly pears). With a touch, they easily become imbedded in skin or clothing, and, because of their light tan or yellow color and barbed surfaces, are most difficult to remove. In other genera, the tiny spines are non-barbed and persistent.

The cactus has become the strange-looking plant it is today because it has evolved in arid and semiarid areas where water is scarce to sometimes nonexistent. Water storage is the greatest problem, solved by the cactus' enlarged stem of thick, fleshy columns or spheres. The root system does not go down deeply into the ground, but rather spreads out just under the surface with a myriad of fine roots that wait for the sudden desert showers, then store much water very quickly in the enlarged stem. As the cactus can swell up when it fills to capacity with water, it can also shrink during times of drought. The arrangement of ribs or tubercles (nipplelike projections) allows this change in size without the plant splitting open or caving in, depending upon water retention or total lack of water.

Since evaporation occurs through the leaves in other plants, and a cactus cannot afford any evaporation, it has eliminated leaves (modifying them into spines, as mentioned earlier), and the green stems are thick and waxy to reduce moisture loss even more. With its tough, stout, and hardy exterior, it is hard to believe that the inside has soft tissue, similar to a cantaloupe, that is moisture-laden and almost "mushy."

Thirsty desert animals know the moisture is there and would eat every cactus in sight if the plant had not also protected itself with a covering of spines so sharp and spreading that nothing can or will bite into it. For those cactus species that cannot stand the full sun, the spines also create the shade they need for protection. The white wool or hair that some cacti have reflects the hot sun and serves as a shading material also.

All cactus blossoms have a waxy surface; they are sometimes large and always showy, bright, and colorful in order to attract insects needed to pollinate them. They bloom for short periods of time and then are gone, which makes it difficult to catch some of them in their prime.

The fruit follows the blossom and is protected initially by spines, or wool, which later drop off. The hungry and thirsty desert animals can finally eat this part of the plant. Eventually the animals drop the seeds elsewhere and help in assuring the plant's regeneration. Cactus fruit is not poisonous, and some species are greatly enjoyed by humans as well as birds and animals.

I feel that I must add a word of caution here against field collecting. It is tempting to dig up and take home pretty cactus plants. In their native environment they appear tough and hardy, but when transplanted, their true delicacy becomes evident, as they often die. Moreover, in the wild, they reproduce slowly, and wide-scale collecting almost assures eventual extinction. Several varieties are already endangered, and a few more are alarmingly close to being extinct; thus it is worth imploring that one should take only photographs and leave the cacti to flourish in their natural environment.

Coryphantha vivipara var. *vivipara*
Pincushion, Spiny Star, Ball Cactus

Plant: Pincushion Cactus has a single stem that grows up in globular or ball-shaped form (never columnar) 2½ inches in diameter. The surface has many tapering, nipplelike projections (tubercles) that spread upward. Each tubercle has a groove from the tip back down toward its base. The color of the stem and its tubercles is a dark green.

The areoles, on the tip of each tubercle, are round and filled with white wool while the tubercle is young. As they mature and grow longer, the wool disappears.

There can be 12–21 radial spines on the various forms of this cactus. They are straight, slender, and firm, ⅜–⅝ inch long, and usually very white or with brown tips. The 1–8 central spines, which stick straight out, are dark reddish brown and ½ to ¾ inch long.

Flower: Bright magenta blossoms, about 1½–2 inches across, burst into bloom around the top of the ball-shaped plant. The 30 or more narrow outer petals are greenish or brownish in color and have pink fringed edges; the 30 or more narrow inner petals are brighter and more vividly pink or magenta. All the petals taper to a sharp point. The filaments are green at their bases, pink in their upper parts; the anthers are bright orange, and the stigma lobes are

deep rose. This cactus blooms from May to July on the Western Plains.

Fruit: The fruits are oval and ½–1 inch long. The dried perianth continues to stay intact, even remaining green or brown when very ripe. The seeds can be light or dark brown and are nearly round with a finely pitted surface.

Range: This cactus has a wide range of distribution, growing from Canada down through the Dakotas, Nebraska, Kansas, Oklahoma, and northwestern Texas, eastern Colorado, and northern New Mexico.

Remarks: One rarely pays any attention to these little green balls covered with "nipples," or tubercles, as they grow preferably on sandy hills and plains. But when the blossoms appear in the spring, you can't miss them, as they advertise their presence from afar. In the bright sunshine, their color almost hurts the eyes.

This is the cactus found in parts of Canada and northern areas where other cacti refuse to grow. It must be more resistant to freeze damage than its cousins. It is easily rotted by too much water, which may be why it prefers hills to valleys. It also seems to do better growing almost hidden in the prairie grasses of the Western Plains, possibly needing the protection from extreme summer sun.

Echinocactus texensis
Devil's Head, Devil's Pincushion, Horse Crippler

Plant: The stem is in a broad hemisphere-shape, growing to a maximum of 12 inches across, but rising only about 2–5 inches tall. This cactus is dark green and has 13–27 very prominent ridges or ribs. The center, at the apex where all the ribs meet, is filled with long white wool.

The areoles are triangular in shape and are covered with white wool also. They are located on every other rib, or ridge, sometimes skipping 2 ribs, usually spaced about 1–1¼ inches apart.

The spines are reddish in color, turning white with age. They have ringed ridges that can be seen with the naked eye. Six or 7 tough, hard spines radiate from each areole, measuring from ½ inch to 2 inches long. One central spine, the longest and strongest, sticks out straight, then curves down.

Flower: The showy flower opens to a spread of up to 2½ inches. The edges of the petals are fringed and feathery looking out to the ends. Their color is a soft pink, and each petal has a darker red midline. The base of each petal becomes an even darker rose-red. In the center are numerous reddish filaments with yellow anthers, a yellowish style, and a stigma with up to 17 yellowish lobes. The plant blooms from late April to early or middle May.

Fruit: A slightly oval fruit, bright red and fleshy, about 1½ inches long, develops where each flower previously bloomed. One or more fruits grow from the apex, or center, of the cactus. The seeds are flat and black, about ⅛ inch long. They are dispersed when the fruit splits open down 1 side later in the summer.

Range: Most of western Texas, southwestern Oklahoma, southeastern New Mexico, and into Mexico.

Remarks: This tough, hardy cactus is cursed by ranchers, and farmers have virtually eliminated it from their fields. It has the largest and toughest spines of any of the cacti that grow on the Western Plains. "Horse Crippler" is an accurate common name, for it certainly can cripple a horse if stepped on just right. Driving over an unseen older plant can puncture a pickup tire, and running over one in a tennis shoe is painful indeed.

But one must forgive all those bad points about this cactus in the spring when it blooms, for then it gives us lovely, delicate, feathery pink blossoms to appreciate. Later in the summer, it offers a vivid splash of red as the fruits ripen.

Echinocereus reichenbachii var. *reichenbachii*

Lace Cactus, White Lace Cactus, Brown Lace Cactus, Hedgehog Cactus

Plant: Stems are ball-shaped when they first come up from the seed, but change to cylinder-shaped as they reach maturity (in about 3 or 4 years). The average adult height is about 4–8 inches, and thickness is usually 2 inches. There are 11–17 narrow ribs on each deep green stem. This species tends to grow in clumps or clusters more often than others.

The areoles are small and very woolly when the plant is young, becoming bare as it ages. In each areole are 10–36 slender spines, lying nearly flat and spreading out in "sunburst" fashion (radially). These spines can be all white or white with the tips turning to brown, black, or even a shiny purplish color. The spines on any one plant are usually all colored the same, and the color never varies on the spines in a single areole. The spines up and down the ribs may sometimes be close enough to interlock, making the plant appear "lace-covered."

Flower: The flowers are large, about 2–5 inches tall and 2–4 inches across. They are a vivid rose-pink. The base of each petal is narrow and a deeper reddish color. The petals (30–50) broaden to be ¼ inch wide at the outer tips and are fringed or ragged on the extreme ends, which are usually pointed. The many anthers are yellowish or cream-colored. The style is long and topped by 8–22 bright green stigma lobes. Lace Cactus blooms in late May and early June.

Fruit: When the flower dries, the egg-shaped ovary remains, containing the seeds. It is entirely covered with small spines and wool. It stays green until it dries and splits open, dropping the seeds to the ground. The tiny black seeds are difficult to see with the naked eye.

Range: Most of northwestern Texas, central and western Oklahoma, southeastern Colorado, eastern New Mexico, and northern Mexico.

Remarks: A little Lace Cactus is not an eye-catching plant until it blooms; then it is dazzling. The large "passionate pink" blossoms dwarf the stems. One wonders how that squatty, short-stemmed cactus could produce such a flower.

On the Western Plains, the Lace Cactus is not overly abundant. Because of its lovely blossom, lacy spines, and adaptability, it is one of the most heavily collected of the Cactus Family. Unfortunately, this could lead to its eventual extinction.

The common name Hedgehog comes from the first part of its generic name, *Echino-*, which is Greek for "hedgehog." This could refer to the spiny look of the fruit.

Mammillaria heyderi var. *heyderi* (= *M. gummifera* var. *applanata*)
Nipple Cactus, Little Chilis, Biznaga de Chilitos

Plant: This single-stemmed cactus grows as a more or less flattened hemisphere, up to 5 inches in diameter and to about 2 inches tall. Each stem is covered by a system of nipplelike projections, called tubercles. Usually they are arranged in spiral rows. Thus there are many little nipples all over the surface of the plant. At the tip of each tubercle is an areole. There are 20–26 radial spines, radiating like spokes, in each areole.

Flower: The creamy-pink (sometimes shading to white) flowers are ¾–1½ inches tall and wide. They grow in a circle like a crown around the newer growth in the center of the plant. The outer petals have a line down the center that is greenish or brownish shading into whitish. These petals have a smooth edge and are pointed at the tip. The inner petals have brownish-

pink to pale rose midlines and are slightly ragged on the edges toward the pointed tips. The filaments range from whitish to dark pink. The anthers are yellow, and the stigma has 5–10 light green to tan lobes. Blooms appear in May and June.

Fruit: Bright red in color and waxy-looking, the fruits lack the tiny spines found on other cactus fruits. They are ½–1½ inches long, pointed at the end that attaches to the plant, and rounded on the opposite end or tip. They ripen 1 year after their inception; so it is not uncommon to see a ring of red ripe "cactus berries" on the plant at the same time as the flowers. The seeds are less than ⅟₁₆ inch long, reddish-brown, and pitted.

Range: North out of Mexico to Texas, Oklahoma, New Mexico, Arizona, and southeastern Colorado.

Remarks: This shy little cactus is always found somewhat hidden in tall grass or at the base of trees and shrubs, where there is partial shade, as it cannot stand the full sun. It goes virtually unnoticed most of the year, except in the spring, when the lovely crown of pale pink blossoms and/or bright red fruit makes it more visible. A plant, with its delicate crown of blossoms, that has another ring of bright red fruit (from last year's blossoms) outside the ring of flowers, is a truly gorgeous sight.

The "cactus berries" are quite delicious, having a sweet/tart taste which is worth sampling whenever found. Often the birds find them first, for the berries are a favorite food of theirs. Our parents and grandparents, living on the Western Plains, were often starved for fresh fruit after a long, cold winter. This tasty red berry was among the first fresh fruits of the season and was used in cobblers and eaten with pleasure.

This cactus has a milky sap, which is unusual among cacti.

Opuntia engelmannii var. *engelmannii*
Engelmann Prickly Pear, Prickly Pear

Plant: An upright, rather compact cactus 2–5 feet tall. It can form large thickets. The stems are a series of flattened joints, commonly called "pads." The pads are circular to a broad egg shape, 12 inches long when mature, and almost as wide. They are ½–¾ inch thick, fleshy, unribbed, covered with a bloom (somewhat like a cabbage leaf), and soft pale green in color.

The areoles are oval, usually widely spaced, 1¼–2 inches apart (except on the edges, where they are closer together), filled with a tan wool and many tan glochids. On the younger pads, there are no spines; as they mature, one and then others develop (usually up to 4) growing in the lower portion of each oval areole. The most mature spines are the longest, reaching lengths of 1½–2 inches. These spines are not barbed but smooth, rather flattened, extremely sharp on the tip, and varying in color from deep yellow or tan at the base to lighter toward the tip (pale yellow to opaque white).
Flower: The flowers are large, showy, and a clear, bright yellow (which can fade to orange before wilting); occasionally they can be a clear bright orange. They are 2½–3 inches in diameter with 10 or fewer green stigma lobes evident in the center. The many petaloid perianth parts are soft yet waxy-looking. This cactus blooms in June to early July.
Fruit: The pear-shaped fruits develop on or near the edges of the pads, where the flowers bloomed. They can be up to 3 inches long with small clumps of glochids over their surfaces. The umbilicus is wide and almost flat on top. The fleshy, seed-filled fruits (tunas) turn a deep red or burgundy color when ripe.
Range: This species is more abundant in Mexico and southern Texas, but has spread northward up into the Southern High Plains of Texas and eastern New Mexico.
Remarks and Recipe: In the spring, I see many local Mexican-American friends out in the large thickets of Engelmann Prickly Pear, gathering "nopalitos." The tender newly forming green pads (which do not yet have spines) can be cut in strips, boiled twice, throwing the water away, then cooked in stews or with scrambled eggs and onions. In Mexico, these strips are pickled and canned.

The ripe fruit, or tunas, have several delicious uses also. The Native Americans preserved them by squeezing the juice out, then drying them in the sun. They can also be eaten fresh or made into a tasty jelly. The recipe for Prickly Pear Jelly is as follows:

In the late summer or early fall, when the tunas are ripe, plump, and deep burgundy in color, they can be gathered (very carefully, using heavy leather gloves, kitchen tongs, and a bucket). When back at home, hold each tuna (in the tongs) over a candle or gas flame to burn off the many glochids. Scrape the tuna with a knife to remove the burned glochids. Wearing rubber gloves (or the juice will dye your hands purple), you can now peel the tunas, after which they can be cut into pieces and put, seeds included, into a saucepan with enough water to nearly cover the fruit. Cover the saucepan and simmer for 45–60 minutes. Strain the juice through cheesecloth, discarding the pulp and seeds. Measure 3 cups of juice and add ½ cup fresh lemon juice and 1 box of Sure-Jell or other powdered pectin. Bring this to a boil, then immediately add 4–5½ cups sugar (depending upon your preference). When the mixture again boils, let it boil hard for 3 minutes, remove from heat, skim the foam off the top, pour into sterilized jars, and seal with hot lids. The jelly will set in several days. The flavor will vary from plant to plant and depending upon the ripeness of the tunas when they are gathered.

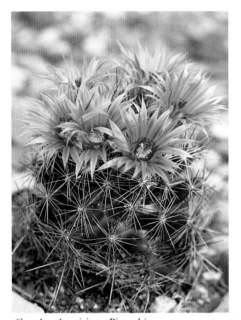

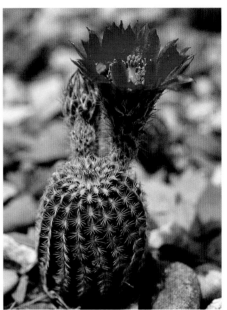

Coryphantha vivipara Pincushion

Echinocereus reichenbachii Lace Cactus

Echinocactus texensis Devil's Head

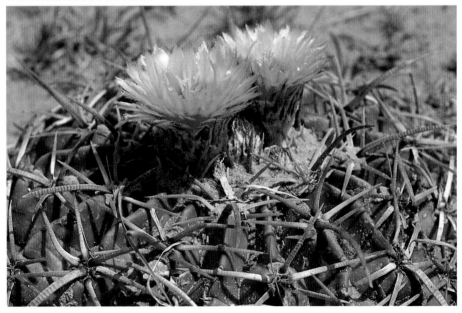

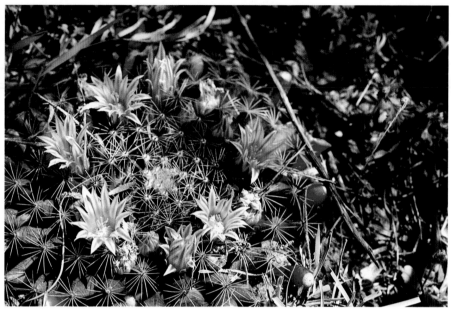

Mammillaria heyderi Nipple Cactus

E. texensis close-up

Opuntia engelmannii Engelmann Prickly Pear

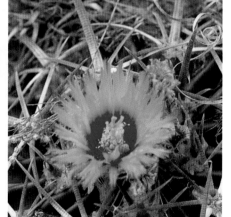

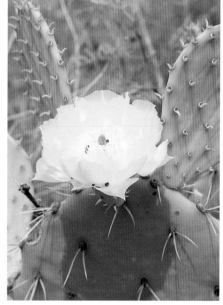

Opuntia imbricata
Tree Cactus, Cholla, Cane Cactus, Velas de Coyote (Coyote Candles)

Plant: Tree Cactus grows tall and upright, sometimes bushy but usually treelike, 3–8 feet tall. The stems are jointed and cylindrical. The main trunk is round and can reach 3–4 inches in diameter with age. It is covered with a rough bark and has elongated areoles.

Each year's new growth consists of tender cylinder-shaped joints 2–8 inches long and about 1 inch in diameter. These joints are covered with rather elongated tubercles, ¾–1¼ inches long and about ¼ inch high, appearing almost rippled.

The spines vary in number from 2 to 10 on the current year's growth, with 20–30 on older portions of the plant. There are 1–8 central spines, ½–1¼ inches long, round, yellowish, and covered by loose sheaths. The other spines are exterior ones, smaller (¼–⅝ inch long), white to brownish, and partly covered by tight white sheaths. There are very few, if any, glochids.

Flower: The showy flowers of the Tree Cactus grow to 3 inches in diameter. The petals open out wide and are a deep wine-red or pale pink in color. The filaments are red at the bases and greenish pink above. The anthers are creamy colored, the style is red, and there are 6–8 fat, pinkish stigma lobes. The blooming period is May and June.

Fruit: The fruit is about 1 inch long and ovate. The scar that is left after the flower parts dry and drop off (umbilicus) is a deep pit on the tip. The rest of the surface has pronounced tubercles which give a bumpy effect. The color is yellow when ripe. The fruit is not fleshy or juicy and usually remains on the plant until the next blooming season. The smooth seeds are ⅛ inch in diameter.

Range: Southern Colorado, most of New Mexico, Arizona, southwestern Kansas, western Oklahoma, the plains and panhandle of Texas, and into Mexico.

Remarks: Tree Cacti are pretty common on the Western Plains, but especially below the Caprock area of Texas. There are large stands of them across many a ranch pasture. They are so numerous, one doesn't pay much attention to them through the year. Then in late May and into June, they bloom the typical wine-red blossoms and the rangeland sings with color, not on the ground where the wildflowers grow, but up higher in the "trees."

Occasionally there will be a plant covered with soft pink blossoms instead of the deep wine-colored ones. These plants, growing alongside the others, offer a lovely contrast.

In the winter and early spring, the fruits, still on the plant, are bright yellow. People often mistake them for blossoms from a distance. They do offer a spot of color at that time of the year, but the plants will be much more spectacular when the actual blossoms appear later.

Old plants that have died dry up and leave wooden skeletons of these large straight trunks and branches. Where the areoles once were, there are long oval holes in the skeletons. Walking canes are made from the hard wood, and the smaller pieces are used in flower arrangements and table decorations.

Opuntia kleiniae
Candle Cholla, Klein Cholla

Plant: Candle Cholla grows erect up to 6 feet tall. It branches from woody trunks, 1–1½ inches in diameter. The current year's tender cylindrical joints grow up to 12 inches long and up to ½ inch in diameter. The tubercles on the joints are indistinct, not large enough to be "bumpy" or "rippled," and ½–⅜ inch long.

The areoles are almost triangular in shape with white wool and 1–4 spines in each one. There is 1 main spine, ½–2½ inches long, and 2 or 3 shorter ones. Glochids grow in a small clump on the upper portion of the areole.

Flower: The flowers are small, 1–1½ inches in diameter, and a soft pinkish-red. The filaments are pink, and the stigma has 6 or 7 white lobes. This flower opens nearly flat when in full bloom, in May.

Fruit: The fruit is small, ¾–1½ inches long, and red (or sometimes orange) in color. There are clusters of glochids on it when ripe. Smaller fruits have "bumpy" ridges (they are tuberculate), while the larger, fuller ones can be almost smooth-surfaced. The seeds are ⅛–³⁄₁₆ inches in diameter.

Range: Parts of Texas, Oklahoma, Arizona, New Mexico, and into Mexico.

Remarks: Like its larger cousin the Tree Cactus, Candle Cholla also grows fairly tall and treelike. Its stems and joints are much smaller and more straggly looking, however. The flowers are also smaller.

Thoughtless cactus collectors are eliminating many species of rare and beautiful cacti from their natural habitats as they illegally dig them up and take them away. This one should continue to flourish, for no one wants it in a cactus garden at all.

In parts of Mexico, Candle Chollas grow in dense thickets and are a real problem to maneuver through. Over the Western Plains, they are usually not found in thickets, just a solitary plant here and there.

Opuntia leptocaulis
Tasajillo, Rat-tail Cactus, Pencil Cactus, Desert Christmas Cactus, Slender-stem Cactus

Plant: A small shrublike upright plant that can grow up to 5 feet tall, Tasajillo is usually 2–3 feet in height with many branches. The slender cylindrical joints of each spring's new growth are 1–12 inches long, but only ⅛–¼ inch thick. The color of the new growth is a deep green. With age, the stems and trunk develop a scaly bark and turn a pale tan.

The areoles are rather oval or nearly diamond-shaped and contain short white wool.

There is usually only 1 long spine growing from each areole. Perpendicular to the surface of the plant, it grows up to 2 inches in length. Sometimes there are 1 or 2 other short spines with the long one.

There are only a few (1–3) small bunches of short yellowish glochids in the upper part of the areole.

Flower: The flowers are small, ½–⅞ inch wide and ¾–1 inch tall. They are greenish-yellow or greenish-white in color, opening up very wide, with many on a plant when in full bloom. The stamens are greenish-yellow, and the long style has up to 6 greenish-yellow stigma lobes. Bloom season is April and May.

Fruit: The small pear-shaped, bright scarlet fruit is only ⅜–1 inch long, but there are many to a plant. The outer skin is smooth, but there are many brown glochids in the areoles. Each fruit bears up to 12 seeds.

Range: From Mexico into Arizona, over into the northwest part of New Mexico and most of Texas and Oklahoma; especially prevalent in sandy soils.

Remarks: Tasajillo grows hidden in other bushes and tall grasses, making it difficult to see. It is not very attractive until it blooms. The little blossoms are neat and crisp-looking, almost pale green in color, and quite pretty.

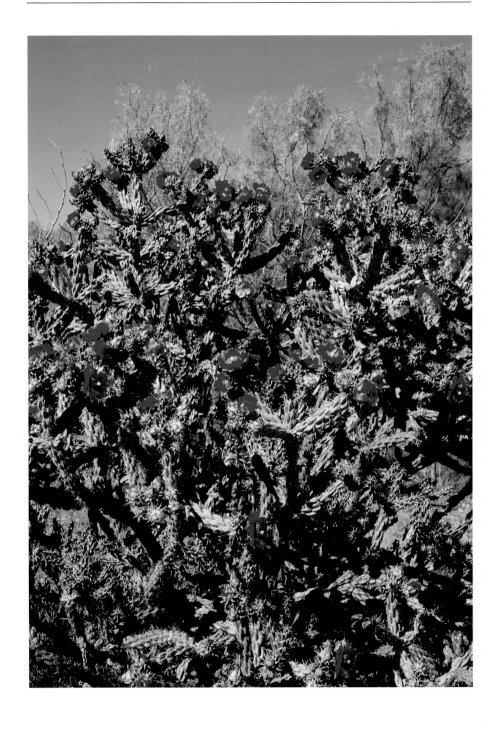

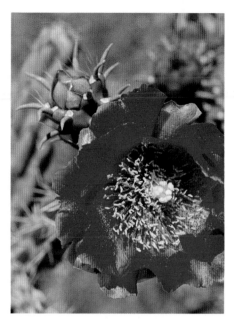

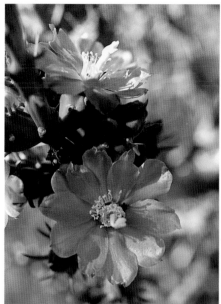

O. kleiniae flower

Opposite and above: *Opuntia imbricata* Tree Cactus
O. kleiniae Candle Cholla

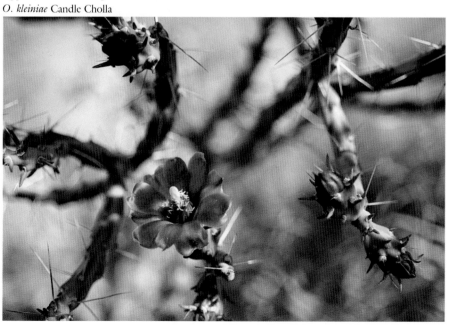

Another point in its favor is that during the bleakness of winter, the fruit stays on the plant and offers a wonderful red splash of color. It is especially nice, when snow blankets the pastures, to see that one bright note of color on a monochrome of white; hence its more romantic name, Desert Christmas Cactus.

Quail love to eat the little red berries. We have watched coveys of blue quail beneath this cactus bush jumping up and picking the fruit, eating it as fast as possible. An entire covey doing this looks like "jumping jacks."

Opuntia polyacantha
Hunger Cactus, Starvation Cactus, Teddy Bear Cactus

Plant: A small cactus whose pads lie prostrate on the ground, rarely growing over 6–8 inches high. Since each almost circular pad can root from its edge, the plant often sprawls out, rooting and growing to form dense mats close to the ground. The pads vary from 1½ to 5 inches long and from 1½ to 4 inches wide. They are pale green and rather thick for their size.

The areoles are small and elongate. When the pad is young, they are filled with fine white wool, which disappears later.

The number of spines in each areole varies greatly. A typical plant can have central spines (none or up to 5) and outer radiating spines ¼–1¼ inches long. They can be yellow, white, brownish, red-brown, or even variegated in color. Sometimes, on an older plant, the radial spines will increase in number and even grow longer (2–8 inches).

Glochids are few and short (1/16 inch) on young pads but become longer (3/16 inch) and more numerous on older pads.
Flower: Clear, bright yellow is the color of this blossom, which grows 2–3½ inches in diameter and up to 2½ inches tall. The petals have the waxy look of all cactus

flowers. There are 5–10 green stigma lobes standing erect in the center of each flower. The plant usually blooms in May and June.
Fruit: Varying in shape, the fruit can be spherical, egg-shaped, or oval, and up to 2 inches thick and long when ripe. The top is often slightly pitted, but not concave as in other cactus fruit. In fact, the top can be flat. Some slender spines appear on the upper third. The ripe fruits dry, and the skin becomes paper-thin as it covers the mass of seeds. The seeds vary in size from ⅛ to more than 3/16 inch.
Range: This may be one of the widest-ranging members of the Cactus Family, for it is found almost to the Arctic Circle. It grows into Canada, the northwestern United States, the Oklahoma panhandle, the Texas plains, Colorado, New Mexico, and Arizona.
Remarks: Because the pads of this cactus do not grow tall on top of each other, but spread on the ground by rooting from the edges, it is not a very conspicuous plant. Preferring sandy soil, it is often half covered by blowing sand and debris. Yet the dense mats it forms help prevent soil erosion. Grass often grows in the sand around the Hunger Cactus, rendering it almost invisible. The plant is easier to locate when in bloom. The blossoms are a true clear yellow with no hint of orange.

Opuntia sp., aff. O. phaeacantha
Prickly Pear, New Mexico Prickly Pear, Brown-spined Prickly Pear, Tulip Prickly Pear

Plant: This cactus has no trunk, just flat, broad, club-shaped pads that grow from the ground, either tall (2–3 feet) or lying low, with the edges of the pads on the ground. They can form large thickets 10–12 feet across. The pads are 4–9 inches long and 3–7 inches wide. Their surface is a bluish-green color, changing to yellow-green as they become older. The areoles on these pads are rather far apart (¾–2 inches) and can be about ¼ inch in diameter when mature.

One to 8 spines grow from each areole on the upper portion of each pad; the lower areoles bear fewer and smaller spines. These spines are ¾–3 inches long, spreading out in all directions. There are some smaller spines under the larger ones. Mostly yellow on the tips, the spines change toward their bases to darker brown, red, or black. Reddish-brown glochids are numerous on the edges of mature pads and grow to be sometimes ⅜ inch long.

Flower: Prickly Pear produces bright golden or sometimes yellowish-orange blossoms 2–3 inches in diameter. They have a colorful deeper orange center and 6–10 green stigma lobes sticking up. The stamens are creamy yellow. The petals have the typical waxy look of all cactus flowers. Blooms appear in May and early June.

Fruit: The fruits (or tunas) are perched on the edges of the pads where the flowers previously bloomed. They are oval with a concave umbilicus (the scar at the tip of the fruit after the flower has dropped off). This concave end makes the fruits look like miniature goblets. They are bright red, cherry red, or deep burgundy red and contain a juicy, fleshy pulp, with many dark seeds, when ripe. The surfaces of these fruits have clumps of minute glochids interspersed over them. Their length ranges from 1 to 3 inches.

Range: This fairly common cactus grows over nearly all of New Mexico, the western parts of Oklahoma, most of Texas, and in Utah and Colorado.

Remarks: Many wild animals utilize this cactus for either food or shelter. Wild turkey eat the seeds, quail and small animals use the sprawling thickets for shelter, and I hardly ever see a blossom that does not have beetles or honey bees frantically at work among the anthers getting pollen all over themselves. Cactus honey is quite flavorful.

Texas cattle have been saved in times of extreme drought when ranchers burned the spines off the pads with butane burners. Since that was all there was to eat, the cattle would follow the fellow with the "flame-thrower" and quickly devour the green Prickly Pear pads as soon as the spines were gone. Other closely related species of Prickly Pears have been utilized in this way also.

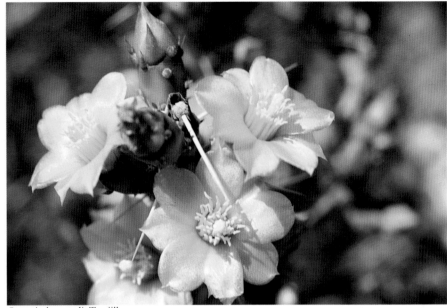

Opuntia leptocaulis Tasajillo

O. polyacantha Hunger Cactus

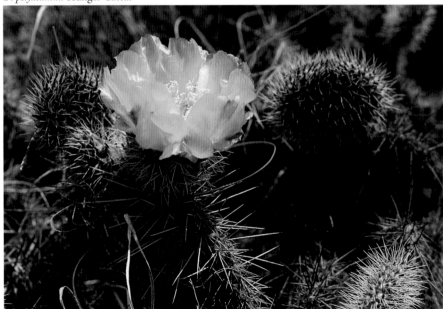

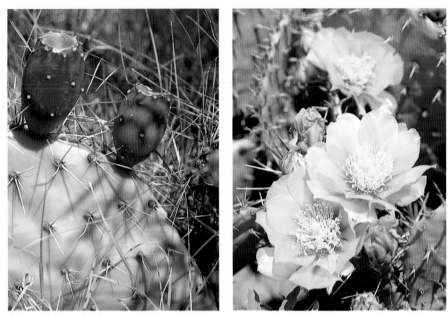

Above, right, and below: *Opuntia* sp., aff. *O. phaeacantha* Prickly Pear

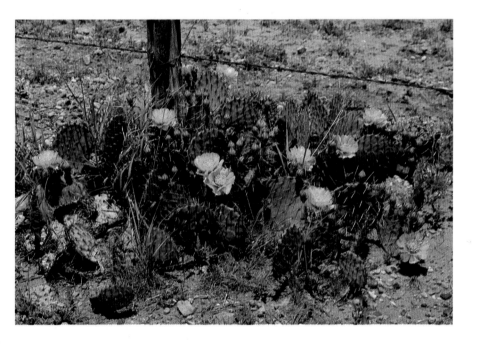

Opuntia tunicata var. *davisii*
Jumping Cholla, Jumping Cactus

Plant: This bush with many branches grows low (usually not exceeding 18 inches tall) but can reach 2 feet or more. It is a jointed cactus with new growth cylindrical in shape, 3–6 inches long. Each joint is narrower at its base than at its tip.

The areoles are less than ¼ inch in diameter with 6–13 spines in each one. Of these, 4–7 are large main spines sticking out in all directions. They are from ¾ inch up to 2 inches long and are thick and round. The largest spines are a brownish-red color, but each is covered by a light yellow sheath so that the spine color is not clearly evident. The sheaths are shiny and loose. There is a cluster of small yellow glochids on the top of the areole.

Flower: The flowers are difficult to see, for they do not open very wide, only about 1½ inches in diameter. The blossom is a deep green, the center is yellow, and the outer surfaces of the petals are reddish-brown. The filaments are greenish-red and the anthers are yellow. The short style has 4–7 big creamy-colored lobes. The plant blooms in June.

Fruit: Egg-shaped, 1–1½ inches long by ⅝–¾ inch wide, the fruit is very bumpy-looking and turns greenish-yellow when mature. Jumping Cholla reproduces largely by vegetative propagation from scattered joints.

Range: Eastern New Mexico to the mountains, southwestern Oklahoma, and most of Texas.

Remarks: If there is such a thing as a "platinum blonde" in the Cactus Family, it is this Jumping Cholla. The straw-colored sheaths that cover the largest spines all over the plant glisten in the sun and from a distance give it a "blond" look even though the surfaces of the stems and joints are green.

This is the greenest flower I have photographed. Since it does not open widely, it is difficult to detect the blossom in its prime. By aiming the camera at it straight-on, the waxy, stiff, green petals can be seen. What a treat from a plant so unbecoming at first glance.

Its common name, Jumping Cholla, comes from the ease with which the joints break. Cattle and other animals walking by get these tangled in their tails or stuck in the hair on their legs and transport them to distant places where they fall to the ground and start new plants.

Incidentally, the spines are difficult to extract. Since they come from different angles, pulling some out pushes others in.

CAMPANULACEAE
Bluebell or Lobelia Family

The Campanulaceae are a family of perennial, biennial, and annual herbs. The simple leaves are without stipules, attached alternately on the stem, and arranged spirally. The bluebells of this family have 5 petals that are joined, then spread out into a 5-lobed bell or funnel shape (usually blue or fading to white). There are 5 stamens and an inferior ovary (2–5-celled or rarely 1-celled).

Some botanists have placed the lobelias of this family in a subfamily, while others have created for them a family of their own, Lobeliaceae. They have done this because of the distinctive bilaterally symmetrical corolla of the lobelias. There are the 5 petals, but they form 2 lips. Two small lobes form an upper lip while 3 somewhat larger lobes form a lower lip. These bilaterally symmetrical flowers are not "bell-shaped" or "funnel-shaped" and are not always blue (the species discussed here is bright red).

Bell-shaped flower

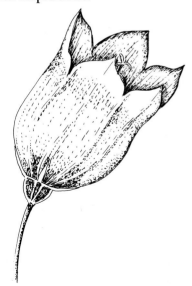

Lobelia cardinalis
Cardinal Flower

Plant: Perennial with usually an erect, single, unbranched stem growing 1–5 feet tall. The many leaves are thin, ovate to lanceolate in shape, irregularly toothed around their edges, 2–5 inches long, and ¼–1½ inches wide.

Flower: The brilliant scarlet-red flowers grow in terminal racemes (4–15 inches long) along the upper third of the plant. There are 5 sepals united at the base of each individual flower and 5 petals that are united forming a straight-tubed corolla about 1¼ inches long. The corolla is split at the tip, becoming 2-lipped, the upper lip notched into 2 small lobes and the lower lip having 3 slightly larger lobes. The 5 stamens are united and extend beyond the upper lip between the 2 lobes, which are split almost to the base of the corolla. The united anthers are a light gray color definitely contrasting with the vivid red corolla. This wildflower blooms in August–September.

Fruit: From an inferior ovary the fruit develops in a 2-celled, many-seeded capsule, ⅜ inch long. At maturity, the capsule splits open at the apex with each half curving down, dropping the seeds to the ground.

Range: This plant is infrequent on the Western Plains, growing in moist soils, stream edges, meadows close to water, roadsides, and boggy places with partial sunlight. It can be found from Canada through Michigan, Wisconsin, and Minnesota, west through Oklahoma, most of Texas, parts of Nevada, California, and into Mexico.

Remarks: Cardinal Flower has been placed on the "Watch List" for those species of plants whose populations have been significantly reduced during the past 100 years. It has been overgrazed by livestock, thus reducing its ability to reproduce itself. Also the moist soils and close proximity to water that it prefers are few and far between on the Western Plains. Please do not collect!

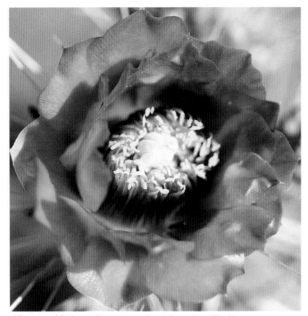

Above and below: *Opuntia tunicata* Jumping Cholla

Opposite: *Lobelia cardinalis* Cardinal Flower

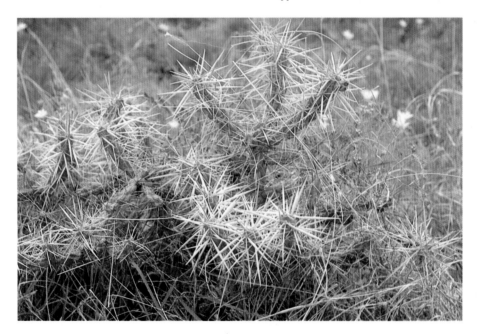

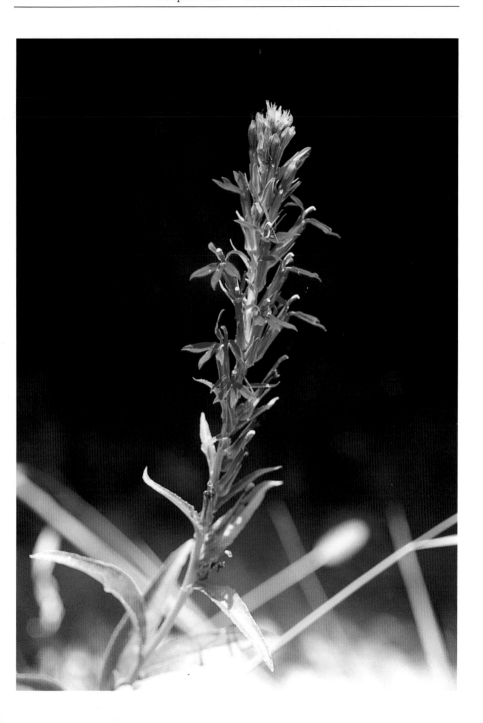

CAPPARIDACEAE
Caper or Spiderflower Family

Members of the Caper Family can be herbs, shrubs, or trees. They resemble mustard plants and usually have a strong odor. The leaves alternate on the stem and can be undivided or divided into 3–7 segments. Flowers grow singly or in many-flowered racemes at the top of the stem. They have 4 petals, 4 sepals, and 6–27 stamens that are exserted, which is to say they extend out longer than the petals, giving them a "hairy" or "spidery" look.

Polanisia dodecandra
Clammyweed

Plant: An upright annual that grows to 2 feet in height, Clammyweed has leaves that are divided into 3 segments, ½–1½ inches long. The stems and leaves have gland-tipped hairs that are sticky or clammy to the touch.

Flower: The flowers are in clusters at the tips of the stems. Four white petals grow upward and are notched to look almost torn at the tip. They can be ½–1 inch long. There are many dark pink or purple stamens (up to 28) that grow much longer than the petals (up to 2 inches long). They grow unequally in length, maturing at different times and giving the flower head a "hairy" or "spidery" appearance. Clammyweed blooms in August and September.

Fruit: Clammyweed develops erect fruit pods that are 2–3 inches long and glandular. The broad seeds are about ⅟₁₆ inch wide, dull brown in color, and wrinkled. The 2-valved capsule allows the seeds to fall free at maturity.

Range: Found throughout Texas, New Mexico, Arizona, and northward to Iowa.

Remarks: Although pretty, this is one of our more rank-smelling wildflowers, which also leaves a sticky residue on the hands (hence the common name, Clammyweed). Found in various soils, it prefers open waste places, fields, and roadsides. The capers we buy in the grocery store are flower buds from a distant cousin, which grows in the Mediterranean area.

CHENOPODIACEAE
Goosefoot Family

The Goosefoot Family consists of mostly weedy plants with inconspicuous, non-descript green flowers. The flowers have 4 or 5 sepals with the same number of stamens. There are, however, no petals. The pistil has 2 styles, or stigmas, and develops 1 seed.

Beets and spinach, which are such good table fare, are related to the Tumbleweed, all being in this family.

Salsola kali
Tumbleweed, Russian Thistle, Russian Cactus

Plant: Annual herb with many branches growing from the base. As it grows, it becomes a large hemisphere-shaped plant sometimes 3–4 feet tall. The bluish-green stems become hard and prickly as they mature. The leaves, which are borne singly, are very linear in shape, and each is tipped with a needle-sharp spine.
Flower: Inconspicuous greenish-white flowers grow in the axils. The almost microscopic flower has a 5-parted perianth, 5 stamens, short anthers, and 2 or 3 stigmas. It blooms in the summer (usually July, sometimes earlier) but goes unnoticed because the flowers are so nearly invisible.
Fruit: In the fall, from about October until frost, some Tumbleweed plants produce very colorful seedpods. In the axils, where the flowers were, stiff pink flower-shaped seedpods have developed. The fruiting calyx, $1/8 – 3/8$ inch wide, resembles 5 pink petals or papery wings with rose-colored veins. Of course they are not petals, but an unusual receptacle that holds the small, black seed (about $1/32$ inch in diameter).
Range: The Tumbleweed has spread across this country depositing its seeds over wastelands and cultivated places alike. It is common along roadsides and fencerows. Typi-cally a plant that grows well by the seashore, this one has spread from the prairie states through western North America, especially in areas with disturbed alkaline or saline soils.
Remarks: Tumbleweeds get their name from the fact that in the late fall the entire globe-shaped plant breaks off at the ground and, driven by the winds, tumbles and rolls across open prairies, cultivated fields, highways, and small-town streets and yards. Thousands of seeds are deposited and will grow nearly anywhere, being very drought resistant, much to human dismay. Farmers on the Western Plains continually fight it in and around their fields.

It is known that Tumbleweed, or Russian Thistle, seeds came to this country from Russia in 1873 or 1874. They came, by accident, to South Dakota in a shipment of flax seed.

The Native Americans called it the "White Man's Plant," recognizing that it was not native to their land and seemed to grow wherever the whites went.

The pretty pink, papery, flower-looking seedpods can be used in fall dried arrangements. Care should be taken and gloves worn when cutting and gathering the stems, with their rough spine-tipped leaves. The pink color will remain for months.

Recent taxonomic revisions have been made concerning the Latin name of this plant. The authorities, however, do not agree on which one to use. It is possible that 2 new names for this Tumbleweed, *S. iberica* and *S. australis*, may be found in future references.
Recipe: Young, fast-growing shoots about 5 inches tall that have not yet developed spines make a very good potherb. Snip them at the ground, wash them, and boil about 15 minutes. There is no need to change the water. Serve with salt, pepper, and butter as you would spinach, or add vinegar or lemon juice for a more zesty taste, since this plant is rather bland naturally. Try it and enjoy it as my family has.

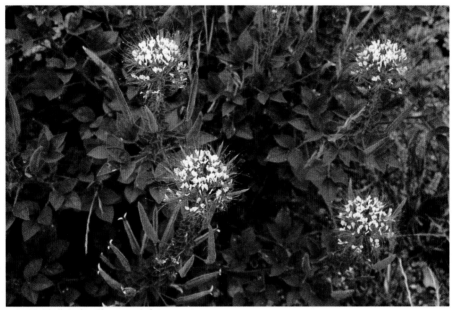

Polanisia dodecandra Clammyweed

Opposite: *Salsola kali* Tumbleweed; seedpods below

P. dodecandra close-up

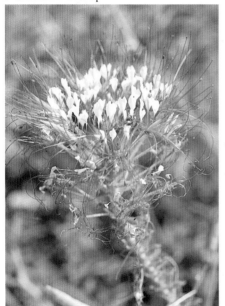

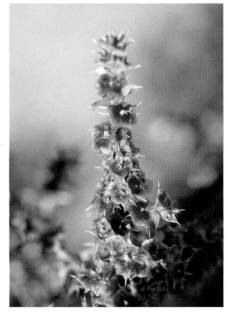

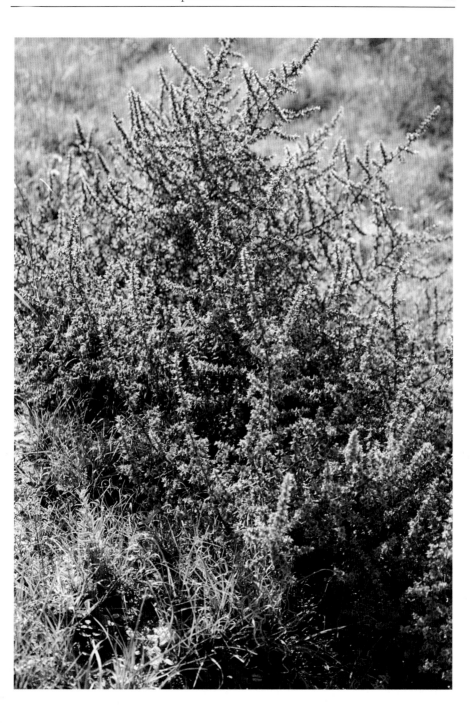

COMMELINACEAE
Spiderwort Family

The Spiderwort Family includes flowers with petals arranged in a radially symmetrical pattern as well as flowers with bilateral symmetry. The roots are thick and tuberous, the leaves are succulent, or fleshy, and sheathing the stem. The plants are perennial or annual with 3 sepals, 3 petals, and 6 or 3 or fewer stamens that are joined with the style. The flowers emerge from 1 or 2 "boat-shaped" bracts that surround them and resemble small leaves. The ovary is usually 3-celled.

Commelina erecta
Dayflower, Erect Dayflower, Widow's Tears

Plant: Perennial with several soft, fleshy, jointed stems that grow from a cluster of thick, tuberous roots, by means of which the plant overwinters. The stems grow upward only if supported by other plants; usually they lie on the ground and can grow to 3 feet long. They are brittle and break off easily. The leaves alternate up the stem, sheathing it at their bases. They are 3–6 inches long and about ⅜ inch wide, linear to lanceolate in shape.
Flower: Two rounded upper petals are bright sky-blue; a third, lower petal is much smaller, inconspicuous and whitish, making the flower bilaterally symmetrical in shape. The flower emerges from an enveloping "boat-shaped" bract that looks like small clasping leaves. The flowers are no more than 1 inch across. There are 3 pollen-bearing stamens and 3 sterile stamens with curious butterfly-shaped crosses on their tips. The flowers only bloom for a day, but there are several buds on a plant that open 3 to 4 days apart. Dayflower blooms from June into early September.

Fruit: A 3-celled capsule with 1–3 seeds per fruit.
Range: This fragile flower prefers sandy soils, shaded areas, moist banks, and roadsides. It grows across most of Oklahoma, from Maine to Florida, Minnesota to Tennessee, Louisiana, and west through Texas, New Mexico, Arizona, and up to Colorado.
Remarks: The genus *Commelina* was named for the three Commelijn brothers who lived in Holland. Two were renowned botanists (represented by the 2 larger upper petals), while a third did nothing (represented by the third hardly noticeable petal).

The common name Dayflower comes from the fact that the flower opens at daylight but is gone by noon on a bright sunny day. It recedes into the spathe, or sheathing bract, from which it emerged, turning into a juicy mass, or "mess." The flower lasts a little longer on cloudy days or in a shady setting.

Tradescantia occidentalis
Purple Spiderwort, Spiderwort, Western Spiderwort

Plant: A perennial with erect stems to 2 feet tall, Purple Spiderwort has alternate leaves with long narrow blades. The leaf blade looks as if it has been folded lengthwise, for there is a crease down the middle. The lower leaves can be up to 20 inches long. The shorter upper 2 leaves enclose the flower clusters like bracts.
Flower: At the top of the stems, the flowers grow in many-flowered clusters. Their color is usually bluish-purple but can be rose-violet, pink, or white. There are 3 small sepals, 3 blue-purple petals (up to ¾ inch long and equal in size), and 6 prominent stamens, tipped with yellow anthers. On the Western Plains, this plant blooms from May into July.
Fruit: A 3-celled capsule that bears 12–15 seeds.

Range: Prefers sandy or fine soils and grows quite well on hills, prairies, and plains from North Dakota to Texas, west to Montana, and Arizona.

Remarks: Purple Spiderwort is the most widely dispersed western (occidental) species of this family. It is characterized by the 3 similar blue-purple petals that last for only a day. However, it produces an abundance; so there are many to enjoy during the blooming season. It resembles the Dayflower (*Commelina erecta*) but has 3 equal-sized petals (radially symmetrical), where Dayflower has 2 large petals and 1 small one (bilaterally symmetrical). The Purple Spiderwort also forms large clumps and produces showier blossoms than its cousin, the Dayflower.

This genus was named for the seventeenth-century English botanist John Tradescant, royal gardener to King Charles I and Queen Henrietta Maria.

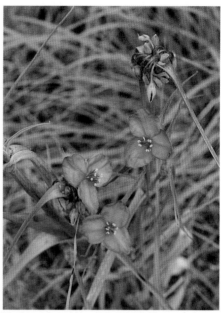

Tradescantia occidentalis Purple Spiderwort

Commelina erecta Dayflower

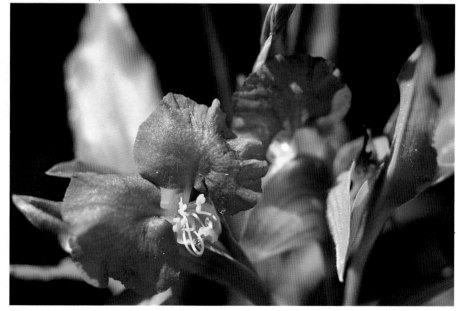

COMPOSITAE (Asteraceae)
Daisy, Sunflower, or Aster Family

The Compositae are the second largest plant family in the world, ranking only behind Orchidaceae in total numbers of species. In climates other than tropical, there are more species of Compositae than any other; it is definitely the largest family on the Western Plains. Of these species, many are old familiar favorites such as daisies, asters, and zinnias. Other well-known members are sunflowers, gaillardias, goldenrods, and coreopsis. Some less-loved ones are dandelions and cockleburs. Most are herbs and shrubs, but worldwide there are a few trees and climbing vines. The leaves are alternate or opposite. They can be simple to various-lobed, divided or compound, often in basal rosettes, or even needlelike in structure. In other words, the leaves are not useful in recognizing this family. What is common throughout this large and diverse family is the presence of an inferior ovary, 5 stamens fused at the anthers, and 5 fused petals.

It is an interesting family, deriving its name, Compositae (meaning "composite"), from the fact that each large flower head is not just one flower but many very small flowers grouped closely together to form a compact inflorescence. These tiny florets generally consist of two kinds, called "disk" (inner) and "ray" (periphery) flowers.

Consider a typical gaillardia, daisy, or sunflower with its dark center and colorful "petals." The dark center consists of many, often minute, disk flowers, each having a corolla of joined petals that form a radially symmetrical tube normally tipped with 5 teeth. An inferior ovary is down inside each one. They are called "disk" flowers

Parts of a Composite Flower

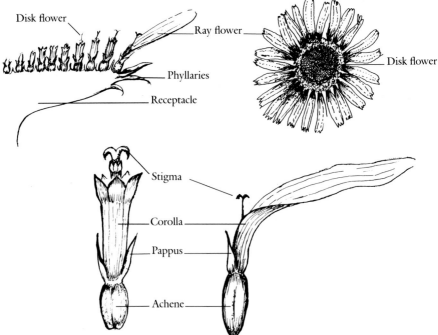

because they are grouped together tightly on the conical, hemispheric, or flattened disk or central part of the flower.

The colorful "petals" are not single petals at all, but small ray flowers, bilaterally symmetrical, with a short tube of 5 joined petals. However, on one side, 3 of these joined petals expand to become the "ray." These little ray flowers are arranged around the outer perimeter of the flower head (like the sun's rays) and have the appearance of petals. Like a disk flower, each ray flower has an inferior ovary.

Of the numerous species, many, such as Gayfeather, have flower heads that lack ray flowers, having only the radially symmetrical disk flowers described above. Others, such as Desert Holly, grow only a mass of modified disk flowers, which are bilaterally symmetrical. Still others, such as Dandelion, Wild Lettuce, and Sow Thistle, lack disk flowers and consist only of ray flowers. These, however, have all 5 petals of each flower involved in the elongated "ray," thus showing 5 tiny points each.

What is usually called the calyx in other families, has evolved to be represented by a pappus in the Compositae. The pappus can be in the form of bristles, stout awns, or even scales (or can be absent) and is found at the base of the corolla. The pappus is easily seen in dandelions and thistles. There are sepal-like bracts that enclose the entire composite head when all its flowers are small buds. These "phyllaries" or "involucral bracts" can usually be found by looking under the head as you would look for sepals under a single flower.

Achillea millefolium
Yarrow, Common Yarrow, Milfoil, Western Yarrow

Plant: Perennial herb that produces 1 to many stems 8–40 inches tall from a creeping root. The straight stems branch near the top. The compound leaves are delicate and fernlike, alternate, twice and sometimes thrice pinnatifid (cleft and those segments then cleft again), and softly hairy, up to 12 inches long on the lower portion of the plant and up to 5 inches long toward the top.

Flower: Numerous flowers are clustered at the top of the plant at the tips of the branches on rounded corymbs. There are 10–20 flowers in a cluster. Each small flower (less than ½ inch wide) has 2–12 white ray flowers and 5–15 white or yellow disk flowers that are 5-toothed and bottle-shaped. Yarrow blooms in the spring through the summer.

Fruit: Flattened, oblong achene without a pappus.

Range: Found growing along roadsides and in pastures over the Western Plains.

Remarks: When this aromatic plant is crushed or broken, it emits a strong but pleasantly spicy odor. It is a native of Europe brought to this country for use as a medicinal herb, since it was believed to cure many ailments. Today it is not popular as a medicine but is used ceremonially by Native Americans. It is lovely by the side of the highways in the spring and summer and often mistaken for Queen Anne's Lace, which is a member of the Umbelliferae.

Acourtia nana (= *Perezia nana*)
Desert Holly, Dwarf Desert Holly

Plant: A perennial herb that grows in patches of several to many plants by means of rhizomes, Desert Holly is a low, leafy-stemmed plant that rarely exceeds 8 inches in height (usually 3–6 inches). The leaves are nearly round, very stiff, and tipped on their edges with spines, similar to holly leaves. They grow to about 2 inches long and wide. These almost circular leaves are, in their early growth, gray-green in color but soon become dry-looking and leatherlike.

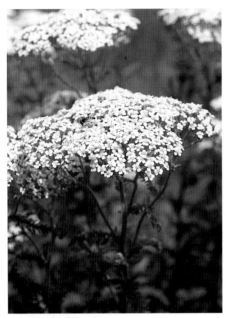

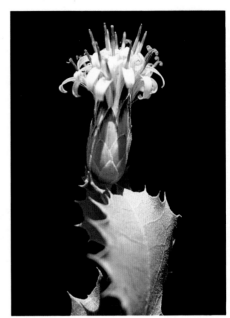

Achillea millefolium Yarrow

Acourtia nana Desert Holly

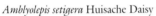

Amblyolepis setigera Huisache Daisy

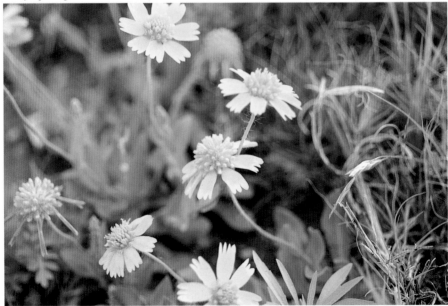

Flower: A single pink flower head terminates each branch and is approximately ¾ inch tall and ½–1 inch across. Many pale pink disk flowers (up to 24) constitute this head, each having a 2-lipped corolla, the outer lip 3-toothed and the inner one 2-lobed. Ray flowers are absent. The subtending bracts, at the base of the flower head, are hairy on their edges. Desert Holly blooms in May and early June.

Fruit: Cylindrical achene crowned with many hairy bristles that greatly resembles a dandelion "puffball."

Range: This plant seems to prefer dry plains, clay-loam soils of canyon breaks throughout Arizona, parts of northern Mexico, New Mexico (except the northern part), and the Western Plains of Texas.

Remarks: Desert Holly is a difficult plant to find in flower. It is small and not very noticeable until it has matured, dried up, and "gone to seed." Even then one has to search for it, usually finding it under shrubs, in tall grass, or hiding in the shade. The flowers are a delicate pale pink, sometimes appearing almost white, and very interesting with their 2-lipped corollas, the bottom lip cleft into 3 lobes and the top lip divided into 2 lobes. They have a faint scent of violets. The leaves definitely have the look and feel of prickly holly leaves; hence its well-deserved common name.

In older references, it can be found listed as *Perezia nana.*

Amblyolepis setigera
Huisache Daisy

Plant: An annual with a slender taproot, Huisache Daisy is a cool-season plant growing from a winter rosette, becoming sparingly branched and reaching a height of 4–18 inches. There are long, cottony hairs on the stems and leaf edges. The leaves are alternate, untoothed, without stalks, and blue-green in color. The lower leaves are ¾–3¼ inches long, oblong to lance-shaped, narrowing at the basal end. The leaves at midstem are more oval, more clasping, and less than 3 inches in length. From these leaves to the top of the plant, the stems are bare, tipped with a solitary flower head.

Flower: The flower heads, on the tips of the naked stems, are hemispheric in shape, ¼–½ inch high in the center and 1½ inches across. The phyllaries are in two rows, the 8 outer ones being long, pointed, and green, the inner ones shorter and inconspicuous, resembling pappus scales. There are 8–10 fertile, pistillate yellow ray flowers, ½–¾ inch long, and 3 or 4-lobed on the tips. The disk flowers are numerous, perfect (having both pistils and stamens), fertile, and yellow. The disk corollas are equally 5-toothed. This plant blooms from late March to May.

Fruit: The fruit is an achene, obconic (upside-down cone-shaped), with the point of attachment at the small end. It is ¼ inch long, has 10 ribs, and is covered with silky-brown hairs. The pappus is 5 thin, dry scales, ⅛–³⁄₁₆ inch long.

Range: Huisache Daisy is a fairly common plant in the southern areas of the Western Plains and down into Mexico. It prefers sandy or gravelly soils and is at home in vacant lots, roadside ditches, and open pastures and prairies.

Remarks: This is another lovely, golden yellow, spring-blooming, sweet-smelling wildflower. It is grazed by livestock and may not be easy to locate in open pastures.

There is only one species of *Amblyolepis.* This genus is included in *Helenium* by some authors.

Amphiachyris dracunculoides
(= *Xanthocephalum dracunculoides*)
Broomweed, Snakeweed

Plant: Bushy annual growing on 1 straight stem branching out at the top and bearing many small flowers singly at the tips of the branches. With plenty of water, plants can grow to 3 feet tall, the bushy tops being sometimes spherical in silhouette. The leaves are narrow, almost threadlike, and lance-shaped (that is, longer than broad and tapering to the tip).

Flower: The yellow flowers consist of 10–12 green bracts on the outer surface of each head, 10 or more disk flowers that have both stamens and pistils but are not fertile, and 8 or more short ray flowers (½ inch long) that are fertile. The pappus, instead of being bristlelike, is joined at the base to form a tube. Broomweed blooms from August to October and sometimes into November.

Fruit: The seed is an inverse pyramid shape, which means the point of attachment to the ovary is on the small end rather than the large end. It is very tiny and covered with stiff white hairs.

Range: From Alabama to eastern New Mexico and northern Mexico, over most of Texas, spreading into Oklahoma, Kansas, and Missouri.

Remarks: There are perhaps 30 species of this genus in America. Usually the annual species is called Broomweed and the perennial shrubby one is called Snakeweed. The ranchers, my husband included, call it several unprintable names, for they cannot find one good use for this plant. It is very prolific, taking over pastures and robbing the grass of precious water. Cattle will not eat Broomweed—nor will goats!

But there are some ways to use and appreciate this otherwise objectionable weed. Since the little yellow flowers are pretty, when they are in full bloom, cut the tall, thickest-blooming ones and fill pots and baskets with them. They dry, retaining some yellow color, and last until they are replaced. Or you can gather the dried plants during the late fall and early winter, cut them apart in small bunches, and spray-paint the dried bunches bright colors to match holiday ribbons on gift packages. A caution to the reader who uses them in dried arrangements: be aware that when Broomweed becomes very dry, it is extremely flammable.

The common name Broomweed comes from the fact that early settlers gathered this plant, tied it in tight bundles around a stick, and used it as a broom.

The name *Xanthocephalum dracunculoides* is considered a synonym in the most recent taxonomic revisions. In older references, it can also be found listed as *Gutierrezia dracunculoides*.

Aphanostephus riddellii
Lazy Daisy, Doze Daisy

Plant: Clump-forming perennial 4–20 inches tall with a rather woody base. If it branches at all, it is in the upper half and only sparingly. The stems and leaves are covered with soft gray hairs. The alternate leaves are simple; the lower leaves are deeply cleft or toothed and ½–2½ inches long, while the upper ones are smooth-edged, more linear in shape, and smaller, ¼–1¼ inches long.

Flower: The flower heads are numerous with long, naked stalks. Each flower is ¾–1½ inches across. There are 40–65 narrow white ray flowers that are fertile, pink or reddish on the underside, and ½ inch long. The center has numerous (200 or more) tiny, fertile disk flowers with yellow corollas. The pappus is alike in the ray and disk flowers, being a rather hairy crown around the achene. Lazy Daisy blooms April through June.

Fruit: Both ray and disk flowers produce achenes that are columnar, grooved, $\frac{1}{32}$ inch long, and have several teeth on the top.

Range: This plant grows from central Texas west through the panhandle and into New Mexico, then south into Mexico. It likes sandy grasslands, prairies, open fields, and pastures.

Remarks: Both the common names, Doze Daisy and Lazy Daisy, are derived from the plant's slowness to open in the mornings. It "sleeps late" and stays tightly closed and drooping until almost noon. When one finds the flower in this stage, the pink or reddish undersides of the ray flowers are very noticeable. As it slowly opens, the flower head becomes erect to display a crisp, pure white "face" to the spring sun.

Aster ericoides
Wreath Aster, White Heath Aster, Frost Aster

Plant: The stems of this perennial are usually much-branched, either erect or sometimes falling over and reclining on the ground. They are covered with minute hairs. The plant grows from rhizomes underground and reaches a height of 1–3 feet. The slender leaves are oblong and rather stiff (½–1¼ inches long and only ¹⁄₁₂–¼ inch wide). There are many crowded smaller leaves at the base of the longer leaves.

Flower: There are numerous flower heads on the upper portion of the stalks. The bracts, if viewed through a 10-power loupe, will reveal green tips with a tiny spine on the end of each. There are 15–18 (or more) white ray flowers about ⅜ inch long. The central disk flowers are tubular, 5-lobed, and brownish-red in color. Bristlelike pappus surrounds each disk flower. This is a fall plant that blooms September–November, or until frost.

Fruit: A small, dry, 1-seeded hard fruit is produced by each disk flower. It is flattened and has 1 or more ribs on the surface.

Range: Growing in open grasslands, roadsides, and dry lands, this attractive plant can be found throughout the northern states, down into Georgia, most of Texas, and parts of New Mexico, Arizona, and Mexico.

Remarks: Wild asters are abundant and may confuse the amateur botanist because they are so numerous and resemble each other in many ways. On the Western Plains, there are only about 6 different ones; half of them bloom in the summer, the other half in the fall.

This fall bloomer can literally cover the pasture with a fluffy carpet of white if given the benefit of late summer and early fall moisture.

Aster subulatus var. *ligulatus*
Blackweed, Annual Aster, Slim Aster

Plant: Annual with a smooth branching stem, growing up to 3½ feet tall. The narrow, lance-shaped leaves have no teeth. They grow ¾–3 inches long, those of the top branches being very small. As the plant branches, these often grow in a zigzag fashion. The stems and foliage are dark green early in the plant's growth, but change to a dark purple as it ages.

Flower: Many small flower heads grow singly at the tips of the numerous branches, measuring only ½ inch or less across. Plants with up to 100 flower heads have been noted. The many ray flowers (¼–⅓ inch long) are white, sometimes varying to a very pale lavender. The more than 20 yellow disk flowers are crowded together in the center. Blackweed blooms summer to fall.

Fruit: Slightly hairy, single-seeded.

Range: A most abundant wildflower, Blackweed grows in poorly drained ditches and around the edges of ponds, lakes, streams, and wastelands. It is found in parts of South Carolina, Kansas, Missouri, Louisiana, Texas, New Mexico, Arizona, California, and Mexico; widespread from Oklahoma to Alabama.

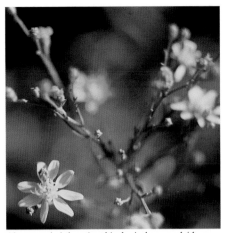

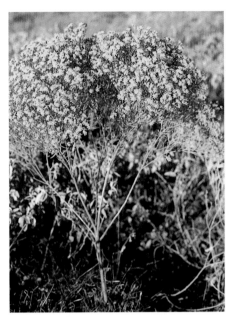

Above and right: *Amphiachyris dracunculoides*
Broomweed

Aphanostephus riddellii Lazy Daisy

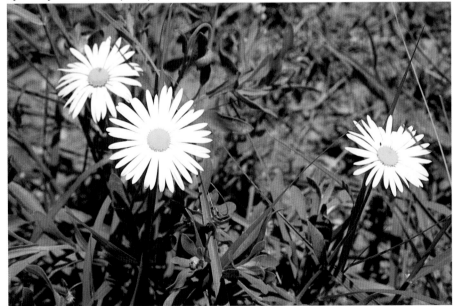

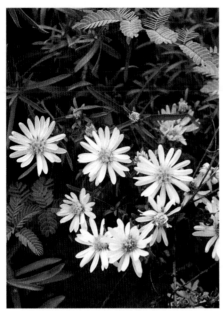

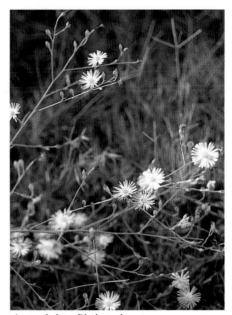

Above and below: *Aster ericoides* Wreath Aster   *Aster subulatus* Blackweed

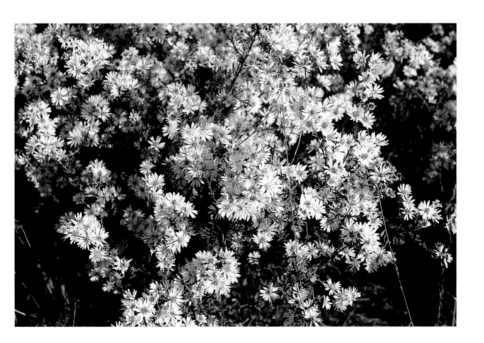

Remarks: Asters are found in nearly all parts of the world except Australia. This annual is the most common one of our native species, forming huge colonies in wet muddy ditches and around the playa lakes of the Western Plains. Viewed from a distance, large colonies of Blackweed in bloom are a dark green with spots of white everywhere, which are the many flower heads. As they reach their peak and begin to decline, the foliage turns dark purple, hence the common name Blackweed.

Berlandiera lyrata
Chocolate Daisy, Green Eyes, Green-eyed Lyre Leaf, Berlandiera

Plant: Perennial plant with a fleshy taproot. The stems are branched and usually erect. The leaves are arranged alternately on the stem, as well as in a basal rosette; they are simple (not divided into segments), with toothed or lobed edges, and velvety-hairy to the touch.
Flower: The plant is multiflowered, quite showy, and each flower head can be up to ¾ inch across. There are usually 8 yellow ray flowers marked with maroon veins on their under surfaces. The many disk flowers in the center are usually a dark red or maroon. The yellow blooms can be found from April to October.
Fruit: Only the ray flowers produce fertile seeds (called achenes), which are small, elongate, and quick-maturing.
Range: Dry rocky soils on the dry plains, mesas, and roadsides from central Texas to Oklahoma, Kansas, Colorado, New Mexico, and Arizona.
Remarks: A large area covered with this plant in bloom smells wonderfully of chocolate. If in doubt, take a whiff of one, up close, to experience a definite chocolate odor—the reason for one of the common names, Chocolate Daisy.

Sometimes the wildflower enthusiast thinks he or she has found an unusual green flower. It is this same daisy, for when the yellow ray flowers ("petals") fall off, after maturing, the very stiff green bracts can be seen. They look like green petals around a green center, hence another common name, Green Eyes. At this stage, the flower has been successfully used in flower arrangements.

It is reported that the Native Americans used the flower heads as a seasoning in their foods.

Carduus nutans
Nodding Thistle, Musk Thistle

Plant: A stout biennial from 16 inches to 6 feet tall, the plant usually consists of a single stem that branches only toward the top. The alternate leaves are pinnately cleft into narrow lobes with serrated, spine-tipped margins. They grow 8–10 inches long and 1–2 inches wide. On the stem are "wings," prickly projections that become part of the leaf edges.
Flower: The large flower heads, up to 2½ inches across, grow solitary at the ends of naked stems. The thick, heavy pinkish-purple flower heads droop over and hang down at the tips of the stems, giving them a bell-like appearance. The phyllaries, beneath the flower head, are wide and spine-tipped, with the outer and middle ones curving down. They are a darker rose-purple in color. There are no ray flowers but many fertile disk flowers, with stamens and pistils and 5-lobed corollas. Nodding Thistle blooms from May to July.
Fruit: An achene is attached basally to the receptacle. There are pappus bristles, but they are not feathery (bearing very fine hairs on each side). The plant is said to be "plumeless" because it lacks these feathery plumes on the pappus bristles.
Range: Nodding Thistle grows well along the roadsides, railroad rights-of-way, hillsides, pastures, and disturbed areas of the Western Plains, thriving in the panhandle

of Texas especially. It has spread to the Western Plains from the northern and eastern parts of the United States.

Remarks: A plant this large and commanding of attention can be called "handsome." The flower heads are a wonderful color of pinkish-purple made even prettier by the bracts, or phyllaries, with their dramatic color and tendency to curve downward. Each fat, rounded head droops slightly beneath the bracts, illustrating one of the common names, Nodding Thistle.

Centaurea americana
Star Thistle, Basket Flower, Thornless Thistle

Plant: An erect annual 1½–4 feet tall on stout, rigid stems, branching a few times near the top. The leaves are attached directly by the base (having no petioles) and are not incised or toothed. They lack the customary spines of common thistle leaves. The leaf blades are oblong or lance-shaped, ¾–2¼ inches long.

Flower: The heads are solitary at the tips of the branches and are 1½–3¼ inches across. A flower head of this plant is composed entirely of disk flowers; there are no ray flowers. The corollas of the disk flowers in the center are a creamy-white; those around the outer edges are pinkish-purple to pink, elongated, and larger than the central ones. The bracts (phyllaries) beneath the colorful disk flowers are feathery looking around their edges. They overlap each other and have a "basket" look. In the fall, they turn straw-colored as they dry. The blooming period is from June to July.

Fruit: A hairy, grayish-brown achene about ¼ inch long.

Range: This plant grows well throughout Texas, except extreme East Texas, also in Louisiana and Oklahoma, from Missouri to Arizona, and Mexico. It seems to prefer undisturbed pasture and areas where rainwater collects, as opposed to hillsides and higher places where rainwater is less likely to be retained.

Remarks: Star Thistle, or Basket Flower, is very showy and lovely with its delicate two-colored flower and basket-woven look. It grows in large stands and is spectacular in full bloom. In the fall, after the colorful flowers have dropped, the plant dries and turns a yellowish tan. The basket-woven look is more apparent, and the stiff pappus bristles give the flower head a "dried flower" appearance. These "dried flowers" are wonderful in winter arrangements and will hold their shape for several years.

Centaurea pollinates in a most unusual way. Since the stamens are even more sensitive to the touch than those of other members of the Daisy Family, when roving, probing insects make contact with them, they contract instantly, pushing pollen out over the insect to be carried to the next blossom.

This wildflower is being cultivated currently for use in native-plant landscaping.

Chrysactinia mexicana
Damianita

Plant: A small, bushy taprooted shrub, rounded in silhouette, 4–12 inches tall. It is very leafy all over except for leafless peduncles, 1–3 inches long, that extend from the tips of the branches, each bearing a solitary flower. The first pair of leaves are opposite at the branchlets; leaves are alternate over the remainder of the stems. Leaves are pinnately parted into 5–7 or more thread-like segments. The leaves, slightly less than ½ inch long, and stems are dotted with microscopic orange-colored oil glands.

Flower: The yellow flowers are borne singly on the tips of the long, naked peduncles. There are many on a plant. The flowering structure (involucre) is hemispheric in shape. Beneath it the 12 phyllaries are pointed on their tips and also dotted with a pair of orange oil glands

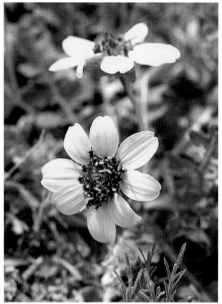

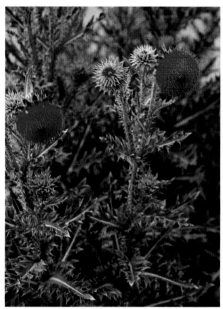

Berlandiera lyrata Chocolate Daisy

Carduus nutans Nodding Thistle

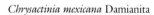

Chrysactinia mexicana Damianita

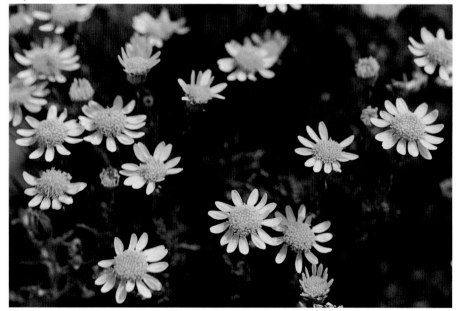

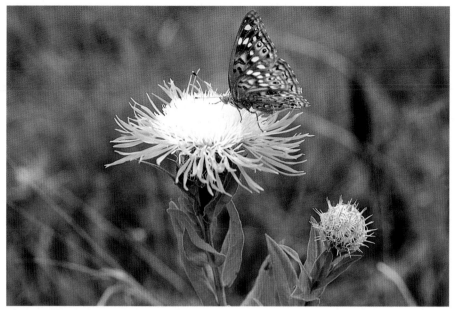

Above and below: *Centaurea americana* Star Thistle

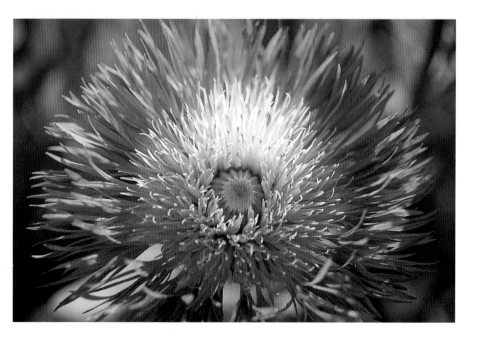

each. Up to 12 yellow, fertile, pistillate ray flowers are narrow and sometimes slightly 3-toothed on the tips. There are 20–25 yellow disk flowers, with stamens and pistils, fertile, with 5-toothed corollas. Damianita blooms from late April into September.

Fruit: Many achenes are crowded together in the center of the flower head. They are narrow, column-shaped, grayish-black, ⅛–³⁄₁₆ inch long. The pappus of unequal bristles dries to a whitish-gray color and remains attached to the tip.

Range: This plant is more common in the arid regions of the southwestern regions of the United States and Mexico than in the Western Plains. It grows in western Texas, eastern New Mexico, and into Mexico.

Remarks: The orange oil glands dotted over this plant are easy to see with a hand loupe. When crushed, any portion of the plant emits a strong, almost piney scent from these glands. When in full bloom, the dark green bouquetlike plant is delicate and showy with its bright yellow flowers extending out from the foliage on leafless stalks. If one's children pick these little flowers in their spring and summer bouquets, their odor is not soon forgotten.

Cichorium intybus
Chicory, Blue Sailors, Succory, Ragged Sailors

Plant: From a large taproot running deeply underground, this perennial wildflower grows 1–4 feet tall. The stems are tall, stiff, and rough, branching only near the top. The dark green leaves are alternate with the basal ones sometimes pinnately divided and 3–6 inches long (resembling dandelion leaves). Those farther up the stem have somewhat serrated edges; toward the top, the leaves become mere vestiges, appearing bractlike and clasping the stem. The plant contains a milky sap.

Flower: The flower heads, 1–1½ inches across, grow from the nodes and on the tips of the stems, bearing beautiful bright blue flowers. (Rarely a white- or pink-flowered plant appears.) There are 12–20 petallike ray flowers, strap-shaped, square-tipped, and 5-toothed on the tips. They bloom from May into September.

Fruit: An achene, somewhat marked with lines or furrows, hairless, unribbed, with a pappus of tiny scales.

Range: Found along roadsides, old fields, and neglected places here and there throughout the United States, Chicory is a European native now common in this country.

Remarks: Clear blue flowers are rare; most tend to be more purple than true blue. These are the color of bright cloudless skies on a hot summer day. This is definitely one of those wildflowers that does "shout its presence from afar," for it is easy to spot by the side of the road, singly or in large stands. However, one must be out early, on a sunny day, to enjoy the "shouting," for Chicory opens at sunrise, facing the sun until it closes by noon. On cloudy days, it usually doesn't open at all.

Several reference books state that the root, dried and roasted, has long been used as a coffee additive or substitute. It was used to make coffee go further in the Civil War and in World War II. In Louisiana, commercial coffee is advertised as special because it has Chicory added to it. The tender basal leaves can be gathered and used as greens if picked early before the flowers appear. Endive, *C. endiva*, a popular lettucelike salad green, is a closely related species. The species name, *intybus*, means "endive" in Latin.

A European legend tells of a beautiful blue-eyed maiden whose lover had left for lands unknown. Daily she waited for him by the side of the road. When he didn't return, her blue eyes filled with tears as the days turned into years. She died of a broken heart, and this gorgeous blue flower sprouted from the spot where she died.

Cirsium ochrocentrum
Yellow-spine Thistle, Bull Thistle

Plant: Perennial 1–3½ feet tall. The undersurfaces of the leaves are covered with grayish-white to yellowish hairs. The leaves are lancelike in shape but cleft deeply, with extremely spiny lobes. The upper portions of the stems, which bear the flower heads, are mostly devoid of leaves.

Flower: The flower heads are solitary on the ends of long, naked stems. The bracts beneath the purplish-pink to pink flowers are tipped with long spines that stick straight out; those on the outer bracts are yellow. The involucre (the whorl of bracts below the flowers) is 1–2 inches tall. As with all thistles, there are only disk flowers (no ray flowers). They look like pink powder puffs on the involucre. Their blooming period is from May to late summer.

Fruit: As is typical for a thistle, the fruit is an achene with a single seed inside, oblong in shape, flat and unribbed. It is attached by its base to the receptacle, the part of the flower head that bears the disk flowers. A pappus of bristles is in a ring at the base.

Range: Open spaces, disturbed soil, roadside ditches, and pastures over the Western Plains, from Nebraska southwest through western Texas and New Mexico, and into Arizona.

Remarks: Thistles are a personal favorite of mine because of their color and shape (like old-fashioned shaving brushes). When photographing them, I am usually in the company of beautiful butterflies and frantically busy honeybees and bumblebees, for thistles are favorites of theirs also.

Recipe: Cut a few stalks at the base. Holding the plant by the flower, scrape the skin off. Cut these cleaned stems into short pieces and boil for 4 or 5 minutes. Season to taste. (After *Papa Stahl's Wild Stuff Cookbook*)

Cirsium texanum
Texas Thistle

Plant: Biennial or perennial, 2–5 feet tall, growing from a taproot. The stems are usually solitary at the base, then branching somewhat at the top. The leaves, 4–9 inches long, are slightly clasping, simple, alternate, with the narrow leaf blades oblong to lanceolate in shape. They have woolly-white microscopic hairs on their undersides. The edges are irregularly toothed and spine-tipped.

Flower: At the tip of each long, naked stalk is a pink to rosy-purple flower head. Totally lacking in ray flowers, this thistle produces only long, slender disk flowers up to 1½ inches across and ⅔–⅘ inch tall. The bracts are tipped with soft, outward-bent spines. Bloom season is May and June.

Fruit: An achene, without hairs, except on top, where it is surmounted by a bristly plume or crown of pappus hairs.

Range: Abundant in disturbed soils by roadsides and in ditches and fields, Texas Thistle grows through most of Texas except extreme eastern Texas and the western Trans-Pecos, north into eastern New Mexico and Oklahoma, and south into Mexico.

Remarks: This lovely late spring/early summer wildflower produces large stands of tall, colorful pink pom-poms. They are spectacular "en masse." Butterflies and bumblebees love the nectar. The entire plant is great in compost heaps due to its rich potassium content.

Cirsium undulatum
Wavy-leaf Thistle, Plumed Thistle

Plant: Perennial 1–3 feet tall on stout branched stems from rhizomes underground. It often produces clumps of stems and appears to grow in colonies. The alternate leaves are cleft into narrow lobes that do not reach to the midrib; the lobes are

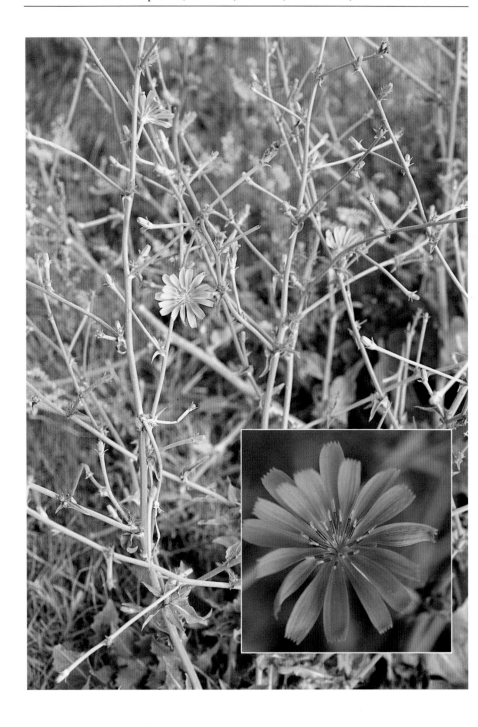

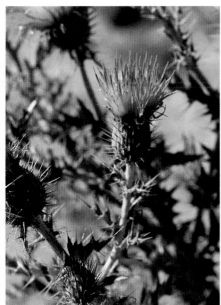

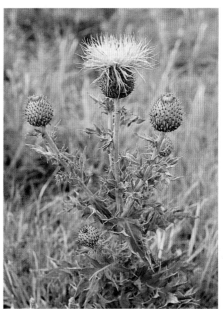

Cirsium ochrocentrum Yellow-spine Thistle
Opposite: *Cichorium intybus* Chicory

Cirsium undulatum Wavy-leaf Thistle

Left and below: *Cirsium texanum* Texas Thistle

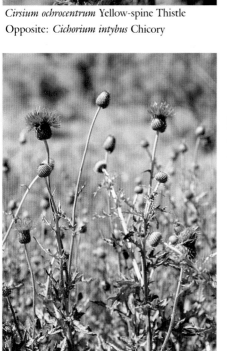

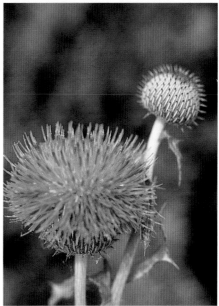

spine-tipped, lanceolate, gray-green in color due to the whitish woolly covering on the surfaces, and 1–8 inches long.

Flower: The single flower heads are thick and 1–2 inches tall (rather cone-shaped), with the numerous disk flowers blooming in profusion at the tip to 1–2 inches across. There are no ray flowers. Each disk flower is perfect (having both stamens and pistil), fertile, with a 5-lobed corolla ranging in color from purplish-pink to white. The bracts that subtend the involucre are overlapping and tipped with rigid spines. Wavy-leaf Thistle blooms in May and June, sometimes extending into September.

Fruit: A flat, oblong achene that has a pappus of feathery-looking bristles.

Range: Canada and Michigan, south to Oklahoma and Texas. It grows well in dry soils of pastures, roadside ditches, and abandoned fields.

Remarks: This is another thistle that, when in full bloom, greatly resembles an old-fashioned shaving brush. The stems and leaves are definitely gray-green in color and stand out against any dark green vegetation nearby. Because the leaves are not cleft deeply, they tend to twist and undulate—hence the Latin name, *C. undulatum.* "Wavy-leaf" is most descriptive.

Coreopsis tinctoria (= *C. cardaminifolia*)
Coreopsis, Painted Daisy, Plains Coreopsis, Tick Seed, Manzanilla Silvestre, Golden Wave, Calliopsis

Plant: Erect, slender annual 2–3 feet tall and branched toward the top. The leaves are opposite on the stems and spaced far apart. The lower leaves, to about halfway up, are once or twice pinnate with very narrow linear segments and are ½–1½ inches long. The uppermost leaves are often undivided.

Flower: There are numerous colorful flower heads bearing 7–8 bright yellow rays ½ inch long and 3-lobed on the tips. Near the center of the flower head, the rays are a red-brown color, giving the flower a "painted" appearance. Numerous fertile disk flowers are 5-toothed with yellow corollas (sometimes red-veined). There are 6–9 rather lance-shaped outer phyllaries that are not united except at the base. Coreopsis blooms in July and August.

Fruit: A tiny black achene, which varies from winged to wingless, only about ¹⁄₁₆ inch long.

Range: Louisiana to New Mexico and Arizona, including most of Texas, north to Nebraska and south to northern Mexico.

Remarks: This is a beautiful, showy, brightly painted–looking wildflower that can cover several acres with magnificent color on the Western Plains. It seems to prefer abandoned fields and low-lying areas that retain moisture, rather than higher, better-drained places. It often can be seen growing in profusion around the margins of playa lakes. For those interested in landscaping with native plants, this wildflower is suggested as a durable and dependable plant for flower beds and borders. The seeds can be sown in the fall and winter.

The common name Tick Seed came from someone's belief that the seeds resembled ticks. Early pioneers stuffed this plant in their mattresses to repel fleas and bedbugs.

It is also known by a synonym, *C. cardaminifolia.*

Echinacea angustifolia
Purple Coneflower, Black Sampson, Blacksamson

Plant: Deep-rooted perennial 1–2½ feet tall. The stems are solitary, rarely branched, and grow in clumps. The leaves are stalked at the base of the plant, becoming stalkless and smaller as they go up the stem. They are 3–8 inches long, covered with stiff hairs, untoothed and have 3 or 5 easily visible main veins.

Flower: The flower heads are borne singly on the long stems. There are 10–15 rose-pink or pale purple ray flowers (¾–1½ inches long) that hang down from the large flower head or "disk." This center, bearing the disk flowers mixed with stiff, pointed chaff, is a dark red-purple dome, rising ¾–1¼ inches tall and ¾ inch wide. The ray flowers are sterile, while the disk flowers are fertile. The corolla of each disk flower is 5-lobed, dark purplish, with 5 stamens and yellow pollen. Purple Cone-flower blooms in May and June.

Fruit: A 4-angled achene ⅛–⅜ inch long. The pappus terminates in a toothed crown.

Range: This wildflower is distributed from Canada south to Oklahoma and Texas. It is found in gravelly soils on the Western Plains, as it prefers dry rocky prairies and hillsides.

Remarks: This interesting plant has a very thick black root that was used by Native Americans in many ways. It was reduced to a juice that was applied to wounds and burns. Toothaches were relieved by placing pieces of the root around the problem tooth. It was also used to treat mumps and even distemper in horses.

Purple Coneflower is a very handsome, stately plant, growing tall, with its delicately colored rays, or "petals," softly drooping.

Engelmannia pinnatifida
Engelmann Daisy, Cutleaf Daisy

Plant: A perennial herb up to 2 feet tall, Engelmann Daisy grows from a tough, woody taproot. It has several stout stems that are branched above and covered with stiff hairs. The basal leaves, also covered with stiff hairs, are 6–12 inches long and deeply pinnatifid (being cleft almost to the midrib). The lobes are round-toothed. Up the stem, the leaves become smaller; some are undivided and smooth on their edges.

Flower: In the upper portion of the plant, the stems branch out and each branch is topped with a yellow flower head, 1–1½ inches wide. The involucre is cup-shaped, with the phyllaries in 3 series: the outer series linear and green, the middle series broader, and the inner series very broad and whiter. There are 8 yellow ray flowers, 3-toothed on the tips, about ½ inch long, and fertile. The many yellow disk flowers are 5-toothed. Engelmann Daisy blooms from April to October.

Fruit: The fertile ray flowers develop flattened, inversely ovate achenes about 3/16 inch long. The pappus consists of a few scales with 2 of them positioned over the achene.

Range: A fairly common plant of the Western Plains, this daisy is found in Nebraska, Kansas, Oklahoma, Louisiana, and throughout Texas, except eastern Texas, as well as Utah, Colorado, New Mexico, Arizona, and Mexico.

Remarks: The genus, *Engelmannia*, is named for George Engelmann, a German-American botanist of the late 1800s.

This bright wildflower can be found blooming somewhere on the Western Plains from early April into the fall. It does well in roadside ditches, vacant lots, ungrazed pastures, and prairies. The flower is expanded to its fullest in the late afternoon, but by the next day, under the hot sun, the ray flowers will curl and turn under at their tips.

Engelmannia is a monotypic genus, meaning one with only 1 species. Its closest relative is *Lindheimera texana*, Star Daisy.

Erigeron modestus
Fleabane Daisy

Plant: Short-lived perennial with a slender, rather woody taproot. The stems are 4–12 inches tall and densely pubescent, or hairy. There are many narrow oblong to lance-shaped leaves, less than 2 inches long,

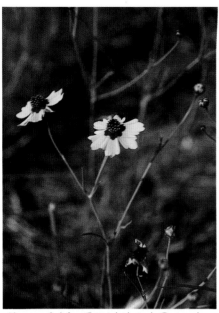

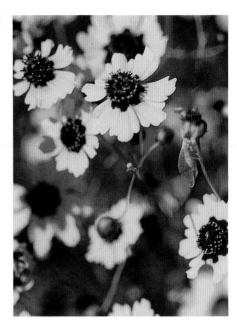

Above and right: *Coreopsis tinctoria* Coreopsis

Opposite: *Echinacea angustifolia* Purple Coneflower

Engelmannia pinnatifida Engelmann Daisy

Erigeron modestus Fleabane Daisy

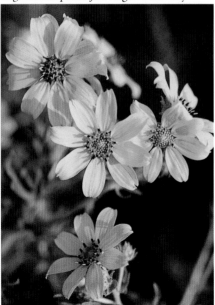

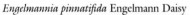

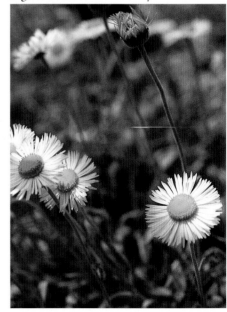

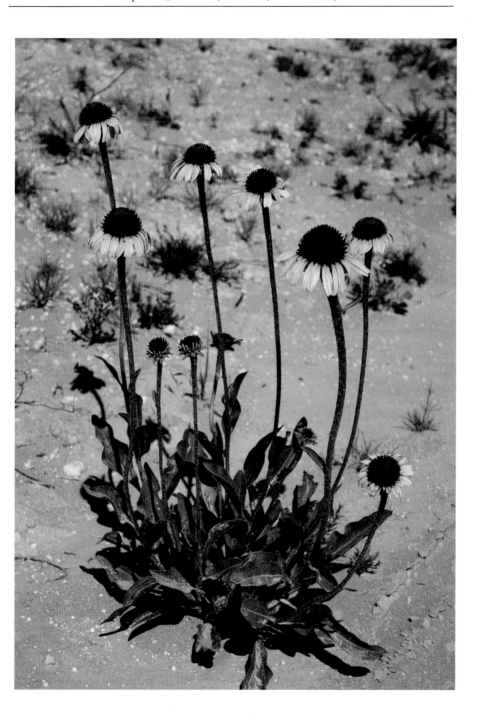

which are broadest at the tip, extremely narrow at the base, occasionally with coarsely toothed edges.

Flower: There are numerous flower heads ½–¾ inch across, with 30–70 white ray flowers, very straight and narrow, less than ¹⁄₁₆ inch wide and about ¼ inch long. The disk flowers have both stamens and pistils and are fertile. The very short corollas (less than ⅛ inch long) are 5-toothed on the tip and bright yellow. The pappus is similar in both ray and disk flowers but of 2 different sizes (referred to as "double"). Fleabane Daisy blooms May–August and sometimes into October.

Fruit: A flat, hairy, 2-ribbed achene crowned with threadlike bristles.

Range: Fleabane Daisy prefers sandy soils, growing abundantly in deep sand hills, grassland pastures, and open plains from Nevada, Arizona, and New Mexico through the plains of Texas into Oklahoma. It also grows in northwest Mexico.

Remarks: With about 200 species, *Erigeron* is often confused with *Aster*. At first glance, the wild asters, daisies, and fleabanes do look alike and are difficult to distinguish from one another. However, most fleabanes bloom earlier than asters, and in general the rays of *Erigeron* are narrower and in greater numbers than the rays of the daisies or asters.

This little fleabane appears to have pink "petals" until it is fully opened because the rays are tinged with pink on their undersides. When it is tightly closed in the mornings, pink is the color that is visible.

The common name came from an ancient belief that the odor in some way repelled fleas. Nowhere have I found any proof that this is more than legend or unfounded rumor.

Gaillardia pinnatifida
Yellow Gaillardia, Slender Gaillardia

Plant: Perennial herb with a slender unbranched stalk up to 2 feet tall. The leaves grow on the lower portion of the plant, near the base, and are oblanceolate in shape and pinnately divided. Under a microscope, tiny hairs can be seen covering the leaf surface like strings of beads (moniliform hairs).

Flower: The flower heads measure about 1½–2 inches across. There are 6–13 yellow ray flowers, purple-veined on their undersides and cleft into 3 lobes. Sometimes the yellow color changes to pale red near the base of the ray. The disk flowers form a sphere ¾ inch across in the center of the flower head. They are a deep purplish-red, appearing brown at times. The disk corollas are 5-toothed and covered with moniliform hairs. The ray flowers are infertile, while the disk flowers are fertile. Yellow Gaillardia blooms in April and May.

Fruit: An achene, ¹⁄₁₆ inch long and partially covered with long, silky hairs. The lance-shaped pappus scales have short awns at their tips.

Range: This wildflower grows from northern Mexico into the Trans-Pecos region of Texas, up on to the plains of Texas, Oklahoma, Colorado, and Utah. It prefers sandy or clay soils of grasslands, open pastures, and roadsides.

Remarks: Yellow Gaillardia is a graceful, slender wildflower. Probably its most unusual feature is the prominent purple veining on the underside of the golden yellow 3-lobed ray flowers.

Gaillardia pulchella
Indian Blanket, Firewheel, Blanket Flower

Plant: Annual 8–16 inches tall. The stems are branched from the base. It is a variable plant that can be hairy or sometimes just downy; the lower leaves may be lobed, toothed, or smooth.

Flower: Stems 2–8 inches tall produce solitary flower heads 1–3 inches broad. The 10–20 ray flowers can be all yellow or all red, but usually are reddish-orange with yellow tips and deeply 3-cleft. The rays are ⅓–1 inch long. The disk flowers in the center are brownish-red and tipped with bristles. Indian Blanket blooms April–June and sometimes later.

Fruit: A small, dry 1-celled seed with moderately coarse, stiff hairs. As the plant matures, the "petals" (rays) fall off and the seeds become drier, stiffer, and lighter in color, as they become part of a sphere on the drying stem. Finally, they fall to the ground.

Range: Indian Blanket grows in pastures, prairies, and along roadsides throughout eastern New Mexico, Texas, Missouri, Nebraska, Kansas, Oklahoma, and Louisiana.

Remarks: This brilliantly colored, plentiful spring and early summer wildflower is a favorite of many people. It is easy to see why some might call it Firewheel, but I prefer Indian Blanket because of the old legend associated with it . . .

Legend: Once upon a time on the Western Plains, when Ancient Man reigned supreme, there lived an old Indian blanket maker. He had been a weaver for his long lifetime. The results of this talent were beautiful blankets. Indians from faraway tribes would travel many moons in order to trade their basketry, jewelry, or pottery for one of his blankets.

The Blanket Maker was an old man and realized that one day soon he would die. With this thought in mind, he began to weave his burial blanket. It would have to be the prettiest one he had ever woven; so he used the browns, yellows, and reds that he loved so well and finally finished this most exquisite of all his weavings. He laid it aside and told his family to wrap his body in this blanket for this was to be his gift to the Great Spirit when they met face to face.

In time the old man died and his family did as they had been instructed. He was wearing his colorful blanket when he met the Great Spirit. Immediately the Great Spirit recognized it as a gift to Him and was pleased. Yet, at the same time, He was saddened that only those in the Happy Hunting Ground would be able to appreciate this lovely gift. So He decreed that the very next spring, on the old man's grave, a wildflower, of the colors and design of his blanket, would bloom forever and a day for us all to enjoy.

Gaillardia suavis
Rayless Gaillardia, Fragrant Gaillardia, Pincushion Daisy, Sweet Gaillardia

Plant: A perennial with branching roots and a basal rosette of leaves that alternate on a very short stem. The leaves are from 2–6 inches long and variable in shape; they can be oblong, lance-shaped, or spatulate (shaped like a spatula), pinnately cleft in narrow lobes or just toothed slightly.

Flower: A single flower head is produced on a tall (1–2½ feet), naked, unbranched, slender stalk. The flower head is usually rayless, but it can have small (or stunted) yellow rays that quickly drop off. The flower head is spherical in shape and ¾–1 inch across. It consists of many small, dark reddish-brown disk flowers that are tubular and 5-toothed or pointed on the tips. These florets have a sweet scent. The plant blooms from April to early June.

Fruit: Downy achene, 5-ribbed and 1⁄16 inch long.

Range: This plant can survive quite well in dry habitats, growing abundantly by the roadsides and in pastures from northern Mexico through western Texas and into Oklahoma, Kansas, and Missouri.

Remarks: When this plant is in bloom, it can be seen in large colonies of tall, swaying, leafless stalks with fuzzy-looking

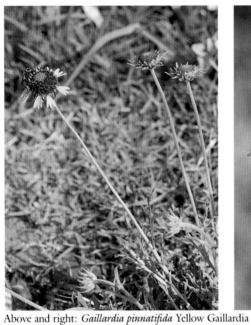

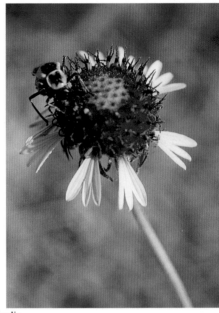

Above and right: *Gaillardia pinnatifida* Yellow Gaillardia

Opposite: *G. suavis* Rayless Gaillardia

Below and right: *G. pulchella* Indian Blanket

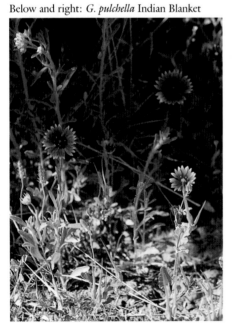

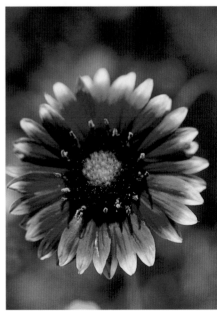

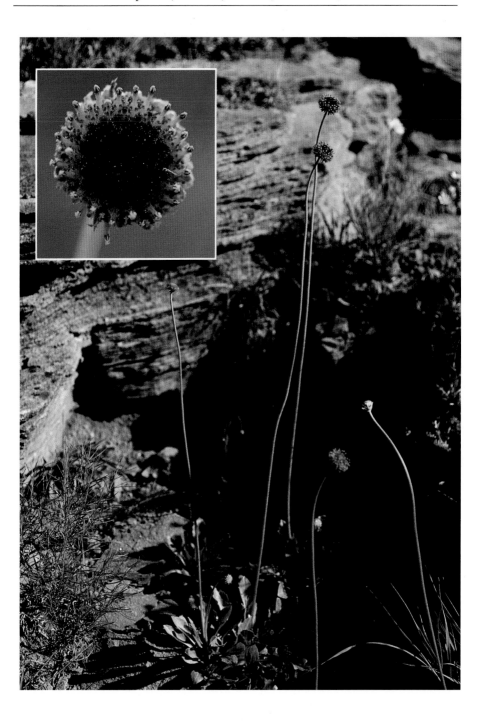

brown heads nodding in the breeze. They inhabit the roadsides on the Western Plains, and one can't help but think they are wildflowers "gone to seed," since they have no colorful "petals" or ray flowers. Examined closely, the round heads look like miniature pincushions. Rayless Gaillardia makes up for its lack of beauty by being most delightful to the nose with its sweet fragrance.

Grindelia squarrosa
Curly-cup Gumweed, Gumweed, Rayless Gumweed

Plant: Perennial taprooted herb with leafy (usually sticky) stems, 1–3 feet tall, and numerous branches. The leaves are alternate, bluish-green in color, and sessile (without a stalk), the base of each leaf partially clasping the stem. Leaf blades are lanceolate to ovate-spatulate (flattened spoon-shaped), 3/4–2 inches long and 1/4–1/2 inch wide. The leaf margins are toothed, with sharp points.
Flower: The flower heads appear on the tips of the stems and are sometimes numerous, 1/2–2/3 inch across, with yellow ray flowers which are not toothed at the tips. Disk flowers are tubular, yellow, and 5-lobed. Beneath the flower cluster is a whorl of bracts (phyllaries) that stick out into slender tips, the lower ones recurving downward. The plant blooms from August through October.
Fruit: An achene with 2 or 3 projections. It is usually smooth but sometimes has a few shallow striations.
Range: Curly-cup Gumweed is commonly found in run-down pastures, roadsides, and open areas over the Western Plains, growing down into northern Mexico. It is also found as far north and east as Minnesota and Illinois.
Remarks: This fall-blooming plant grows quite well on the Western Plains. Livestock find it unpalatable due to the tannin and resins in it. Native Americans and early settlers used it for asthma and bronchitis

relief. For topical use, a poultice of the crushed flowers is said to be helpful in poison oak miseries.

After watching a demonstration of weaving done by some Native American Pueblo women at the Indian Market in Santa Fe, I learned they used *Grindelia* as a dye source for the wools in their blankets. They achieved lovely hues of yellow, gold, and olive-green from this genus. The different colors depended on the methods used in dyeing the wools.

Gutierrezia sarothrae
(= Xanthocephalum sarothrae)
Snakeweed, Broomweed, Turpentine Weed, Matchweed, Escoba de la Víbora

Plant: A small, perennial, many-stemmed, upright shrub 1–3 feet tall. New growth and dead stems from the previous year are found in the same bush. The leaves are linear, 1/2–2 inches long, almost threadlike, 1/16–3/16 inch wide, and have resinous glands on the surface. The entire plant, with its many branches spreading out from the ground and thick clusters of flower heads on the top two-thirds, has a corymb, or slightly convex, shape. It resembles a large, compact, yellow bouquet growing on the ground.
Flower: The numerous small flower heads grow in groups at the thickly branched and rounded top of the plant. Each has 3–7 golden yellow fertile ray flowers about 1/5 inch long. The pappus is several scales, more or less joined. Disk flowers number from 2 to 6 and are also fertile, the pappus on them being 8–10 sharp-pointed, chafflike scales. They bloom from September into November.
Fruit: The tiny fruit is an achene that is reverse pyramid-shaped (obpyramidal). The achene is covered with stiff white pappus.
Range: Like other members of this family, Snakeweed grows well in barren places,

rocky roadsides, dry plains, overgrazed rangelands, and hills over most of western Texas and eastern New Mexico. It is also found as far north as Canada and south into Mexico.
Remarks: This is a rather hated weed and indicator of overgrazing, if you ask any rancher. Not palatable, it is shunned by livestock and wildlife alike. The stems, when picked and placed in baskets, dry to make easy, eye-pleasing arrangements that will last a long time. When crushed, the plant emits a light piney scent. Remember, this is a flammable dried plant.

The name *Xanthocephalum sarothrae* is considered a synonym in the most recent taxonomic revisions.
Folk Medicine: A cup of these stems and leaves can be steeped for about 30 to 40 minutes in a quart of water, then strained to make a concoction, NOT TO BE DRUNK, but to be put into hot bath water. In this way, it can be used to ease the pain of rheumatism and arthritis. It is a common *remedio* of the Spanish-speaking people of New Mexico.

Helenium microcephalum
Sneezeweed, Small Sneezeweed

Plant: Annual 8–36 inches tall, growing from a taproot. At the base, the stem is single, then becomes bushy-branched above. The narrow leaves (1–2½ inches long) are alternate, lanceolate to oblong-elliptical, saw-toothed on the edges, and decurrent (extending down the stem by means of thin "wings" that continue past the point of attachment to the stem). Their surfaces are covered with microscopic droplets of a resinlike liquid, making them somewhat sticky to the touch.
Flower: The many flower heads bloom in the top of the plant, barely emerging above the foliage. The receptacle is domed and covered with numerous disk flowers. Beneath the flower head are 16 bracts, in 2

rows, curving downward. Eight small, 3-lobed ray flowers hang drooping around the disk. They are widest at the ends and only about ¹⁄₁₆–³⁄₁₆ inch long. (They look rather stunted and are sometimes nonexistent.) The disk (receptacle) is about ¼–½ inch across with its many tiny red-brown disk flowers, which are fertile. Their corollas have 5 lobes, pointed on the tips. Sneezeweed blooms throughout the summer into fall (June–September).
Fruit: A small achene (¹⁄₁₆ inch or less) with 4 or 5 angles crowned with short oval scales.
Range: This plant is abundant in western Texas and New Mexico, but extends into northern Mexico also. It does best in fields and ditches, around playa lakes on the Western Plains, and in other low, seasonally moist areas (especially those areas with moist clay soils).
Remarks: Sneezeweed is a fairly common plant on the southern Western Plains, being considered a "noxious weed" by many. Hay-fever sufferers call it much worse names, blaming their seasonal allergy miseries on its pollen. It is not one of our lovelier plants. The blossoms are definitely not showy, with ray flowers that are barely discernible. Add to this its ability to make one sneeze, and it becomes a wildflower often avoided rather than appreciated.

Helianthus annuus
Common Sunflower

Plant: Widely branching, stout, hairy-stemmed and -leaved annual 3–10 feet tall. It has a taproot from which the very thick (sometimes 1½–2 inches in diameter) stem grows. The coarse, hair-covered leaves are alternate, simple, toothed, and triangular-ovate to broadly lanceolate in shape. They can grow up to 12 inches long on the lower portions of the plant.
Flower: The flower heads are large and showy, often 3–4 inches across. The heads

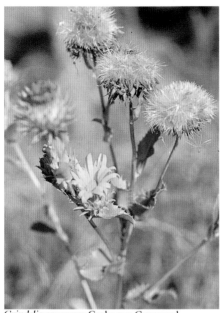

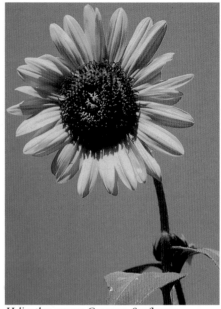

Grindelia squarrosa Curly-cup Gumweed

Helianthus annuus Common Sunflower
Opposite: *Helenium microcephalum* Sneezeweed

Gutierrezia sarothrae Snakeweed

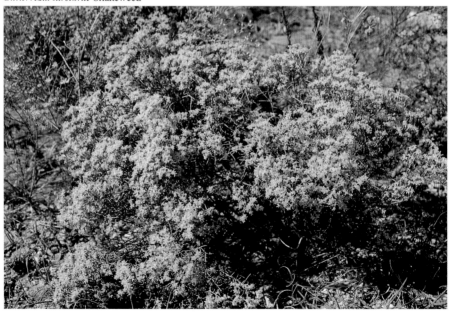

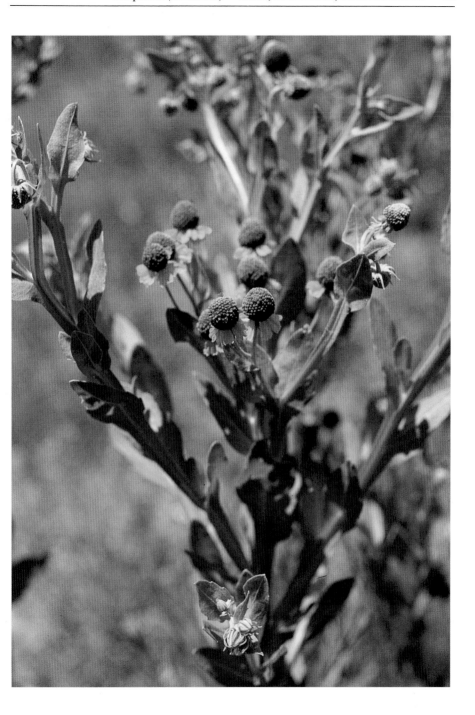

are solitary on the tips of the rough stalks. The center contains many small, dark brown disk flowers; it can measure 1½ inches or more across. The ray flowers are bright to golden yellow. They are sharp-pointed on the tips and 1–2 inches long. The blooming period can span May to November.

Fruit: An achene, rather flat and 4-angled in profile, containing a single seed of the same shape. The achene develops up to ¼ inch in length.

Range: This prolific plant can be found from the plains of south central Canada down through the Great Plains of the United States, through Texas (except the extreme northeastern portions), and into Mexico.

Remarks: The Common Sunflower does well in roadside ditches and pastures. Various cultivars of *Helianthus* are being planted and improved today, as many former cotton fields are being turned into sunflower fields instead. Sunflower oil is widely marketed, as are the tasty seeds.

It is believed that this plant had been in cultivation here, by earlier people, before Columbus arrived. The Native Americans gathered the mature seeds, boiled them, then skimmed the oil from the water and used it in cooking and mixing paints.

Some of the best dove and quail hunting in the fall is close to large stands of sun-flowers. Many birds relish the seeds as a valuable food source. Cattle have a particular fondness for the flowers, with their maturing seeds. The plant is a rich source of protein for birds, people, and animals alike.

Helianthus ciliaris
Blueweed

Plant: Herbaceous perennial growing from underground rhizomes. The stems can be from 1 to 3 feet tall. The blue-green lanceolate leaves are smooth, paired, and noticeably 3-nerved.

Flower: The 12–18 bright yellow ray flowers are ½ inch long. It is not unusual to find occasional flower heads with the rays absent. The disk is about ½ inch across, covered with tiny disk flowers whose corollas are red (but sometimes yellow at the base). Plants bloom from June into September.

Fruit: Typical of the sunflowers, Blueweed produces slender achenes ⅛ inch long and black or dark gray when mature.

Range: Preferring disturbed ground of fields and roadsides, especially muddy wet places, this sunflower can be found from the plains of Kansas through Oklahoma, Texas, New Mexico, Arizona, and into Mexico.

Remarks: Blueweed is not much loved by anyone, especially farmers. Since it prefers disturbed ground, it grows in and around cultivated fields, making it necessary to plow often in order to keep it cut down. It is a tough, hardy plant that also seems to grow in any low-lying place where water ever made a puddle. The flowers are typical sunflowers, the unusual feature of this plant being the distinct blue-green color of the foliage.

Helianthus maximilianii
Maximilian Sunflower

Plant: Perennial to 10 feet tall. Several unbranched stems grow from the base; they are rough and hairy but not extremely coarse. The grayish-green leaves are simple, alternate, up to 10 inches long, narrow (¾–2 inches wide), with a definite fold down the midrib. They are pointed on the tips and often curve down on the ends. The edges are only slightly toothed.

Flower: Numerous yellow flower heads, on their own stalks, grow from the leaf axils on the upper half of the plant. The flower head can be up to 4 inches across. The disk flowers are yellow, ⅗–¾ inch across, with brown anthers. The 15–30 yellow ray

flowers grow up to 1½ inches long. The blooming period is from July to October.
Fruit: A flattened 4-angled achene, up to ¼ inch long, with a flat seed inside.
Range: Southern Canada through the central United States into northern Mexico.
Remarks: This sunflower, named for the Emperor Maximilian of Mexico, is often cultivated today because of its grace, beauty, and ability to produce numerous flowers in the late summer and early fall. Economically, it is growing in importance as the source of an excellent birdseed. In the wild, it is becoming endangered due to overgrazing. But where it does grow, the birds and wildlife are sustained. Maximilian Sunflower is a most useful plant for food and cover for wildlife, livestock forage, landscaping, and erosion control. The Soil Conservation Service has recently released two strains of this species to be used for these purposes.

Helianthus petiolaris
Plains Sunflower

Plant: An annual growing from a taproot, the Plains Sunflower has many-branched, erect stems from 20 inches to 5 or 6 feet tall. The leaves are alternate with blades narrow and lance-shaped to sometimes rather oval, 1½–6 inches long by ¾–1½ inches wide.
Flower: The flower heads grow terminally on the tips of 3–4-inch peduncles. The ray flowers are yellow in color and oval in shape, about ¾ inch long. The disk is about ½–1 inch across and densely covered with red-purple disk flowers. Bloom season is May to October.
Fruit: The achene is swollen, oblong, and rounded on 1 end. A dark seed is inside.
Range: Plains Sunflower grows best in sandy ground. It does well in open prairies and sandy plains. Like the Common Sunflower (*Helianthus annuus*), it grows over much of the Western Plains, down into

western Texas, New Mexico, Arizona, southern California, and Mexico.
Remarks: This is a smaller version of the Common Sunflower. Since it is more branched and usually shorter than its cousin, it is being considered by native landscape enthusiasts as a bedding plant. Sunflowers attract birds, which is another reason people are using them in cultivation more.

I have noticed fields, once planted in cotton and now abandoned, that are covered with this little sunflower. Sandy soil assures it excellent growing conditions.

Hymenopappus flavescens
Yellow Woolly-white

Plant: Biennial from a taproot, 1–5 feet tall on a single stem. At the base of the plant is a rosette of leaves 2½–6 inches long, woolly underneath (less so on the top side), and cleft into many narrow lobes. The fewer leaves growing up the stem are smaller but also cleft into narrow segments. The stem and foliage are a gray-green color because of the minute woolly hairs on their surfaces.
Flower: The flower heads are in clusters at the top with more than 30 to a plant. There are only disk flowers, no ray flowers. (The bracts sometimes are mistaken for rays.) The disk corollas are bright yellow, ⅛ inch long and 5-lobed. From 30 to 90 disk flowers comprise the ½-inch-wide head. The stigma in each disk flower protrudes noticeably from the tip of the corolla. This plant blooms in May and June.
Fruit: Achene, oblong-pyramid-shaped, 4-sided, and somewhat hairy on the corners.
Range: Yellow Woolly-white seems to prefer sandy fields, open pastures, roadsides, and waste places on the Western Plains; Kansas and Colorado south through the Texas panhandle and west into New Mexico.

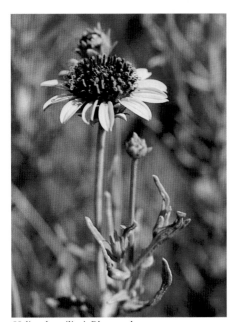

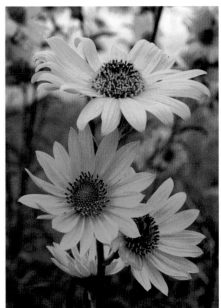

Helianthus ciliaris Blueweed

H. maximilianii Maximilian Sunflower

H. petiolaris Plains Sunflower

Hymenopappus flavescens Yellow Woolly-white

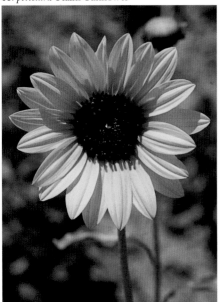

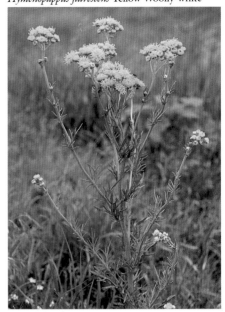

Remarks: The rayless flower heads are pretty with their tiny yellow disk florets clustered together to form an almost spherical shape. They have a somewhat pungent odor that seems to attract a variety of insects. When in full bloom, this plant is almost always covered with many insects, crawling over the flower heads, pollinating as they go.

Hymenopappus tenuifolius
Old Plainsman, Woolly-white

Plant: Biennial 1–3 feet tall from a single taproot. The stem is covered with fine hairs, as are the leaves, creating a soft gray-green overall color to the plant. The leaves, found mostly near the bottom in a basal rosette, are 3–6 inches long, bipinnately cleft into very thin linear segments (somewhat threadlike). A few leaves grow toward the top of the plant, but they are much reduced in size as they advance up the stem.
Flower: The plant is much-branched above and has many small flower heads (20–200) in clusters near the top of the plant. There are no ray flowers. The disk flowers have white corollas ⅛–³⁄₁₆ inch long. There are 25–50 disk flowers in a single flower head. Old Plainsman blooms in May.
Fruit: A 4-sided achene less than ¼ inch long with tiny hairs on the corners and a pappus of 16–18 oblong scales.
Range: This graceful plant seems to prefer the clay and sandy soils of open grasslands, roadside ditches, and canyon breaks. It grows from central Texas northwestward to the Texas panhandle and eastern New Mexico and northward into South Dakota.
Remarks: The soft green plant is very similar to its cousin, Yellow Woolly-white (*H. flavescens*), the main difference being the color of its flowers. Both are leggy, gray-green, and microscopically hairy, with foliage that is nearly the same. From a distance, Old Plainsman does not show up well because it is tall and pale in color.

Large stands of the plant make more of a "statement," but the best way to appreciate the loveliness of this flower is up close and individually. The flower heads are most delicate and interesting.

Hymenoxys odorata
Bitterweed, Yellow Poison Bitterweed

Plant: A much-branched, delicate annual that grows from 4 inches to 2 feet depending upon the rainfall received. The leaves are alternate, 1½–2½ inches long, once or twice pinnately divided into 3–15 very narrow linear segments. Leaves and stems are spotted with microscopic dots of resinlike liquid which impart to the plant its peculiar odor.
Flower: The numerous heads are solitary on 1–2-inch peduncles. There are 6–13 yellow ray flowers, ¼–⅓ inch long (longer than the phyllaries) and oblanceolate in shape. Each ray is 3-toothed at its tip. Disk flowers are yellow-orange, less than ³⁄₁₆ inch tall. Bitterweed blooms early in the spring, from March to May. It sometimes blooms again in September or October.
Fruit: A 5-angled achene, only ¹⁄₁₀ inch long, covered with coarse hairs and crowned with slender pointed scales.
Range: A common plant on the Western Plains, from central Texas to California, from Kansas through Oklahoma, south into Mexico. It also grows in Colorado, New Mexico, and Arizona.
Remarks: Bitterweed is a rounded plant that grows in large stands often covering many acres of pastureland, doing especially well in overgrazed areas. It can begin its growth in December or January and therefore is usually one of the earliest-blooming wildflowers to appear in the spring. Sometimes a carpet of yellow blanketing a pasture will be Bitterweed.

It must truly taste bitter because horses simply will not sample it. Sheep and cattle

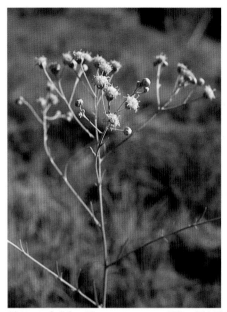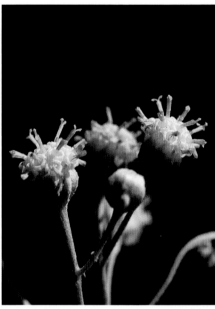

Above and right: *Hymenopappus tenuifolius* Old Plainsman

Hymenoxys odorata Bitterweed

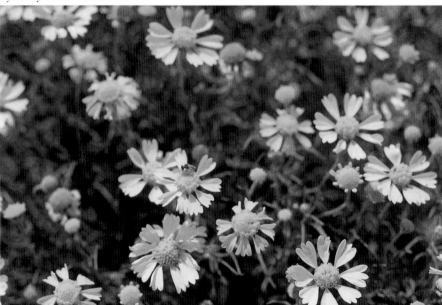

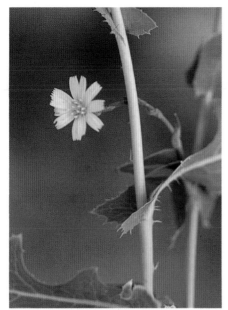

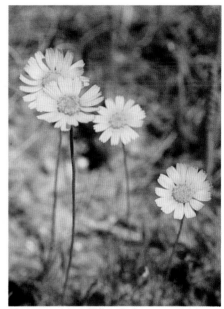

Lactuca serriola Prickly Lettuce

Hymenoxys scaposa Yellow Daisy

Liatris punctata Gayfeather; close-up at right

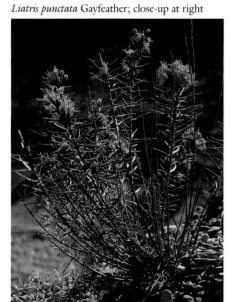

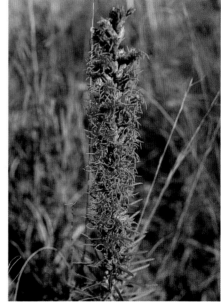

are not as discerning, for they will eat it and be mildly poisoned by it, especially in times of drought when other greenery is not available.

Hymenoxys scaposa
Yellow Daisy, Plains Yellow Daisy, Slender-stem Bitterweed

Plant: A low perennial growing from a slender taproot. The leaves are alternate and crowded basally, 3–5 inches long, silvery-green in color. The shape of the leaf is linear to linear-lanceolate, tapering so that it is narrower at the base. The edges are usually undivided and smooth, but some can have irregular teeth or lobes.
Flower: The solitary flower heads grow on naked peduncles 3–8 inches tall. There are 12–25 yellow ray flowers, about ⅓ inch long, pistillate, fertile, and 4-veined. The tip of each is 3-toothed. The disk flowers are bright yellow and fertile also. They bloom in April and May.
Fruit: Both ray flowers and disk flowers produce achenes that are similarly 4-angled, with a pappus of 5–8 scales.
Range: Yellow Daisy grows best in clay and limestone soils, preferring rocky and gravelly hillsides and canyon breaks of the southern Western Plains. It can be found over most of central and western Texas, from Arkansas to New Mexico, and into Mexico.
Remarks: Wherever Yellow Daisy grows, it usually does so in large stands. The plants are not in a thick, solid carpet but rather dotted here and there with their single stalks topped with delicate yellow flower heads. The 4 dark purple veins (on the rays) are easily visible on both surfaces. The yellow rays remain hanging on the head, after maturity, and turn almost white with age.

This plant has an unpleasant odor when picked. It is known to be somewhat poisonous to sheep.

Lactuca serriola
Prickly Lettuce, Wild Lettuce, Compass Plant

Plant: Tall, with leafy stems that often reach a height of 10 feet. The leaf edges are very spiny and toothed (or serrated). The leaves are arranged alternately up the stem with those near the top often clasping the stem. Each plant has a single, simple stem that branches only in the upper (flower-bearing) portion. It has a long taproot and is an annual, or winter annual (a plant from autumn-germinating seeds that fruits the next spring).
Flower: The flower heads are small but numerous; there can be from 5 to 35 on the upper portion of a plant. The ray flowers are a pale yellow, sometimes turning blue or pale purple with age. There are no disk flowers. The tips of the ray flowers (which really look like petals) are jagged or 5-toothed. It blooms in July and early August.
Fruit: Small, dry, hard achenes with long, narrow beaks. A crown of bristles (pappus) is on the summits of the achenes.
Range: Prickly Lettuce can be found growing in disturbed soils throughout most of the United States.
Remarks: A wild relative of cultivated lettuce (*Lactuca sativa*, a native of Europe), Prickly Lettuce is widely distributed throughout the United States now. The young leaves of all *Lactuca* species are edible and can be used for greens and salads. The name *Lactuca serriola* is sometimes misspelled *scariola;* one must be aware that they are one and the same.

Like members of the Milkweed Family, some members of the Compositae also have milky sap. As with that of the milkweeds, the application of this sap was reported (by our pioneer ancestors) to have cured seed warts. The botanical name for this plant comes from the Greek word for "milk," which refers to this white, milky-looking juice that "bleeds" from any broken part.

One of the common names, Compass Plant, refers to the fact that the leaves twist slightly at their base to face east and west, with their edges pointing in a general north-south direction.

Liatris punctata
Gayfeather, Dotted Gayfeather, Blazing Star, Button Snakeroot, Dotted Button Snakeroot, Cachana

Plant: A perennial that grows from a large corm, or underground bulblike root, to heights of 1–3 feet. This corm is long, brown, and nodular. The plant forms several stems (1–15) from 1 corm. The leaves are numerous, erect, stiff, linear, smooth-edged, and punctate (covered with tiny dots, visible with the naked eye). They are 3–6 inches long and only about ¼ inch wide and crowded along the stem as they intermingle with the flowers.

Flower: There are no ray flowers, but the 4–8 disk flowers form flower heads that grow crowded on a spike of bluish-purple to violet-pink. Each disk flower is ½–⅔ inch long and cylindrical, with a 5-lobed corolla (with 5 stamens) surrounded by purplish bristles, which are nearly equal in length to the corolla. The oblong bracts have triangular points and are fringed with cilia, or hairs. Gayfeather blooms from late August to October.

Fruit: Cylindrical achene, pointed on its base, with 10 ribs covered with hairs. It has a pappus of 12–40 bristles. The achenes are dandelion-like puffs that are carried away by the wind.

Range: This fall-bloomer prefers dry prairies and grasslands at elevations of 2,000–7,000 feet. It also grows along hillsides and roadsides in gravelly soils. From eastern Wyoming and Colorado through northern New Mexico, the Texas panhandle, and western part of Oklahoma, Gayfeather also spreads into the plains states, through Michigan into Canada.

Remarks: In the fall, when all the spring and summer wildflowers have gone, this striking plant is just beginning to dot the plains with tall spikes of color. Its long blooming period makes it possible to continue to find something colorful on the Western Plains up until frost.

The root has been used in the past for different medicinal purposes, but at present it is used by the Hispanics and Native Americans of New Mexico and Mexico as a talisman or good-luck charm. The corm, or root, is halved, and a cross is carved in one half. The two halves are then worn around the neck to ward off the "evil eye" or simply to ensure the wearer good fortune.

In some southern and eastern states, a cousin to this plant is used to ward off snakes and evil spells.

Lindheimera texana
Star Daisy, Texas Yellow Star, Texas Star, Lindheimer Daisy

Plant: Annual wildflower with a slender taproot that produces a plant 6–20 inches tall. The stems are branched, in the upper portion, with the leaves alternate and crowded on the stem. The leaf is oblong to lance-shaped, and narrow on both ends. There are tiny hairs over the surface of the bright green leaves, which are about 1–3 inches long and toothed at the very tip.

Flower: The flower heads are solitary on the 1-inch-long peduncles and are hemispheric in shape. The receptacle is in 2 parts, an outer ring bearing the yellow ray flowers and an inner portion bearing the disk flowers. There are 5 ray flowers, ¾–1 inch long and 2-toothed at the tip. The ray flowers are fertile; the numerous (10–15) disk flowers are infertile, 5-toothed, and yellow or yellowish-brown in color. Star Daisy blooms in April–May.

Fruit: Large incurved achene about ¼ inch long. Near the top are 2 hornlike projections.

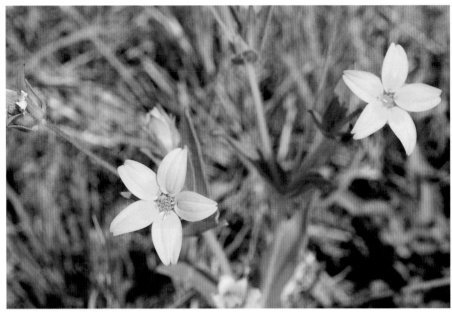

Lindheimera texana Star Daisy

Lygodesmia texana Skeleton Plant

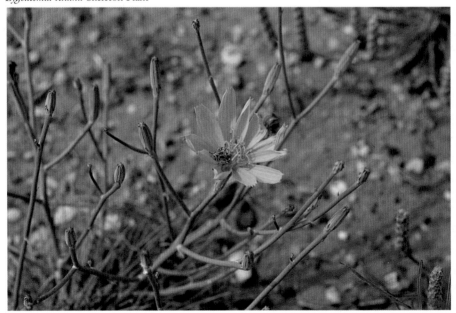

Range: This is not a prolific plant on the Western Plains, but it is found in the sandy soil of fields and roadsides in southwestern Oklahoma, north central Texas, and the Rolling Plains of Texas, as well as northern Mexico.

Remarks: Living up to its common name, the Star Daisy always displays the five points of a star in its 5 yellow ray flowers. It is large enough to be showy and is interesting with the cut at the tip of each "petal," or ray flower, that makes it 2-toothed.

Lindheimera is a monotypic genus, one that has only 1 species. It was named to honor Ferdinand Lindheimer, a German-born botanist who lived in Texas in the nineteenth century.

Lygodesmia texana
Skeleton Plant, Skeleton Weed, Pink Dandelion, Flowering Straw

Plant: Perennial, growing in clumps 10–20 inches tall, from slender, branched rhizomes. The stems are branched (often at odd angles), bare, soft gray-green and smooth. The few leaves, if there are any, are on the ground, alternate and lobed. Typically, the leaves have been reduced to small linear bracts that usually dry and fall off before the plant blooms.

Flower: The flowering heads are solitary, growing on the tips of the branched stems. They bloom only 1 at a time on a stem, and the flowers last for only a few hours. There are usually 11 pinkish-purple ray flowers with 5 teeth on the squared tips. The flower head is 1–2 inches across and has a pleasant fragrance. In the middle of the flower, 11 purple anthers, each with a split style, stick up, then curl to the center. There are no disk flowers. The pappus consists of a number of flattened bristles. Skeleton Plant blooms May through August.

Fruit: Achene, narrow, columnar, with few ribs and no pointed beak.

Range: A prairie-loving wildflower, Skeleton Plant grows in western Oklahoma, throughout most of Texas, and in northern Mexico.

Remarks: Skeleton Plant has a beautiful soft color in its delicate ray flowers. Its stems are brittle, naked, and oddly branched. Possibly it derives its common name from one or all of these stem characteristics. Since the flowers last only a few hours, it is fortunate for the wildflower enthusiast that each plant has several other buds awaiting their turn.

Another common name is Pink Dandelion because the flower resembles a Dandelion, just pinkish-purple instead of yellow. Even the seed head resembles that of the Dandelion. *Lygodesmia* (unlike Dandelion) is never yellow.

Native Americans used to break the stems into short sections, from which dripped a milky, resinous sap, and collect the droplets into a ball which, when partially dried, was then chewed like gum.

Machaeranthera pinnatifida
Spiny Aster, Cutleaf Goldenweed, Yerba de la Quintana, Yellow Spiny Daisy, Spinyleaf Goldenweed

Plant: A perennial that grows from a woody crown, sometimes reaching a height of 20 inches. Over the Western Plains, depending on the rainfall, heights of 6–12 inches are more common. It is a rough plant, branched in the upper part, and covered with minute hairs, which tend to make it gray-green in color. The leaves are threadlike yet pinnately cleft (the leaf has lobes on both sides, cut almost to the midrib, with a bristle tip on each tooth).

Flower: The flower heads, 1 inch across, bloom singly on the ends of the branches. The disk and ray flowers are bright yellow. The 20–30 ray flowers are ½ inch long and pointed at the end. Both disk and ray flowers have a similar pappus, tawny-colored and bristlelike. The plant blooms from about April into November (until frost).

Fruit: A tiny achene, barely ¹⁄₁₆ inch long, linear with very fuzzy hairs. The plant makes a small puffball after the blossom is gone, and each seed in the puffball has its own "hairs" (pappus) to help transport it on the winds to distant places where it will come up next growing season.

Range: This hardy plant grows from Texas into New Mexico, Arizona, southern California, and Mexico; also north into Minnesota and southern Canada.

Remarks: This bright yellow-faced flower grows and blooms almost continually from spring until frost. On the Western Plains, it is usually rather short. It has the ability to bloom and set seed at the same time, so that at most times during its blooming period, one can see blossoms and puffballs on the same plant.

In the past, this plant has been mashed and used as a poultice on open sores. The roots were believed to relieve toothaches.

Machaeranthera tanacetifolia
Tansy Aster, Tahoka Daisy, Tansyleaf Aster, Tansyleaf Machaeranthera

Plant: An annual herb, Tansy Aster is a many-branched, bushy plant growing 8–15 inches tall from a taproot. It is sticky-hairy all over with many dense, almost fernlike alternate leaves that are bipinnately cleft in the lower part of the plant and once-cleft or just toothed toward the top. The small spine that tips each leaf is a distinctive feature of the species. The leaves are 2–4 inches long, becoming shorter toward the top.

Flower: The flower heads grow on the tips of the branches, are not crowded, and are very showy. They are 1–2 inches across when in full bloom. The bracts are long and narrow, with green tips. There are

15–25 ray flowers (pistillate and fertile) which are a violet-blue (or lavender) color and ½–¾ inch long. The bright yellow disk flowers are numerous, fertile, and have 5 short teeth on the corolla tips. Both ray and disk flowers have a pappus consisting of many unequal brown bristles. Tansy Aster blooms in late April through August and occasionally into the early fall.

Fruit: Down-covered, oblong, flat achene about ¹⁄₁₆ inch long.

Range: This colorful wildflower can be found growing in southern Canada through South Dakota, then south into Mexico. It has also been reported in California. Its favorite habitats are plains, open pastures, roadsides and hillsides, vacant lots, and disturbed soils. It is abundant over the western portions of Texas and adjacent New Mexico and Oklahoma.

Remarks: At times in the past, many species of *Machaeranthera* have been labeled *Aster*, because they are so closely related. Botanical authorities recently have separated them according to their differences. *Machaeranthera* species are more abundant in the West and have minutely spine-tipped leaves, which the *Asters* do not have. They are also often confused with *Erigeron* (Fleabanes). However, the Fleabane Daisies have more numerous and much narrower ray flowers than *Machaeranthera*.

This species has retained the name Aster in one of its common names, Tansy Aster. To make it even more confusing, another common name is Tahoka Daisy. It seems that some years ago, some seedsmen found pastures abounding with this lovely flower and received permission to harvest the seeds and cultivate them for commercial purposes. Since they had been collected near Tahoka, Texas, and resembled a lavender daisy, they were labeled Tahoka Daisy by the seed company for retail sales. Because they are available commercially, and are a tough and hardy annual, their popularity as a garden plant is growing.

There are other very closely related lavender-colored species that also grow on the

Western Plains; *M. wrightii, M. linearis, M. tephrodes*, and *M. asteroides* are some.

Melampodium leucanthum
Blackfoot Daisy, Plains Blackfoot, Rock Daisy, Mountain Daisy

Plant: Perennial herb 6–12 inches tall. The plant forms a dense, rounded, bouquetlike mound when in full bloom. The stems are much-branched with the leaves opposite, narrow, linear to oblong; the margins untoothed or sometimes slightly lobed. The surfaces of the leaves are covered with rough hairs. They can be ¾–1¾ inches long and ⅛–¼ inch wide.
Flower: Solitary flower heads grow on slender stalks and are 1 inch across. The subtending bracts are united for about half their length. There are 8–11 white ray flowers about 1 inch long, each being broadly 2- or 3-toothed on the tip. Each ray flower has easy-to-see dark veins on the underside. The numerous disk flowers are yellow, 5-toothed, and tubular. Blackfoot Daisy blooms from April to August.
Fruit: Many curved achenes; the outermost ones have a hoodlike covering.
Range: Preferring calcareous soil, this hardy daisy can be found in western Oklahoma, through north-central Texas, Kansas, Colorado, Arizona, and New Mexico, reaching down into northern Mexico.
Remarks: Blackfoot Daisy is a most drought-resistant plant. It can be found blooming profusely in the middle of hot, dry July, when most other plants are dying for lack of water. It seems to prefer dry, rocky places, often sprouting in the cracks between rocks on slopes and ledges. Because of its low height, round bouquetlike shape, and minimal water consumption, it makes a nice border plant in a garden.

The common name Blackfoot Daisy comes from a foot-shaped bract, subtending each ray flower, that turns dark when it matures.

Palafoxia texana
Palafoxia

Plant: An annual, much-branched plant 1–2 feet tall. The leaves are alternate and rather broadly lance-shaped, ¼–1¼ inches wide. The leaf edges are undivided, not incised or toothed. Minute short hairs lie flat on the surface of the leaves, giving them a gray-green color.
Flower: Up to 30 flowers bloom in the uppermost portion of the plant. There are no ray flowers. The disk flowers are a soft rosy pink to pinkish-white with the corollas deeply cleft into 5 long narrow lobes. They are fertile. The style branches stick up, then split and curl backward, at their tips, on the hemisphere-shaped flower head. The phyllaries (bracts), in 2 or 3 rows, are thick and green, with a reddish tip that adds to the color of the flower head. It blooms in late June–July.
Fruit: A 4-angled achene, upside-down-pyramid-shaped (obpyramidal). The achenes are ³⁄₁₆–⁵⁄₁₆ inch long. The pappus consists of 7–10 tapering scales, variable in length.
Range: Prefers sandy ground or clay loam places beside stream banks. This is a plant of the southwestern United States and northern Mexico, found over most of Texas, southern Oklahoma, and parts of Mexico.
Remarks: Palafoxia, being tall and graceful, is easy to see when in full bloom, and the color is a lovely soft mauve-pink. It somewhat resembles Bachelor Buttons or Cornflower (*Centaurea cyanus*).

Pinaropappus roseus
Rock Lettuce, White Dandelion, Pink Dandelion, White Rock Lettuce

Plant: Perennial with short rhizomes. It has smooth stems and grows 5–12 inches tall. The leaves are alternate, pinnately

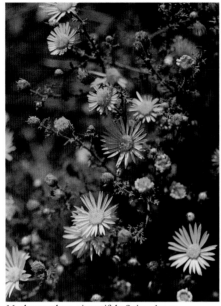
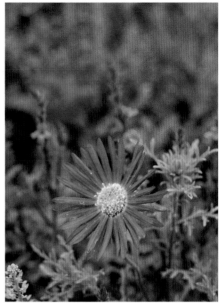

Machaeranthera pinnatifida Spiny Aster   *Machaeranthera tanacetifolia* Tansy Aster

Below and right: *Melampodium leucanthum* Blackfoot Daisy

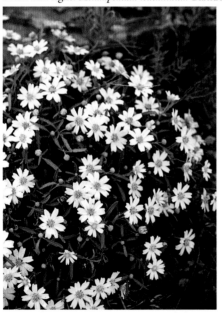
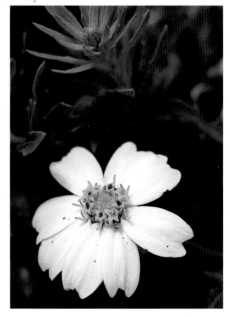

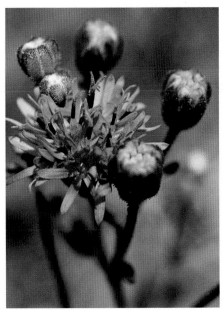
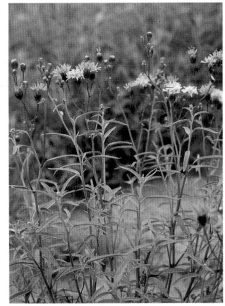

Above and right: *Palafoxia texana* Palafoxia

Below and right: *Pinaropappus roseus* Rock Lettuce

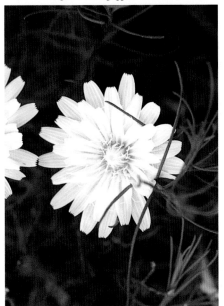
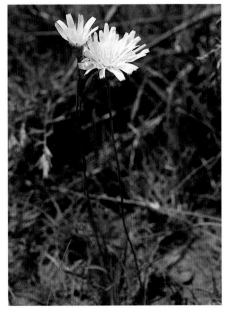

lobed or cleft, and mostly at ground level. A few narrow, slightly toothed leaves grow up the stem. Those at the base are more lobed than the upper ones. The leaves and stems bleed a milky sap when broken.
Flower: The large flower heads grow singly at the tips of the stems and are 1½ inches across. The ray flowers are white, gradually becoming tinged with yellow toward the center of the flower head, about ⅛ inch wide and finely 5-toothed at the squared-off tip. They are fertile, having both stamens and pistils, and bilaterally symmetrical. There are no disk flowers. The bracts have dark tips. A chaffy scale subtends each flower. The blooming period is April and May.
Fruit: Achene, round and 5-ribbed. There is pappus of barbed bristles.
Range: This plant prefers dry and rocky soils and grows over most of Texas, southern New Mexico, Arizona, and Mexico.
Remarks: This pretty little wildflower looks like a white Dandelion, hence one of its common names. I have never observed any specimens that were truly pink or lavender, but the undersides of the rays are often tinged with pink. One of its most unusual features is the presence of dark-tipped involucral bracts on the underside of the flower head.

Prionopsis ciliata
Sawleaf Daisy, Gumweed

Plant: Annual or biennial herb 3–5 feet tall. The stems are erect and stout, only branching near the top into short flowering stems. The leaves are alternate, coarse, spiny-toothed on the edges, thick, and clasping the stem at the base. They are from ¾ inch to 4 inches long.
Flower: The bright yellow flowers, 1¾ inches across, grow on short stems crowded near the top of the tall plant. The bracts have long, threadlike tips. There are many ray flowers, often more than ½ inch long.

The numerous disk flowers in the center are usually sterile, while those near the outside edge are fertile. They bloom from August into October.
Fruit: Oblong, slightly flattened achene with numerous slender bristles.
Range: Found in waste places, fields, and roadside ditches, this plant grows from Missouri and southeastern Kansas to Tennessee and Alabama as well as Texas and eastern New Mexico.
Remarks: Sawleaf Daisy is a very drought-resistant plant. It derives another common name, Gumweed, from the sticky residue that seeps from broken parts of the flower heads. Native Americans used to collect this residue, ball it up, and chew it as we do chewing gum today.

Psilostrophe tagetina
Paperflower, Plains Paperflower

Plant: This much-branched perennial herb grows in clumps with shaggy-haired stems 4–20 inches tall. The leaves are oval to lance-shaped at the bottom of the plant, smooth-edged or pinnately lobed, hairy or shaggy, ¾–5 inches long and half as broad. Toward the top of the plant, the leaves are more linear, smaller, and darker green, also hairy, sometimes lobed, and ½–2¾ inches long.
Flower: The numerous flowers grow in dense clusters on peduncles ¼–1 inch long on the tips of the branched stems. Each flower head has 3–5 bright yellow fertile ray flowers, with 3-lobed tips, and 6–12 fertile yellow disk flowers. Each tiny corolla is 5-toothed around the rim with a stigma that protrudes above the corolla. Each flower is ½–¾ inch across. They bloom from spring into the fall.
Fruit: Small linear achene.
Range: Paperflower grows well along highways and in pastures and wide open plains of Kansas, Oklahoma, New Mexico, Texas, Arizona, and into Mexico.

Remarks: This hardy, drought-resistant plant blooms off and on from spring into fall, often in large stands. The bright yellow clusters at the top of the bushy plant dazzle one's eyes in the sunlight, when they are blooming in profusion. It gets its common name from the fact that when the flowers have reached their peak and faded, they do not wither and fall from the plant. Instead they become dry, rather paperlike, and remain on the stems. They can easily be used in dried fall arrangements.

Pyrrhopappus multicaulis
False Dandelion, Texas Dandelion, Many-stem False Dandelion

Plant: A slender annual plant with several stems up to, but usually less than, 18 inches tall. The leaves are alternate, 2–6 inches long, crowded at the ground in a rosette when young, on curving stems as the plant ages and flowers. They are oblanceolate and usually cleft into narrow lobes, but can also be only slightly toothed.
Flower: The solitary flower heads grow on the tips of the stems and are ¾–1½ inches across. They are composed of ray flowers that are very bright yellow, fertile, with bilaterally symmetrical 5-toothed corollas, ¾ inch long. The anther tubes are unusual in that they are dark purple in color and contrast markedly in the center of the yellow flower. The blooming period is April into June.
Fruit: Plump brown achene tipped with parachute-like bristles which are off-white or tawny-white. Each achene has 5 ribs.
Range: Florida to Arizona and into northern Mexico.
Remarks: This Dandelion "look-alike" is often mistaken for the Common Dandelion (*Taraxacum officinale*). It is related, but is a separate species with several differences that are worthy of note. It is larger than the Common Dandelion, has a more intense yellow color, and has the unusual purple to black anther tubes in the center of the flower head. The bristles (pappus) that tip each achene are off-white or sometimes reddish-brown, instead of the clean white of the Common Dandelion. On the underside of the involucral bracts are keels, or ridges, that help to identify the plant as *Pyrrhopappus multicaulis*.

Its Latin name translates as Fire- (*pyrrho-*) bristles (*pappus*) Many (*multi-*) stem(s) (*caulis*). The reference to "fire-colored" bristles may be a bit exaggerated when describing the pappus; however, in some plants, it can be more reddish-brown than white.

Ratibida columnaris
(= *R. columnifera*)
Mexican Hat, Thimbleflower, Long-headed Coneflower

Plant: Perennial growing from a deep taproot to heights of 1–3 feet. It has branching stems with alternate leaves, deeply cleft to the midrib into 5–13 very narrow segments (almost threadlike). The leaves are 2–4½ inches long and rough, being covered with coarse hairs.
Flower: The flower heads grow 1 to a stem with the upper portion of the stem bare of leaves. There are 3–7 broadly elliptical, oblong ray flowers ¾–1 inch long and infertile (they have no styles or stamens). They vary in color from solid yellow, red-brown, or copper-toned, to ones with a deep reddish-brown base and a yellow tip. Sometimes the yellow ray is streaked with the red-brown color from the base toward the tip. The ray flowers droop and hang softly down around the center of the flower, which is a cylindrical or columnar receptacle. This fingerlike column (1–2 inches tall and 5/16–¾ inch thick) is gray-green and bears the many tiny, fertile disk flowers, each with a 5-lobed dark red-brown corolla. As they open, they begin to

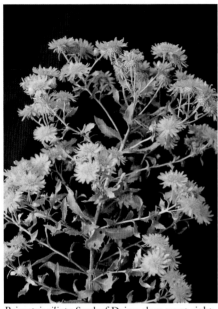

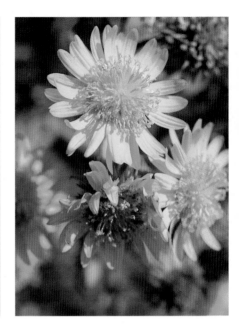

Prionopsis ciliata Sawleaf Daisy; close-up at right

Psilostrophe tagetina Paperflower; close-up at right

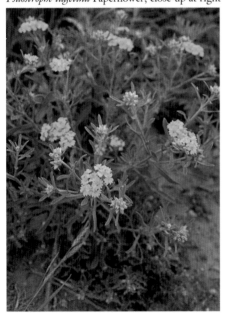

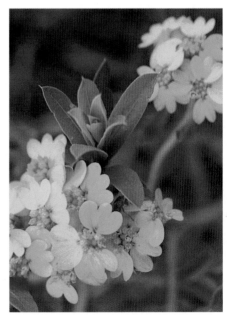

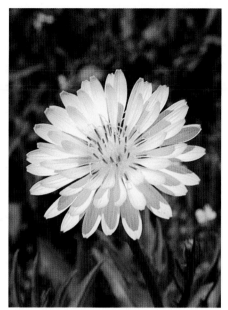

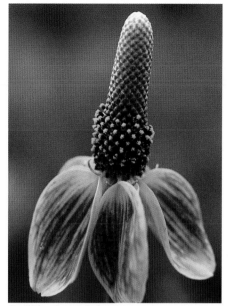

Pyrrhopappus multicaulis False Dandelion

Ratibida columnaris close-up

Ratibida columnaris Mexican Hat

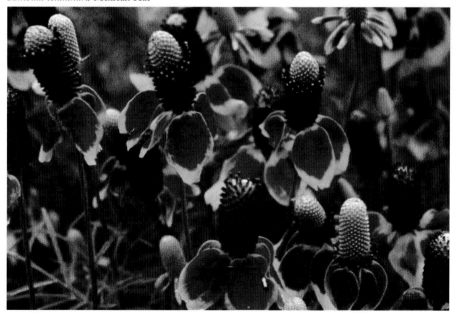

cover the column, from the base toward the top, replacing the gray-green color with brown and yellow (tiny yellow-tipped stamens). Blooms appear in May–June, and later if there has been summer rain.

Fruit: Achene with wings on its margins. Each achene is barely $\frac{1}{16}$ inch long.

Range: Mexican Hat can be found from Alberta, Canada, to northern Mexico, growing in fields, open pastures, and roadside ditches, in the states of North and South Dakota, Minnesota, Illinois, Missouri, Tennessee, Nebraska, Kansas, Oklahoma, Texas, Montana, Wyoming, Colorado, Arizona, and New Mexico.

Remarks: This is one of my personal favorites. It is an abundant roadside flower, and traveling through miles of its various colors is a splendid experience. It is a graceful plant, bending and swaying with the wind, yet tough enough that the colorful "petals" (ray flowers) never shred from nature's winds nor from the gusts of wind caused by traffic on the highway.

The unusual copper color often seen in the ray flowers is lovely and not encountered often.

This plant can be used as a dye source, imparting a bright yellow or olive-green color depending upon the method used.

It is also known by a synonym, *R. columnifera.*

Senecio douglasii var. *longilobus*
Threadleaf Groundsel,
Felty Groundsel

Plant: Perennial with several erect or spreading stems from the base which then branch out toward the top. It grows $1\frac{1}{2}$–3 feet tall and can be somewhat woody at the base. The leaves are alternate, numerous, up to 5 inches long, and pinnately divided into 3–7 linear lobes. The stems and leaves are covered with minute soft woolly hairs which impart a grayish-green color to them.

Flower: The flower heads are numerous in flat-topped clusters at the tips of the branches. Each one is about $\frac{3}{4}$ inch across and a butter-yellow color. There are 6–8 slender yellow ray flowers, pistillate, fertile, and 3-toothed on the tip ends. The disk flowers are yellow, perfect (having both stamens and pistil), fertile, and 5-toothed on the corolla tips. Phyllaries are in 1 row and usually number about 21. Threadleaf Groundsel blooms in April and May and can bloom again in the late fall (November or December).

Fruit: Small, narrow, flat-topped, columnar achene (about $\frac{1}{8}$ inch long) topped with spreading white pappus bristles. The whiteness of the pappus is one of the features used to readily identify members of *Senecio.* The ray and disk flowers alike produce achenes.

Range: Widespread in the drier areas of the Western Plains: western Texas, the prairies of southwestern Oklahoma, northern New Mexico, and northern Mexico; also found in Nebraska, Wyoming, and Arizona. It seems to grow better in pastures that are heavily grazed due to overstocking.

Remarks: Approximately 2,000 species of *Senecio* have been described worldwide, making it one of the largest genera of flowering plants. About 14–20 of these species grow on the Western Plains. The plant is considered to be toxic to cattle and horses, causing liver lesions when ingested in abundance. However, I have never observed them eating it. It is possible that they don't, unless there is absolutely nothing else to graze upon.

Threadleaf Groundsel is sometimes found listed as *S. filifolius.* It is also known by the synonym *S. longilobus.*

Sonchus asper
Sow Thistle

Plant: Winter annual with a long, slender taproot and a hollow, leafy stem. It can grow to 5 or 6 feet in height but usually is shorter (10–36 inches) on the Western Plains. The stem is solitary, becoming branched toward the upper portion. It "bleeds" a milky sap when cut. The leaves are prickly on the edges, with large rounded lobes at the ends. They are alternate on the stem and 2–8 inches long. The lower leaves are deeply cleft, lobed, and clasping the stem. The upper leaves are smaller, less lobed, and less prickly.

Flower: There are many flower heads on short stalks near the top of the plant, sometimes so many that they appear to be growing in clusters. They are slightly cup-shaped and ⅔–1 inch across. There are numerous bright yellow ray flowers (in several concentric rows), but no disk flowers. The blooming period is usually in the spring, but can last even up to frost.

Fruit: Achene about 1/12 inch long, flat, ribbed, grayish to red-brown in color, and topped with a tuft of white pappus hairs.

Range: A native of Europe, this plant thrives throughout Texas, Oklahoma, and most temperate and subtropical regions of the United States. It prefers disturbed ground close to inhabited areas and loves lawns, gardens, and cracks in sidewalks.

Remarks: The prickly leaves on this plant are not painful to touch, although they look as if they might be. It is often mistakenly called a Dandelion because the flowers resemble Dandelions and the little puffballs (which are the achenes) look like the sphere of "parachutes" of the Dandelion.

In Europe, Sow Thistle is used as a potherb and in soups and salads. Since this plant grows everywhere, and because I had a recipe, I gathered a large sack of the tender leaves. After washing them several times, I boiled them in salted water for 5 minutes, poured the water off, and seasoned the greens with lemon juice, margarine, salt, and pepper. Maybe it was the lemon juice, but my family found this lowly thistle quite palatable, which was saying a lot for meat-and-potatoes men!

Taraxacum officinale
Dandelion, Common Dandelion, Blowball

Plant: Winter annual or perennial herb from a long taproot. The root can be ¼–⅜ inch thick. The deep green leaves are crowded at the base in a rosette. There are many leaves, each 2–9 inches long, spatulate to oblong in shape (the blade being wider at the tip), and irregularly cleft or dentate along the margins.

Flower: The flower heads are solitary (growing 1 to a stalk) and terminal, on a leafless and hollow stalk that grows from the center of the rosette of leaves. There can be 1 to a plant or there can be many, appearing in succession. The stalks, or scapes, are very short when they bear the yellow flower head, which is ½–1½ inches across; then, as the flower matures and the seeds appear, the stalk becomes much longer (up to 12 inches tall). The bright yellow flower head is composed of all ray flowers (no disk flowers) which are fertile (or in some races, parthenogenic—lacking fertile stamens). Each tiny corolla is 5-toothed on the tip. (Plants of this particular subgroup, or tribe, of the Compositae always have a flower head bearing only ray flowers, each with a 5-toothed tip. Plants in other tribes, either with or without disk flowers, have ray flowers with 3-toothed tips, if ray flowers are present.) Dandelion blooms January–December, preferring cool, damp weather.

Fruit: The seed, or achene, is a slightly flattened, round one with pappus of many whitish capillary bristles or hairs. The color of the achenes can vary from greenish-tan to brown to reddish-brown. As the ray flowers mature, they change from a bright yellow flat involucre to a sphere of seeds with tiny white "parachutes" on their tips, producing a white "puffball" or "blowball."

Range: This hardy plant grows virtually all over North America as well as portions of Canada. It is a frequent flower of disturbed

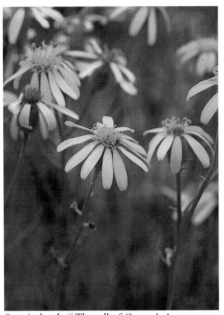 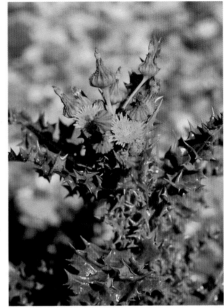

Senecio douglasii Threadleaf Groundsel   *Sonchus asper* Sow Thistle

Taraxacum officinale Dandelion
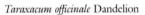

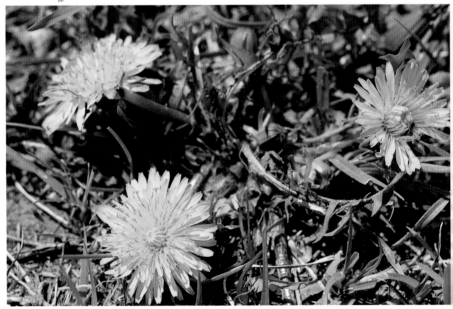

fields and roadsides, lawns, city parks, and playgrounds.

Remarks: Dandelion may be one of the most recognizable wildflowers worldwide. A native of Europe, it was brought to America by the Pilgrims, who believed it to be good medicine for many ailments.

It is usually cursed, poisoned, dug up, and killed because people are not fond of it growing in their well-manicured lawns and parks. But there are others who appreciate this plant as a delicious potherb. Vineland, New Jersey, bills itself as "the dandelion capital of the world," where "more dandelion is grown as a salad green than anywhere else in the nation." A Dandelion recipe book can be ordered from the Mayor's Special Events Office, Vineland, New Jersey.

Dandelions can be a very tasty part of an enjoyable meal. If picked for greens, the leaves should be cut early when they pop out of the ground, before the buds appear. A bitter taste accompanies the buds. At the earlier stage, they are good for salads or for cooked greens.

When the flowers appear, a light yellow, sherrylike wine can be made from the flower heads mixed with citrus juices, sugar, yeast, and water. The blossoms can be sautéed and added to pancake or waffle batter.

For centuries Dandelions have been used for drink, food, and even medicine. Europeans have long claimed they are good for everything from tired blood to toning up the internal organs. The very name that science has given this little wildflower, *Taraxacum officinale*, means "the official remedy for disorders" in Latin.

The leaves are credited with more food value than tomato juice or spinach, being very rich in vitamins A and C, iron, calcium, phosphorus, and protein. A pound of raw dandelion greens has only 200 calories.

Historically, dandelions have been one of the world's great free vegetables. So, why curse them? When our children blow the parachute-tipped seeds to the four winds,

and the resulting plants sprout in our yards in abundance, if we can't beat 'em, let's just eat 'em.

Thelesperma filifolium
Greenthread, Golden Wave, False Golden Wave, Threadleaf Thelesperma

Plant: Taprooted annual up to 30 inches tall on slender, branched stems. The leaves are much divided into threadlike segments, ⅓–1 inch long, and are scattered on the stem. The leaves on the lower portion of the plant can be up to 4 inches long.

Flower: There are several flower heads on the upper branches. While they are in bud, they droop down; when fully opened, they are erect and upright. There are usually 8 bright yellow ray flowers, 3-lobed at the tips, ½–1 inch long and ⅜–⅞ inch wide. The ray flowers surround the numerous disk flowers, which are yellow to reddish-brown in color, tubular, and 5-toothed on their tips. The flower head is about 1½ inches across. The flowering period is April–June.

Fruit: Narrow achene about ⅛–1/16 inch long, green to black in color. The pappus is of 2 bent-back, barbed yellow awns.

Range: South Dakota to Mexico, including parts of Arkansas, Oklahoma, and Louisiana, and throughout Texas.

Remarks: During the month of May, this is one of the most prolific wildflowers growing in the southern part of the Western Plains. It does well by the roadsides and in the pastures but can be a "city dweller" too, filling vacant lots, alleys, and some yards with bright yellow splashes of spring color. Closer inspection reveals urn-shaped buds that hang drooping until they open. When the colorful flowers appear, the miniature "urn" seems filled with a "bouquet." Then, as the ray flowers shrivel and fall, the involucre, or "urn," begins to bulge as the seeds form inside.

Thelesperma megapotamicum
Cota, Indian Tea, Navajo Tea, Colorado Greenthread, Rayless Thelesperma

Plant: Perennial growing from horizontal rhizomes. There can be 1 to several erect stems branching from the base and then branching once or twice again farther up. They are soft blue-green in color and grow to 3 feet tall, with threadlike leaves sparsely arranged up the stem. The upper third of each stem is nearly bare of leaves.
Flower: The flower heads are solitary on the tips of the bare stems. The involucre is a smooth, round, cup-shaped receptacle from which the disk flowers grow. There are no ray flowers. The disk flowers are yellow to yellow-brown, turning darker as they mature; they have reddish-brown veins. Each tiny corolla is irregularly lobed to nearly its entire length, which is about ½ inch. The flower heads are approximately ½–¾ inch across. The best blooming time is May and June, but Cota can bloom sporadically through the summer and even into October.
Fruit: Slim achene, only about ¼ inch or less, dark brown in color, and each standing erect in the cup-shaped receptacle. Each achene has a pappus of 2 barbed awns, or bristles, on the tip. This gives the once yellow flower head a fluffy, white appearance when it has "gone to seed."
Range: The harsher the land and the more alkaline the soil, the better this plant grows. It is widespread and common on the plains of Texas and eastern and northeastern New Mexico. From there, it goes into Arizona, Colorado, Utah, Nebraska, and up into Wyoming.
Remarks: I have a good friend who is a Native American and lives at San Ildefonso Pueblo in New Mexico. One fall, while I was visiting her, she pointed to a stand of Cota growing at our feet and commented that it was her favorite tea, confessing that she never bought commercial tea but gath-

ered this in yearly supply. I was rather dubious until she gave me a book, *Medicinal Plants of the Mountain West* by Michael Moore, a good friend of hers. In it was the complete description with directions for gathering, drying, and ultimately brewing this interesting plant.

Cota, or Indian Tea, is difficult to identify positively until it blooms, as there are other plants that resemble it before the yellow tufts appear. When it blooms, the delicate, graceful, swaying blue-green stems are tipped with round, yellow, "petal-less" flowers, indicative of the species. Large areas of this plant are easy to gather and one does not need to worry that the species may become extinct because of a fondness for "wild tea," since it is quite abundant. Cota has a nice piney taste and is well worth the time and effort involved in getting it from the pasture to the teapot.

Among the Pueblo peoples of New Mexico and Arizona, its use as a tea has continued from ancient times to the present day.

Townsendia exscapa
Easter Daisy

Plant: Dwarf perennial growing from woody roots that protrude to just above the ground. The leaves are in a dense rosette at ground level. They are 2 inches long with narrow, straight sides, somewhat wider toward the tip, and gray-green in color.
Flower: The stems barely extend up and out of the ground. There is a large solitary flower, 2 inches across, on the tip of each short stem. The numerous ray flowers are white (never yellow), fertile, and ¼–½ inch long. The many disk flowers have yellow corollas and are usually fertile. This daisy blooms in the very early spring before anything else has turned green; March–May.
Fruit: Achene, oblanceolate, with 2 ribs and dense hairs sticking up.
Range: Easter Daisy is not very common,

but does grow infrequently on the Western Plains. It prefers short-grass pasturelands and can be found from northern Mexico through Arizona, New Mexico, western Texas, and northward into Canada.
Remarks: Aptly named, this wildflower blooms sometime around Easter. The showiest part is the large flower head, which appears to be growing on the ground in the center of a tuft of green foliage. But because of its size and the fact that it blooms while the surrounding flora is still dry and brown, it is easy to see and a definite harbinger of spring.

Tragopogon major
Goatsbeard, Star of David, Salsify, Oyster Plant, Noonflower, Jerusalem Star

Plant: Biennial with a deep, turnip-shaped taproot. It grows about 2–3 feet tall. The stems branch from near the base of the plant. They contain a milky sap and are smooth and tough, becoming swollen and hollow just beneath the flower head. The gray-green leaves, which clasp the stem at their base, are long and grasslike, tapering to a point.
Flower: Each stem bears a single flower head, consisting only of ray flowers (15 or more on each head), which are bright yellow. The bracts, behind the ray flowers in 2 rows, equal the length of the rays, with some extending well beyond the tips of the ray flowers. The bracts are narrow and pointed and almost 2 inches long. The ray is also narrow and 5-toothed on the tip. The flowers are fertile and bilaterally symmetrical. The blooming period is April–July.
Fruit: Achene about 1 inch long (including a slender beak), 5-ribbed, and rough. Each seed is equipped with parachute-like fibers (much like those of Dandelion but larger). The "puffball" is spherical and 3–4 inches across when fully mature.

Range: Favoring waste grasslands, roadside ditches, fields, backyards, and vacant lots, Goatsbeard grows well in the western half of Oklahoma, central and western Texas, and the Texas panhandle.
Remarks: Three species of this genus grow in North America. Two of them have yellow flowers, and the other has purple. The plants came to this country from Europe and have naturalized quite well here.

On the Western Plains, *Tragopogon major* makes its presence known in extensive stands by the roadside. The large yellow flowers are easily visible from a moving vehicle, and the larger "puffballs" are even showier. However, one must observe the flowers before noon, for they close shortly thereafter; hence one of the common names, Noonflower.

Goatsbeard was brought to this country for its edible root, which is reported to taste somewhat like oysters and can be cooked as a stew or eaten raw in salads. The root can be dried, ground, and used as a coffee extender. I have not yet experimented with the culinary aspects of this wildflower.

Verbesina encelioides
Cowpen Daisy, Butter Daisy, Golden Crownbeard

Plant: A much-branched annual that grows 1–4 feet tall from a taproot. Minute hairs on the leaf surfaces give it a gray-green color as well as a coarseness. The leaves are opposite or alternate and rather triangular in shape, toothed on the edges, with prominent veins on their undersides. The leaf stalks are broadly winged on either side at the base of the leaf, giving it something of an "arrowhead" shape. The leaves are 2–4 inches long.
Flower: The flower heads grow singly on the tips of leafless stems. They are 1–1½ inches across. There are 12–15 fertile yellow ray flowers (about ⅜ inch long) that

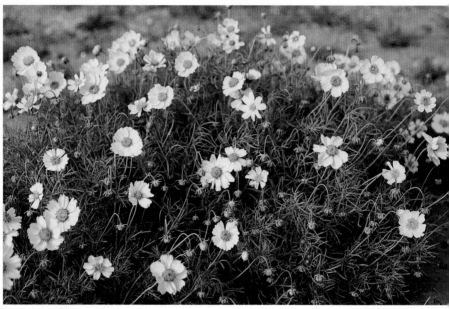

Thelesperma filifolium Greenthread

Thelesperma megapotamicum Cota

Townsendia exscapa Easter Daisy

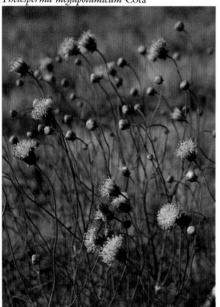

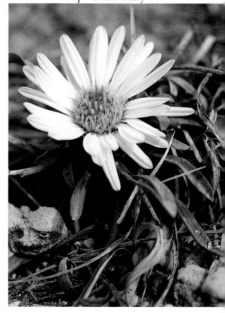

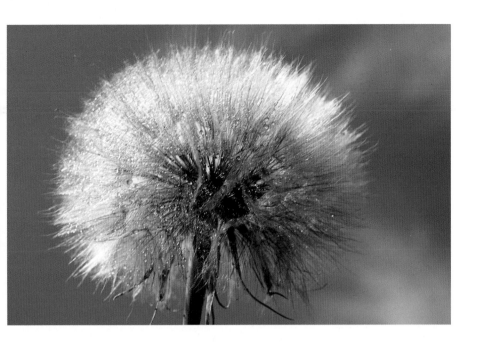

Below and right: *Tragopogon major* Goatsbeard; puffball above

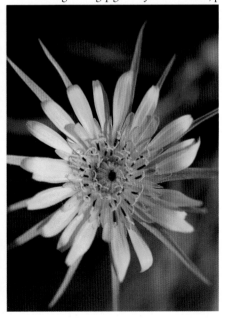
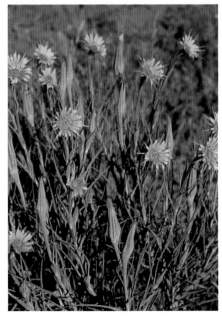

are deeply 3-toothed on the tips. The many disk flowers are yellow or yellowish-orange with outer green phyllaries that often stick up noticeably beyond the disk flowers. Cowpen Daisy blooms from July into October and even November.

Fruit: Winged achene, broad and flat, with 2 stiff teeth on the end (pappus).

Range: This hardy plant can be found growing best in disturbed sandy soils of old fields, pastures, roadsides, dry stream banks, and around cow pens and horse lots. It grows over all of Texas except the far eastern portion, west to Arizona and north to Montana, as well as throughout most of the southeastern states and into Florida.

Remarks: Cowpen Daisy often grows in the same areas that the sunflowers prefer, making it difficult to distinguish between the two. It has a strong, pungent odor when one walks through it (some might consider it almost unpleasant).

Under a microscope, the disk flowers resemble little bottles packed tightly together.

Native Americans as well as early settlers used this plant to treat skin problems and boils. It has been said that they bathed with the leaves to ease the discomfort of insect bites.

Vernonia marginata
Plains Ironweed

Plant: Stately perennial 1–4 feet tall. The stems are erect, branching only at the top. The leaves are alternate, linear, and narrow, 3–4 inches long and ½ inch or less wide. The surfaces of the leaves are minutely hairy to almost smooth and pinnately veined. The edges are smooth to faintly toothed.

Flower: The plant is branched at the top, where many flower heads grow at the tips of the separate branches. They form a flattish inflorescence of dark purple. Each head bears 10–20 flowers; the individual flowers

are less than ½ inch wide and ½ inch tall. There are no ray flowers, but the numerous 5-lobed disk flowers have both pistils and stamens and are fertile. Plains Ironweed blooms in June–September.

Fruit: The fruit is an achene, ³⁄₁₆ inch long, with 6–10 ribs. In the furrows between the ribs are microscopic resin-tipped glands. The dirty-white pappus is in two rows of irregular bristles.

Range: This species of Ironweed grows well in the panhandles of Texas and Oklahoma, as well as in New Mexico, Colorado, and Kansas. It flourishes in dry stream bottoms and low roadside ditches, in pastures, and on prairies and hillsides.

Remarks: Plains Ironweed is a hardy, drought-resistant, handsome wildflower that is very eye-catching when a large colony is in full bloom. The dark purple color is massed at the tops of the plants. The plants spread both by seed (with their dandelion-like "parachutes") and by runners underground.

Being bitter and unpalatable, Plains Ironweed grows ungrazed in pastures with livestock.

Xanthisma texanum
Sleepy Daisy

Plant: Annual herb 8–30 inches tall, branched from about midstem to the tip. The leaves are alternate and directly attached to the stem (lacking a petiole). The basal leaves are narrow and linear in shape, deeply toothed, and 1–2½ inches long. Those toward the upper portion of the plant are less than 1 inch long and untoothed or smooth on the edges.

Flower: The lemon-yellow flowers are borne singly on the tips of the slender stems. When fully open, they are almost flat and measure up to 1½ inches across. The several ray flowers are bright yellow, fertile, ³⁄₈–½ inch in length. The many disk flowers are also an intense lemon-yellow color and fertile. Sleepy Daisy blooms May–July.

Fruit: Achene covered with stiff, whitish hairs. It is only about $1/10$ inch long.

Range: Prefers the sandy and clay soils of open rangelands, neglected fields, pastures, and dry stream banks throughout the Western Plains.

Remarks: The common name, Sleepy Daisy, is derived from the fact that this wildflower does not open fully until into the morning and then closes tightly by late afternoon, well before dark. When it is fully open, it has brilliant yellow color with the 18–22 rays extending out in a neat and erect fashion, not easily blown about by hot summer winds. It is regularly visited by insects.

and with awns (bristles on the tips). The disk flowers produce flat achenes, $3/16$ inch long, with or without awns.

Range: Plains Zinnia grows well on dry, rocky hillsides, preferring calcareous soils of the Western Plains; Colorado, Arizona, New Mexico, Kansas, and the plains of Texas.

Remarks: The Plains Zinnia does not resemble cultivated zinnias in any way. This little desert plant grows low and crowded in a mound shape, looking like a tight bouquet on the ground. After the flowers fade, they remain on the stem in a paper-dry state. This is another example of a drought-resistant native plant that likes gravelly, harsh terrain. It covers areas (where few other plants will) with yellow mounds of color in the summer.

Zinnia grandiflora
Plains Zinnia, Prairie Zinnia, Rocky Mountain Zinnia

Plant: Perennial rarely over 8 inches tall; a rounded, low-growing, many-branched, woody shrublet that grows from a woody taproot. The leaves are 1 inch long, very narrow ($1/8$ inch wide), opposite, linear, and 3-nerved for at least half their length. The edges are smooth (untoothed).

Flower: There are numerous flower heads, growing 1 or 2 to a stalk. They are $3/4$–1 inch across with 3–6 (normally 3 or 4) yellow ray flowers. The ray flowers are untoothed, broad, almost round in shape, and tend to droop a bit. The disk flowers number 18–24 and are red or green in color and $3/8$ inch long. The ray flowers do not drop off when the plant matures; instead, they remain on the stem, turning dry, papery, and light brown in color. The plant blooms in the early summer and sometimes again in the fall.

Fruit: The ray flowers produce achenes that are oblanceolate, straight, 3-angled,

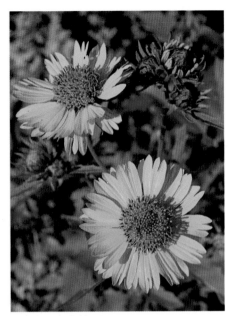

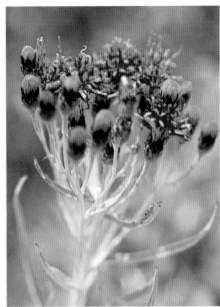

Verbesina encelioides Cowpen Daisy

Vernonia marginata Plains Ironweed

Xanthisma texanum Sleepy Daisy

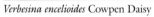

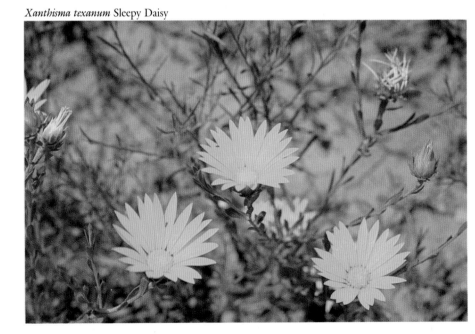

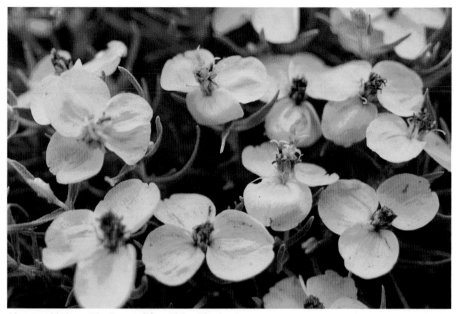

Above and below: *Zinnia grandiflora* Plains Zinnia

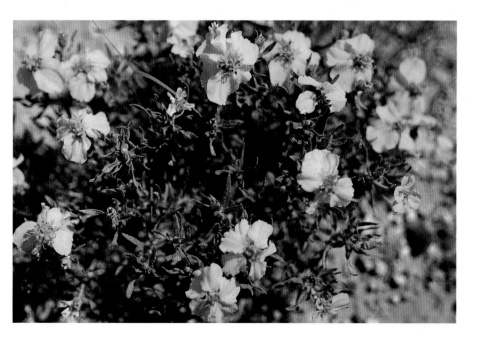

CONVOLVULACEAE
Morning Glory Family

Members of the Morning Glory Family are usually twining or trailing plants with brightly colored flowers that look like funnels or bells. The petals are joined to form this funnel or bell shape, and there may be 5 lobes, or teeth, around the edges or none at all. The corolla is twisted in the bud stage, unfurling as it opens to full bloom, then often twisting back again as it withers. When untwisted but not fully opened, the corolla looks "pleated" like an accordion. The 5 sepals often overlap and can be separate or united at their base. The ovary has 2 (but sometimes 1, 3, or 5) chambers, and 2 seeds form in each.

Calystegia sepium
Hedge Bindweed, Bindweed

Plant: The stems of this perennial plant trail and twine along the ground to lengths of 6 feet. They grow from rhizomes creeping underground. The leaves are variously shaped, some heart-shaped with notches at the base, then abruptly narrowing down the length to the pointed tip, while others have fewer notches and smoother edges. They are 1½–2½ inches long and bear microscopic hairs on both surfaces.
Flower: Solitary (or sometimes paired) flowers grow from the leaf axils on short peduncles, which grow longer with maturity. There are 2 bracts, which overlap and conceal the calyx. The corolla is funnel-shaped, slightly 5-angled on the rim, white or pale pink in color. The 5 stamens are borne on the inner surface of the corolla tube. A 1-celled ovary has a style with 2 linear-oblong stigmas. The plant blooms from May to October.
Fruit: A 2- to 4-seeded capsule.
Range: This creeping vine can grow almost anywhere in abandoned places, along rail-road tracks, highways, flower beds, and cultivated fields. It ranges throughout the United States as well as other countries.
Remarks: Because the nature of this plant is to creep and twine, it tends to climb up any supporting plant that it can, eventually choking out large areas of cotton and other crops, if they are left untended. It is difficult to eradicate and farmers really hate it. Just don't tell them it is a pretty little wild morning glory.

The flowers usually open in the morning and close in the afternoon, and when a lush carpet of Hedge Bindweed is in full bloom, the bell-shaped flowers are rather showy.

Convolvulus equitans
Texas Bindweed, Bindweed

Plant: Perennial from a taproot, with stems that trail on the ground and grow to 6 feet in length. The leaves vary in shape, ranging from oval-round to narrow and oblong; they are sometimes toothed or lobed. They have microscopic hairs on both upper and lower surfaces and are ½–2 inches long and ⅛–1¼ inches wide.
Flower: The flowers, growing on stalks from the leaf axils, usually occur singly but can be in 2's or 3's. They are funnel-shaped (the 5 petals are fused to form a funnel), with each corolla being rather narrow at the base, then flaring out on the tip and becoming 5-angled; the angles are sometimes so pronounced as to have slight points at each one. The white to pale pink flower has a deeper red center, or throat, and is 1–1¼ inches long and ½–¾ inch across. There are 5 sepals, and the stamens are borne on the inner surface of the petals (epipetalous). The ovary is 2-celled; there are 2 flat, linear stigmas on a simple style. Texas Bindweed blooms from April or May into September and October.
Fruit: A 2- to 4-seeded capsule.
Range: This plant flourishes in disturbed ground of cultivated fields and lawns, road-

sides, and prairies of western Oklahoma, Texas, Kansas, Colorado, and Arizona; also into Mexico.

Remarks: This, like the other bindweeds, is a generally hated and cursed plant because of its ability to "take over" large areas usually intended for profitable crops such as cotton, feed grains, sunflowers, etc. However, the symmetry and color of its funnel-shaped flower with the distinct red center is worthy of praise.

Cuscuta squamata
Dodder, Love Vine

Plant: Dodder is a true parasite. It has no leaves or roots, just a tangle of yellow or orange stems twining around a host plant. Actually, the seeds do germinate on the ground, but when the slender stems attach themselves to nearby plants, they lose their connection with the ground, and the Dodder begins to derive its livelihood from these neighboring plants. By means of suckers attached to the stems of the other plants, Dodder feeds on the nutrients provided by its neighbors (to the detriment of the neighbors).

Flower: The flowers are small (⅛–¼ inch long and ¼ inch across) and in a few- to several-flowered cyme. Each flower in the cluster is white, 5-merous with the perianth parts partially united, and subtended by 2 to several compact bracts. The 5 sepals are rather pointed on the tips. The corolla is 5-lobed with each lobe somewhat pointed on its tip also. The 5 stamens arise from the corolla throat. There is 1 pistil with 2 styles. Dodder blooms in July and August.

Fruit: Somewhat cone-shaped capsule that opens near the base to drop the 1–4 seeds.

Range: Often found twining over plants around the margins of playa lakes or along the roadsides, Dodder grows in southern New Mexico, northern Mexico, and parts of Texas. It is not a common plant on the Western Plains.

Remarks: Dodder is a most unusual plant. When observed by the roadside, it looks like discarded yellow twine or plastic string clumped and matted over the existing vegetation. Instead it is a parasite, sucking and absorbing the life from the green plants growing nearby.

Evolvulus nuttallianus
Silky Evolvulus, Shaggy Evolvulus, Hairy Evolvulus, Dwarf Morning Glory, Ojo de Víbora

Plant: Low perennial, growing from a stout root, with erect stems 2–9 inches tall. It is densely downy, being covered with long, silky hairs. The alternate leaves are lanceolate to oblong-elliptic, ¼–¾ inch long, ¹⁄₁₆–¼ inch wide, and hairy on both the upper and under sides. They are smooth-edged with short petioles.

Flower: The pale lavender flowers grow in the axils of the leaves, being spirally twisted in the bud, as is typical of morning glories. There are 5 sepals united at the base and 5 petals united to form a shallow, funnel-shaped flower ⅓–½ inch across. There are 2 styles, each having 2 branches; the stigma is threadlike. The bloom season is from April into July.

Fruit: A 1–4-seeded capsule about ⅛ inch long.

Range: From North Dakota and Montana down to north central and western Texas, Arizona, and Tennessee, Silky Evolvulus can be found growing in sandy or rocky soils, preferring poor, dry conditions in open pastures.

Remarks: The many common names of this wildflower accurately describe it as being silky, shaggy or hairy, and a dwarf. Its color is a soft lavender, fading to almost white in the center, but it is difficult to see and hardly showy since it is so small and pale. It does not climb or twine around other plants; therefore it is not disliked as are the other wild morning glories.

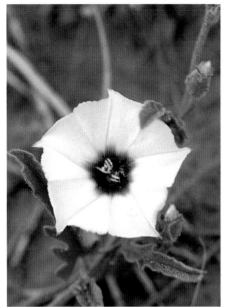

Convolvulus equitans Texas Bindweed

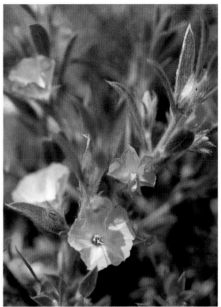

Evolvulus nuttallianus Silky Evolvulus

Calystegia sepium Hedge Bindweed

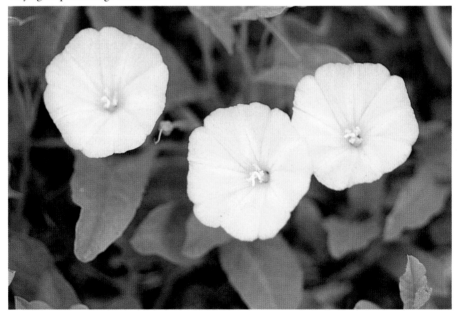

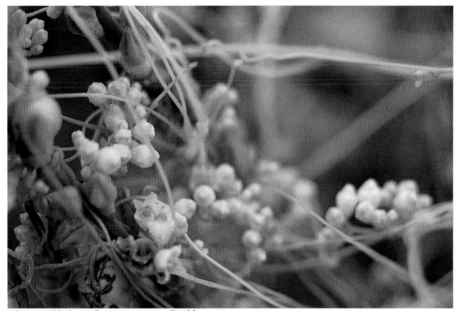

Above and below: *Cuscuta squamata* Dodder

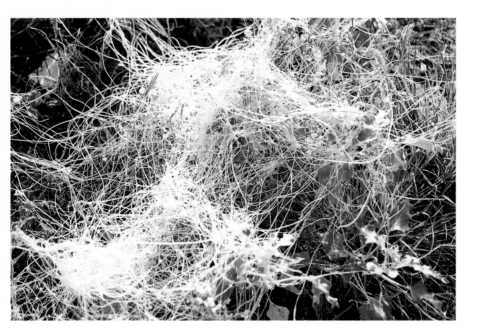

CRUCIFERAE (Brassicaceae)
Mustard Family

Flowers in the Mustard Family are generally easy to recognize. There are always 4 sepals and 4 petals, which can be pink, white, yellow, or purple. The petals are radially symmetrical, forming a cross, from which the name is derived. (Latin *cruci-* means "cross.") The primarily spring-blooming flowers are usually in a raceme, with the youngest flowers, at the tip, continuing to bloom while the ones beneath are forming fruit. Generally, there are 6 stamens (4 with longer filaments than the other 2). The leaves vary greatly in this family, but the fruit is always a pod, either long and thin or short and wide, with a partition down the middle dividing the seeds into two individual chambers.

Cauliflower, turnip, radish, cabbage, broccoli, rutabaga, watercress, and alyssum are all members of this large family.

Descurainia pinnata
Tansy Mustard

Plant: Annual with several stems growing from the base and branching above. The stems and leaves are grayish-green in color because of the dense and minute hairs on the surfaces of both. The plant can grow up to 2 feet tall. The leaves are bipinnate (cut into many very narrow segments with these segments often deeply incised).

Flower: The sepals and petals are about the same length (up to $\frac{1}{10}$ inch). The petals are whitish to bright yellow and clawed (which means they have a very narrow base, almost petiole-like in shape). The sepals have a soft rose color to their surfaces. As with most Cruciferae, there are 4 sepals, 6 stamens, and 4 petals forming a cross-shaped structure (crucifix). Their blooming period is from very early spring through early summer, February–June.

Fruit: Narrow, cylindrical pod usually $\frac{1}{4}$–$\frac{3}{4}$ inch long and very slightly larger at the apex than at the base (giving it a somewhat clublike shape). Tiny seeds are arranged in 2 rows and crowded in the pod. The seedpod is so slightly curved that it appears to be growing straight.

Range: This plant can be found in nearly every waste place throughout the Western Plains as well as Canada and northern Mexico. It appears to be more prolific in yards, vacant lots, and ditches in towns than in rangelands and pasturelands farther from civilization.

Remarks: Actually, Tansy Mustard is considered just an ordinary weed. The flowers are definitely not showy, fragrant, or usable for bouquets, fresh or dried. The plant is not suitable at any time in its life cycle for human consumption. It is included as part of this collection because in the very early spring, it is sometimes the first and only plant blooming. When no other color can be seen, this plain plant stands out with its delicate, pale yellow flowering tips.

Dimorphocarpa wislizeni
(= *Dithyraea wislizeni*)
Spectacle Pod

Plant: An erect annual herb, grayish in color, Spectacle Pod grows 1–3 and sometimes as much as 5 feet tall. There are 1 to several stems, branching at the base. The leaves are broad and lanceolate and, like the stems, are covered with microscopic whitish hairs. They are somewhat toothed to nearly smooth on the margins.

Flower: The flowers grow in racemes (each flower, with a tiny stem or pedicel, is borne along a straight axis with the younger flowers near the tip). They form large flower heads. The 4 sepals, which are closed tightly when the flower is in the bud, are a delicate gray-mauve color and covered with tiny hairs. When the bud opens, the 4 petals are white (³⁄₁₆–⁵⁄₁₆ inch long), but the mauve sepals can still be seen below the petals. The plant has a long blooming period starting in late April and lasting until October.

Fruit: A flat, 2-seeded, peculiar-looking seedpod develops on the ends of the pedicels after the petals have dropped off. The seeds resemble 2 tiny lenses of old-fashioned spectacles protruding at right angles to the stem.

Range: Preferring sandhill country and grasslands, this plant ranges from northern Mexico through New Mexico, Colorado, Nevada, up into Utah, over to western Oklahoma, and western and southwestern Texas, as well as Arizona.

Remarks: A striking plant, Spectacle Pod is easily visible on the roadsides and in pastures beginning in the early spring. When one zips along the highway at 55 miles per hour or more, the grayish plant appears to have white flowers. Only when one stops and takes the time to examine them closely, does one discover the delicate grayish-mauve color throughout the flower head and the little "spectacles."

In northern Arizona, the Hopi are reported to have used this plant to treat wounds.

This plant has been known by a synonym, *Dithyraea wislizeni.*

Lesquerella gordonii
Bladderpod, Popweed, Beadpop, Gordon Bladderpod

Plant: An early-blooming annual spring flower with horizontal stems that curve upward. Its leaves grow alternately up the stems and also up to 4 inches long in rosettes at the base of the plant. They are narrow and lanceolate, usually not toothed as they grow up the stem. The stems are from 2 to 12 inches long at flowering. (They grow 2–8 inches tall on the Western Plains, depending upon the winter moisture they have received.)

Flower: Many loose clusters of bright yellow 4-petaled flowers. The petals are ¼–⅓ inch long. They begin to bloom in late February or early March and continue into May. During warm winters they can bloom even earlier.

Fruit: Spherical, inflated pods (about ⅛ inch in diameter) grow on S-shaped pedicels. The pods are partitioned in half with 5–10 round, flattened seeds on each side of the partition.

Range: Northern Mexico north through New Mexico, Arizona, and Utah, then west into California; also in Texas and western Oklahoma.

Remarks: A vivid yellow, low-growing carpet of blossoms appearing in the early spring is nearly always Bladderpod. Winter-weary cattle relish it as a delicious forage plant. When the seedpods mature and become dry, they "pop" when stepped on, hence one of its common names.

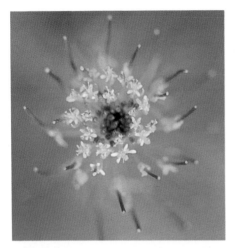

Descurainia pinnata Tansy Mustard; close-up above

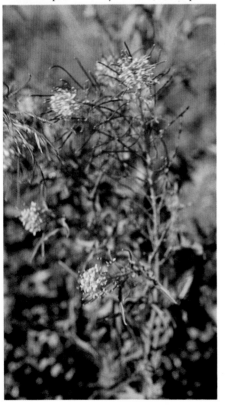

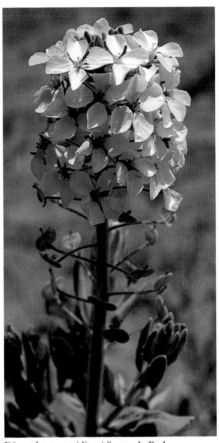

Dimorphocarpa wislizeni Spectacle Pod
Opposite: *Lesquerella gordonii* Bladderpod

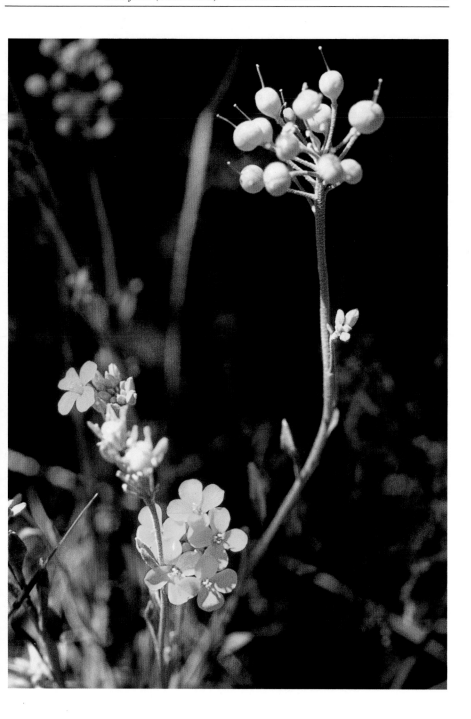

CUCURBITACEAE
Gourd or Melon Family

The Gourd Family consists of herbaceous plants, both annuals and perennials. The stems have coiling tendrils and climb or trail as vines do. The alternate leaves are borne singly, varying from simple to compound. The unisexual flowers (either male or female) grow on the same plant in all species except *Ibervillea*. The flower is bell-shaped, with 5 spreading lobes forming the "bell." Usually its color is yellow, yellow-orange, greenish, or white. Generally there are 3 stamens, but sometimes 5. The ovary is inferior, forming the bulbous gourd (or berry) at the base of the flower where it attaches to the stem.

The Gourd or Melon Family, as the name implies, contains many important foods used worldwide, including watermelons, cucumbers, squash, cantalopes, pumpkins, and gourds.

Cucurbita foetidissima
Buffalo Gourd, Stinking Gourd, Common Gourd, Wild Gourd

Plant: Coarse perennial trailing vine that grows from very large roots deep underground. The thick stems can reach out to 20 or 30 feet in length. The gray-green leaves are thick, triangular-ovate, 4–12 inches long, and rough to the touch. Their margins are irregularly toothed.

Flower: The flowers are unisexual, meaning each is either male (staminate) or female (pistillate), and both are on the same plant. They are yellow to orange in color and 2–4 inches long. The flaring, bell-shaped blossom is 5-lobed to about the middle, then united to the base. Each flower is solitary in a leaf axil. The male flower has 3 stamens pressed together, and the female flower has 3 aborted stamens, a sticky 3-lobed stigma, and an inferior

swollen ovary well below the sepals. They bloom from May to July or later.

Fruit: Round or globular, about 2–4 inches across. When immature, fruits are green with dark green stripes. As they mature, they turn yellow, then light brown as they become drier. The gourd, or berry, is filled with many flat, tawny-colored seeds.

Range: This fast growing vine is widely distributed in waste places (especially railroad rights-of-way) and seems to be spreading rapidly. It can be found in Nebraska, Missouri, California, Arizona, Texas, Oklahoma, New Mexico, and Mexico.

Remarks: The common names Buffalo Gourd and Stinking Gourd come from the fact that when the stems or leaves are bruised, they smell awful! The experience of walking through a dense mat of this large vine will "linger" with you, on shoes and clothing, for a long time.

Children have always gathered the dried gourds to make craft items, to play with, or just to throw at one another. My boys preferred the latter.

The thick root is high in starch, and the seeds are rich in protein and oil. Buffalo Gourd is considered to be a potential new crop plant for dry areas.

Ibervillea lindheimeri
Balsam Gourd, Globe Berry

Plant: Slender climbing vine with unbranched tendrils. The thick leaves are smooth, simple, and alternate on the stems, deeply 3- to 5-lobed, with the lobes coarsely toothed and bearing tiny, almost microscopic warts.

Flower: The unisexual flowers (either male or female) are found on different vines. They are greenish-yellow in color, sometimes striped with green. The staminate (male) flowers grow in short racemes, while the pistillate (female) flowers are borne singly. There are 5 sepals, united at the base, and 5 petals, united to form the corolla tube but flaring out to an almost flat surface on the end in 5 separate petals. There are 3 stamens deeply inserted in the tube of the male flower. The female flower has a 3-lobed stigma with an inferior swollen ovary well below the blossom. Balsam Gourd blooms in May and June.

Fruit: A bright orangy-red ball, or berry, about 1–2 inches in diameter. It has a smooth skin and is filled with plump seeds.

Range: Balsam Gourd grows in open pastures but really prefers fencerows, low shrubs, or trees to climb. It can be found in southern Oklahoma, Texas, New Mexico, southeast Arizona, and Mexico.

Remarks: This vine is often found in wild plum thickets, if there are wild plums in the area. Otherwise, it climbs other trees and shrubs. The flowers are hardly noticeable, but the bright orange-red fruit is easily visible at eye level, or higher, in the trees.

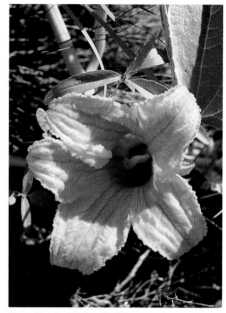

Cucurbita foetidissima Buffalo Gourd: flower above, fruit below

Ibervillea lindheimeri Balsam Gourd

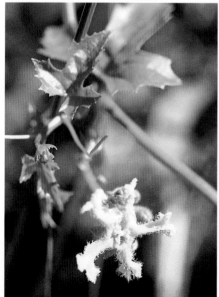

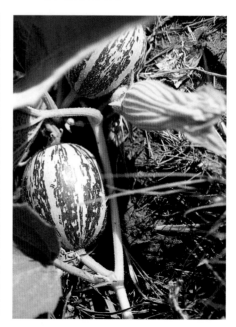

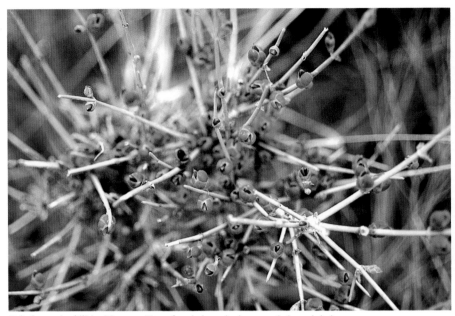

Ephedra antisyphilitica Mormon Tea: female branch above, male branch below

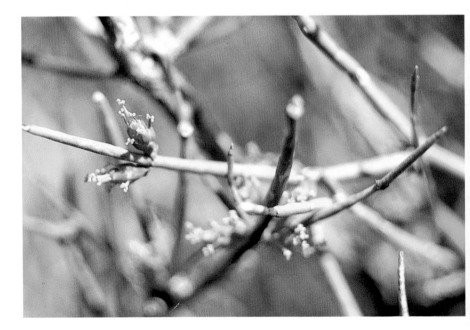

EPHEDRACEAE
Ephedra Family

Members of the Ephedra Family are Gymnosperms, thus not true flowering plants (Angiosperms). They are commonly found on the Western Plains. The family consists mostly of shrubs with jointed branches and leaves that are scalelike (not typically leaflike) and are opposite or whorled, usually having been reduced to sheaths that are united at their base. The reproductive parts (not technically flowers) are unisexual, either male or female. The staminate (male) ones have stamens that are united by their filaments. Beneath these stamens is a 2-lobed, calyx-like perianth. The ovulate (female) ones have 1 or 2 erect ovules wrapped in an urn-shaped perianth which hardens when mature.

A single genus with several species, it is usually found in the more arid and semiarid regions of North America.

Ephedra antisyphilitica
Mormon Tea, Squaw Tea, Cowboy Tea, Desert Tea, American Ephedra, Joint Fir, Clapweed, Popotillo

Plant: Spreading shrub that grows to about 40 inches tall. There is seldom a pronounced central trunk. The branches are hard and stiff, alternate or whorled at the nodes, and ⅜ inch thick. The segments of stems, or branches, between the nodes are ¾–2 inches long. The new stems are smooth, green, and have tiny grooves. With age they become yellow-green, then grayish-green. The tiny grooves become cracks in the grayish bark. The leaves are in pairs, only ¹⁄₁₆–⅛ inch long (actually reduced to scales), and located at the nodes. They soon split and fall off.

Reproductive structure: The reproductive organs are in several cones emerging at the nodes of the branches. They are unisexual, with the male and female cones growing on separate shrubs. The staminate cones are elliptic in shape and ¼–⅜ inch long with 5–8 pairs of thickened bracts, the margins pale green to reddish in color. The staminal column is ¼ inch long and protrudes about half its length (from the tip of the cone). It has 4–6 anthers. The ovulate cones are elliptic in shape, ⁵⁄₁₆–½ inch long, with 4–6 pairs of ovulate bracts. These pairs of bracts become bright orange-red and fleshy when ripe. Mormon Tea blooms in May and occasionally in September and October.

Fruit: The ovulate cones produce a single seed, or rarely a pair, 3-angled or sometimes 4-angled, light brown, smooth, ¼–⅜ inch long, and ¹⁄₁₆–⅛ inch wide.

Range: Found in rocky, gravelly soils of rimrocks, canyon ledges, arroyos, and ravines from southwest Oklahoma through the western two-thirds of Texas, including the panhandle, up through the Four Corners area of New Mexico, Colorado, Utah, and Arizona, then into south central California. It also grows down into Mexico.

Remarks: This can hardly be considered a "wildflower." It is a straggly, jointed, occasionally creeping, medium-sized shrub. It has, for all practical purposes, no leaves. The overall appearance is that of a weather-beaten, gnarled or sickly pine tree. However, the strange-looking red-orange reproductive structures are striking. They are very different in their appearance, fascinating under a microscope, and worthy of note here.

The young, slender branches, gathered and dried, make a tasty tea that is used today by many Native Americans and Spanish-speaking people of the Southwest. I have brewed tea from this plant and found it refreshing.

An Old World species of *Ephedra* is the source for ephedrine, a compound useful in the treatment of nasal colds, asthma, and hay fever.

FUMARIACEAE
Bleeding Heart Family

The Fumariaceae typically have 2 tiny sepals, 4 petals, and 6 stamens (in 2 sets of 3 each). They are herbaceous plants with watery sap. The leaves can be in the shape of a rosette or alternate on the stem and usually are much divided. The flowers can be terminal or axillary.

In this family, the 4 petals are of 2 different sizes and shapes, with the 2 outer ones wrapped around the inner 2 (which adhere by their tips). Some genera have outer petals that extend backward like "spurs." This arrangement makes these flowers bilaterally symmetrical.

As common names of wildflowers are often misleading, do not be confused by this one; the domesticated bleeding hearts (genus *Dicentra*) of flower beds are not found wild on the Western Plains.

Corydalis aurea Scrambled Eggs

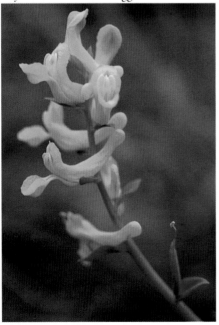

Corydalis aurea var. *occidentalis*
Scrambled Eggs, Golden Smoke, Curvepod

Plant: A winter annual or biennial, this plant branches from the root and has stems that can be erect or prostrate and 4–14 inches long, containing a watery sap. The leaves are pinnate (leaflets arranged feather-like on each side of a common petiole), with the 5–7 pinnae again cleft into narrow lobes and those again incised. This incising gives the leaf its "feathery" or shaggy look.

Flower: The 2 minute sepals are rather oval in shape, toothed on their edges, and about ⅛ inch long. The bright yellow flowers are ½–¾ inch long. The upper petal has a saclike spur at the base and is slightly incurved and blunt on the end. The flowers grow in a raceme or spikelike arrangement. The 6 stamens are in 2 sets of 3 each. The blooming period is March–May.

Fruit: Elongated bivalved capsule with several tiny black seeds. The style remains attached to the fruit capsule. The fruits are strongly curved, stout, and erect.

Range: Preferring a prairielike habitat, Scrambled Eggs grows in open pastures and along roadsides that are sandy or gravelly. It usually grows in small colonies from northern Mexico through the western half of Texas to southern Nevada, then northward to Alaska. It also grows in New England.

Remarks: This is one of the many bright yellow wildflowers that can be found on the Western Plains in the very early spring.

The common name Scrambled Eggs is comical and thought-provoking. The petals are unusual in their design and placement, and it is possible that some imaginative person perceived that a plate of scrambled eggs thrown out to land on green vegetation might, indeed, look like this yellow flower.

Members of this family are often united with members of the Papaveraceae, or Poppy Family, because of basic similarities.

GENTIANACEAE
Gentian Family

Worldwide, the Gentian Family is quite large, but on the Western Plains there are not that many to be found. They prefer more temperate regions.

The flowers of this family can be small or large and are borne solitary or in clusters. There are 4 or 5 corolla lobes, which spread out at the end of a tube, giving it a bell shape, but in some species the tube is so short that the bell shape is not evident and the corolla lobes look like separate petals instead. They range in color from white to greenish, pink to purple and blue.

There are 5 stamens that are attached to the corolla. The ovary has 1 cavity with ovules on the inner surface, arranged either in 2 lines or all over it. It has a 2-lobed stigma.

The leaves are usually paired or sometimes whorled in a circle on the stem. They are smooth-edged and not lobed. Except in 1 genus, they are undivided.

Eustoma exaltatum
Bluebell, Prairie Gentian, Lira de San Pedro

Plant: Annual, 1–3½ feet tall, with more or less branched stems. The leaves are very smooth, paired, and clasping (the leaves have no stalks, so they partly surround or clasp the stems). They are 1–3 inches long and 1 inch wide, ovate or egg-shaped in outline, attached at the wide end, and tapering to the tip. They are also noticeably 3-veined.

Flower: The flowers are solitary, large, and deep blue or bluish-purple. The color blends to a lighter shade at the base of the tube, or throat, of the large blossom. The 5 or sometimes 6 petals join at the base to form a tube about ⅜ inch long. The corolla lobes are 1 inch long or less, and only

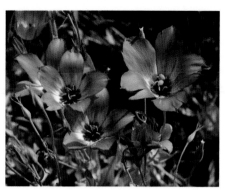

Eustoma exaltatum Bluebell

½–⅝ inch wide. The ovary produces a threadlike style with a 2-lobed stigma at its tip. There are 5 or 6 stamens joined to the throat of the corolla tube. Bluebell can bloom from June to September, but on the Western Plains it usually blooms in July and August.

Fruit: Oblong capsule ½–¾ inch long.

Range: This plant is found in moist places by the roads, in fields, on the prairies around watering holes, and on riverbanks. It does well in salty, wet places on the Western Plains and grows over most of the southern United States, western Texas, and into Mexico.

Remarks: Even though I have been searching for, studying, and photographing wildflowers for over 20 years, I still find plants that I have never seen before. Bluebell was one of these, discovered on the bank of a sometimes wet, usually dry river. A greater than average rainfall had rendered it continually wet through the spring and summer of 1985. It was well worth the walk through tall weeds, grassburs, flying biting insects, and deep mud to meet this beautiful "new friend" face to face.

Incidentally, *eustoma* means "open mouth" and refers to the large throat area of the flower.

Because of their popularity and beauty, Bluebells are becoming more infrequent in the wild. PLEASE DO NOT PICK.

GERANIACEAE
Geranium Family

The Geranium Family is characterized by its 5-merous parts. In other words, there are always 5 petals, 5 or 10 stamens (arranged in 2 series), and a pistil that has 5 parts. The strange-looking seedpod (which resembles the head and beak of a stork or crane) is a most unusual feature of this family. The seeds are contained in the short, thickened "head," and the style elongates into a pointed "beak." The flowers are radially symmetrical and usually purplish or rose-pink. The leaves are either palmately or pinnately divided, cleft, or lobed.

The word "geranium" is derived from the Greek word *geranion*, meaning "crane."

Erodium texanum
(Stork's-bill)

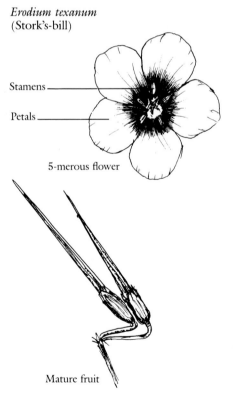

Stamens ——

Petals ——

5-merous flower

Mature fruit

Erodium cicutarium
Cranesbill, Stork's-bill, Pin Clover, Filaree, Alfilaria

Plant: This annual plant lies prostrate on the ground with horizontal stems up to 20 inches long. In this semiarid area, the many stems arising from a dense rosette of leaves usually are 2–8 inches long, depending upon winter moisture in the ground. The leaf blades are finely dissected, with the divided segments toothed and cleft. They have a fernlike or featherlike appearance and grow up to 4 inches long.

Flower: The 5 sepals (only 1/16–1/4 inch long) have white hairs on their surfaces, linear green veins, and are tipped with 1 or 2 bristles. The small pink or rose flowers have 5 petals and grow longer than the sepals (about 1/4–1/3 inch long). There are 10 (rarely 5) stamens, a pistil with 5 united carpels, and 5 stigma tips showing. The flowers bloom in clusters of 2–5 during the months from February to May.

Fruit: The style column can grow to 2 inches long. The dull brown seed is about 3/16 inch long with a "tail" extending to 1½–2 inches inside the style column. This elongated part of the pistil, with its seeds enclosed, looks like a miniature replica of a crane, heron, or stork head and bill. The 2–5 clusters of these seedpods usually grow pointing straight up. As the style column dries, it splits open, exposing the seeds and their long "tails" to the drying air. Each one coils up spirally, as it dries, and breaks loose from its enclosure, then eventually is blown away to rotate or "screw" itself into the ground and thus be ready for germination later.

Range: Cranesbill prefers rocky or sandy soils and can be found in fields, open places, roadsides, waste places, and lawns. It grows from Canada through Michigan and Illinois, south to Virginia, Tennessee, Arkansas, Texas, and Mexico.

Remarks: This plant, with its delicate leaves and small pink blossoms, is among the first wildflowers to bloom in the spring. The leaves have been growing during the winter months, and even with scant moisture in the ground, the plant can still produce blossoms that last only a day. The seedpods look like hungry baby birds with their beaks up.

Originating in Europe, *Erodium cicutarium* is doing quite well as a naturalized American plant today.

Erodium texanum
Stork's-bill, Filaree

Plant: Annual, or sometimes biennial, forming rosettes with spreading leafy branches. It has horizontal stems up to 16 inches long. The leaves are opposite, ovate in outline, round-toothed and 3-lobed.
Flower: The flowers are in clusters of 2–7. The petals are purple or rose-violet, nearly 1 inch long and twice as long as the sepals. Typical of the Geranium Family, there are 5 sepals, 5 petals, 10 stamens (in 2 circles), and a pistil that has 5 parts. The plant blooms from March to May.
Fruit: The style column, which contains the seeds, greatly resembles the head and beak of a miniature stork. It is 1¼–2½ inches long and contains 5 tan seeds, each with a long beak. As they dry in the low humidity of the Western Plains, each seed is freed. The beak, which is bearded on the inner surface, coils up (corkscrew fashion) as it dries. The seed is smooth, slender, and pointed on the end. As each blows away and falls to the ground, the beak straightens or coils back up, according to the humidity. The minute hairs on the inner surface catch on the dirt and drive the pointed tip of the seed into the ground. This action, together with the wind, actually "screws" this tiny corkscrew into the ground.
Range: Preferring clay and sandy loams of grasslands, Stork's-bill grows from Texas to southern Utah and southeast California.

Remarks: One of the earliest plants to bloom in the spring, Stork's-bill is relished by grazing livestock. It was introduced to this country from the Mediterranean countries.

Geranium carolinianum
Carolina Geranium, Wild Geranium, Cranesbill

Plant: Annual or biennial herb 6–12 inches tall. The stems are much-branched and rather sprawling. The 2½-inch-wide leaves are palmately 5-parted, these divisions being cleft or lobed again and round-toothed on their edges. The plant is covered with short hairs.
Flower: The flowers are in a loose terminal cluster with 5 petals of pale pink or white, ¼–⅜ inch long and oblanceolate in shape. The underlying sepals are usually longer than the petals. There are usually 10 stamens, 5 of them longer than the other 5. The plant blooms in April and May.
Fruit: Similar to that of *Erodium texanum*, or Stork's-bill, being elongated (the style column almost ½ inch long) and resembling a tiny stork's or crane's beak or bill. The 5 seeds are oblong and ⅟₁₆ inch long. The "tails" on the seeds do not coil spirally but curl upward.
Range: This little geranium prefers dry, hard ground, wastelands, gravelly or clay soils. It is found from Alaska, Canada, and New England south to Florida and Mexico.
Remarks: With sepals as long as or longer than the petals, the flower appears nestled in a green cup at the tip of the stem of a rather low-lying or sprawling plant. The large leaves are eagerly grazed by livestock, causing this to be a hard-to-find spring wildflower. When the seedpods develop, it is easy to recognize and fun to discover the miniature "storks' bills" so similar to those of its cousins, *Erodium texanum* and *E. cicutarium*.

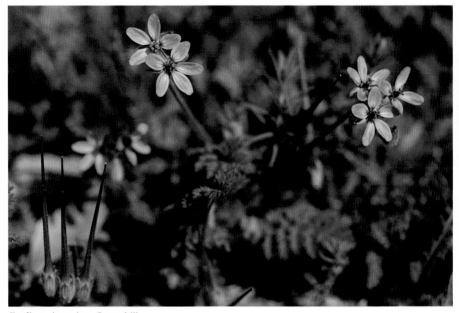

Erodium cicutarium Cranesbill

Opposite: *Erodium texanum* Stork's-bill

Geranium carolinianum Carolina Geranium

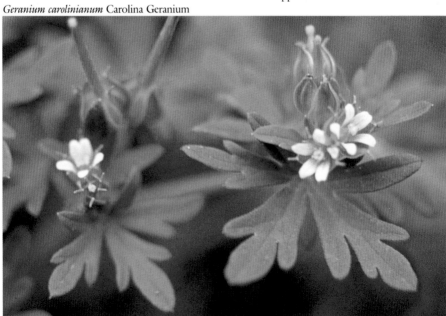

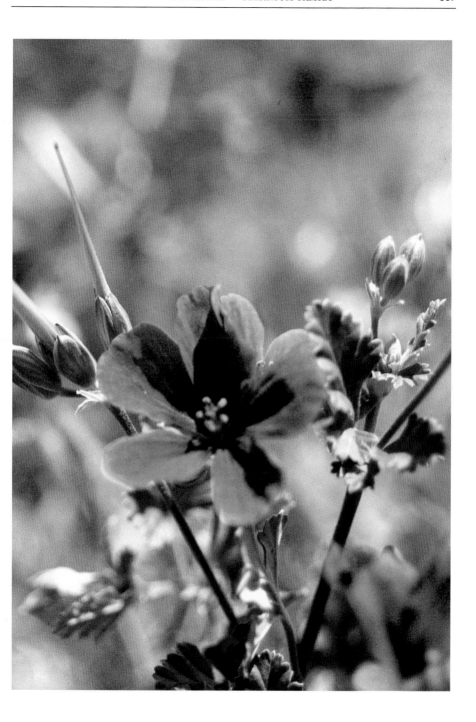

HYDROPHYLLACEAE
Waterleaf Family

The Waterleaf Family is mostly composed of large and small herbs with an occasional shrub. The leaves are either in a rosette at ground level or borne singly. They are pinnately lobed, cleft, or divided. The flowers are 5-merous, regular (radially symmetrical), and have both stamens and pistils. The color is usually blue, lavender, or purple with a very few being white or yellow. The 5 petals join to form a bell, funnel, or narrow tube, flaring at the end. The calyx is deeply lobed. The stamens are borne upon the petals; so there are only as many stamens as petals. The ovary is 1- or 2-celled, maturing into a capsule bearing few to many seeds.

Nama hispidum
Waterleaf, Nama

Plant: Small annual herbaceous plant growing barely 6 inches tall. The narrow leaves are not divided, nor are they deeply cleft. Somewhat succulent and ⅜–¾ inch long, they are borne singly and scattered over the erect, bristly gray stems.
Flower: The blue-purple flowers grow in crowded clusters at the tips of the branches. The 5 petals are fused to form a little bell about ½ inch long. The stamens are unequal in length and do not project beyond the corolla. There are 2 styles. Waterleaf blooms in April, May, and June.
Fruit: From a superior ovary, several yellow seeds develop in a capsule.
Range: This plant prefers sand and gravel but grows in many habitats throughout Texas, spreading north to Oklahoma and west to Arizona and California.
Remarks: A lovely small spring-bloomer, Waterleaf would be expected to have fat fleshy leaves, judging from its name. Actually, they are not as fleshy as one would anticipate, but are somewhat succulent-

looking. In the spring, with some early rains, this plant can be covered with rich purple bell-shaped flowers, low to the ground, but colorful and easy to locate.

Phacelia congesta
Blue Curls, Spike Phacelia, Spiderflower

Plant: Annual or biennial 4–24 inches tall. The leaves, which are covered with minute gray hairs, are alternate, ovate, and 2–4½ inches long. They are once or twice pinnately cleft with round-ended lobe segments (appearing almost fernlike).
Flower: The flowers are perfect, meaning they have both stamens and pistils, and are arranged along 1 side of a progressively uncurling raceme. Blossoms open progressively from the base of the inflorescence to the terminal end. Only 2–3 flowers are open at any one time, located at and just below the curve of the raceme. The 5 sepals are united, as are the 5 bluish-purple petals. Their lobes are rounded and half as long as the tube. The corolla is ¼–⅓ inch across. The 5 stamens arise straight up and out (exserted) from the corolla. The blooming period is March–June.
Fruit: Oval capsule, 1/16–⅛ inch long, containing 2 or 4 seeds. The seeds are smooth and unwrinkled (not corrugated).
Range: Blue Curls grow well in sandy or gravelly soils and prefer rocky places. Sometimes they can be seen in roadside ditches in Texas, New Mexico, Arizona, and Mexico.
Remarks: This plant's most unusual characteristic is the tightly coiled inflorescence with 2 rows of buds on the same side. (It makes one think of octopus tentacles.) When the buds open and the blue-purple blossoms appear, the exserted stamens look like antennae tipped with yellow. The plants often are found growing in colonies, enhancing the rich color of the flowers.

IRIDACEAE
Iris Family

Members of the Iris Family include perennials and annuals, with rootstocks that are short in some cases and long in others. The leaves are folded lengthwise down the midrib. (They look like grass except for this crease down the middle.) A distinctive feature is that each leaf enfolds the next younger leaf, which faces toward it. The flowers contain both pistils and stamens and grow from spathelike bracts.

Members of this family, although diverse, share certain botanical characteristics: a perianth with 6 parts (inner and outer series with 3 segments each), 3 stamens, and an inferior ovary. The 3 stamens and inferior ovary are the characteristics that separate the Iris Family from the Lily Family, with which it is often confused. There are few to many ovules, and the fruit is a 3-valved capsule.

The garden varieties of Iris are the best-known members of this family, but there are other domesticated ones such as Crocus and Gladiolus.

Sisyrinchium scabrum
(= *S. ensigerum*)
Blue-eyed Grass

Plant: Perennial herb that grows in compact bunches from fibrous roots. Grasslike tufts of flat, broadly winged stems grow 6–18 inches high. The leaves are flat, erect, almost as long as the stems (8–10 inches), folded lengthwise, and only ¼ inch (or less) wide.

Flower: The flowers are on individual stalks as they emerge from a flattened sheath. There are 1–3 in each sheath, blooming 1 at a time. They are blue to blue-purple and are composed of an outer and inner floral bract (the outer being longer than the inner) with 3 segments each. The flower is ¾ inch across, with a bright yellow center and a stigma that sticks up prominently. It blooms in April and May and has been noted blooming in August and September as well.

Fruit: A 3-valved capsule, ⅛–¼ inch tall, produced on a curved pedicel (or stem) that protrudes from the sheath. The pods and the plant turn light green as they dry.

Range: This delicate-looking plant prefers low-lying wet areas in disturbed ground of pastures and prairies. It grows in portions of Oklahoma and New Mexico; also over most of Texas, except the southern area.

Remarks: Blue-eyed Grass is not a member of the Grass Family at all, but bears its common name because of its grasslike leaves and bright blue "eyes" (with yellow centers). It is a pretty plant that often hides in the shade of tall grass or beneath trees, in low-lying areas that retain moisture, and is the only member of the Iris Family that grows well on the Western Plains.

It is also known by a synonym, *S. ensigerum*.

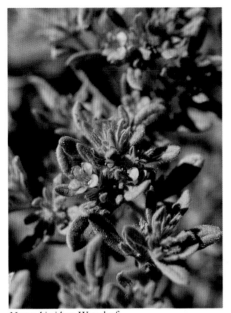

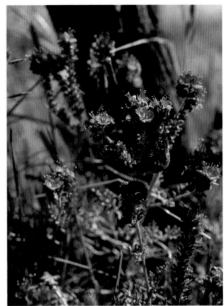

Nama hispidum Waterleaf

Phacelia congesta Blue Curls

Opposite: *Sisyrinchium scabrum* Blue-eyed Grass

P. congesta close-up

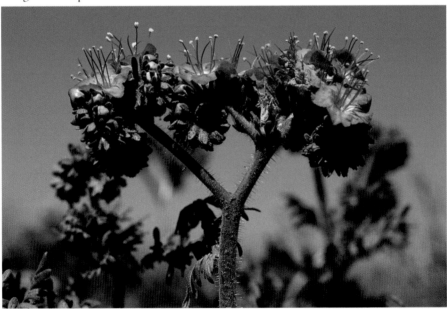

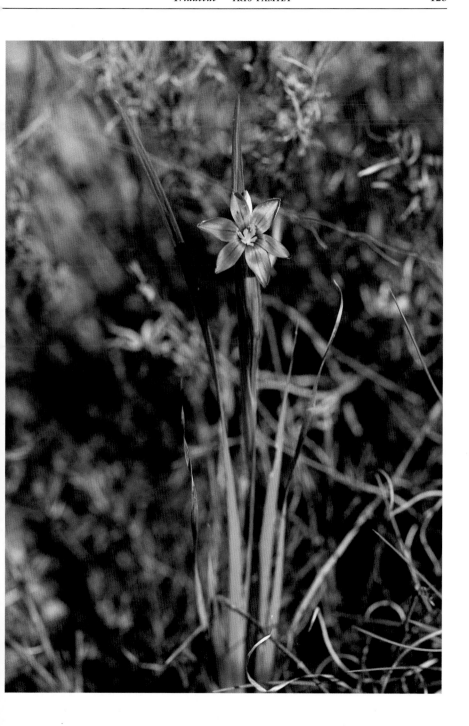

KRAMERIACEAE
Rhatany Family

The Rhatany Family includes only 1 genus, *Krameria*. It is an American genus of about 25 species and ranges from Chile to the southern United States. Once included in the Leguminosae, it is now given its own rank.

The plants in this family can be low shrubs or perennial herbs. The leaves and stems are grayish in color and minutely hairy. The leaves are alternate on the stems, linear, and pointed on the ends. The flowers have both stamens and a pistil. In different species, they are either deep crimson or white in color. A most peculiar characteristic that sets them apart is the arrangement of the 5 petals; the 3 upper, long-clawed ones appear as normal petals, but the 2 lower ones are broad, fleshy, and greenish. The petals are smaller than the 4 or 5 sepals, which are often mistaken for petals because their color is the same crimson. There are 4 stamens that are freestanding or grown to the claw of the upper petal, depending upon the species. The fruit is a 1-seeded pod that is hairy and prickly.

Krameria lanceolata
Prairie Bur, Crameria, Trailing Rhatany, Sandbur

Plant: Perennial herb growing from woody rootstocks with trailing, vinelike stems 12–18 inches long. Covered with minute silky hairs, it is a gray-green color. The leaves are simple (not compound as in most of the Leguminosae), alternate, linear (⅜–¾ inch long), hairy on their undersides, and pointed on the ends.

Flower: The flowers have both stamens and pistils, 4 or 5 deep crimson sepals of unequal length, and 5 bilaterally symmetrical petals, also of very unequal length. Of the 5 petals, 3 stalked ones on the upper portion have long claws. The 2 lower ones are much smaller, glandular, fleshy, and a lighter greenish color. The sepals are larger than the petals and, since they are the same color, are often mistaken for petals. There are 4 stamens that are somewhat joined to form a stalk. This flat-on-the-ground wildflower blooms May–August.

Fruit: A fat, woolly 1-seeded capsule that bears soft, barbless spines, ¹⁄₁₆–⅛ inch long. The seed is ½ inch thick.

Range: Prairie Bur grows from Arkansas through Kansas, over most of Texas, to Arizona, then south into Mexico. It prefers open prairie habitats, slopes, canyon walls, grasslands, and stream banks.

Remarks: This plant appears to be fairly drought-resistant, for it often blooms when other wildflowers have failed to germinate. Because it is a trailing plant and the foliage is rather sparse, it is not easy to see. The color of the flower is such a deep wine-red that it almost appears brown at times, which makes it blend with the ground. Fortunately for the barefoot, the spines on the seedpod (bur) do not puncture.

LABIATAE (Lamiaceae)
Mint Family

The plants of this large family are typically very aromatic, providing the world with herbs used as food flavor enhancements as well as medicine.

Members of the Mint Family have square stems and leaves that are paired (2 arranged opposite each other at the same point on the stem). These leaves can be entire or lobed.

The botanical name Labiatae refers to the unusual corolla shape with its 2 "lips" (*labia*). Five petals are joined at the base, forming a funnel, then usually flaring out into a 2-lobed upper lip and a 3-lobed lower lip (there are variations, however). This lower one, sometimes spreading, has a middle lobe which often looks rather like a dipper.

The stamens vary from 2 to 4, usually in 2 unequal pairs. The ovary has 4 lobes, which ultimately form 4 small nuts. The style terminates in a split or forked stigma (which looks like a snake's tongue).

Numerous members of this family have been widely cultivated for their aromatic oils: rosemary, sage, lavender, thyme, marjoram, peppermint, and basil to name a few. Many of their wild cousins have characteristic odors of their own and were used by the Native Americans as teas as well as for medicinal purposes.

Lamium amplexicaule
(Henbit)

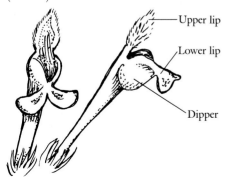

Upper lip

Lower lip

Dipper

Lamium amplexicaule
Henbit, Dead Nettle

Plant: Winter annual or biennial herb with several stems growing from 1 root. The stems are low and branching, occasionally even prostrate, 4–16 inches long. The lower leaves have petioles and are about ½ inch wide. The upper leaves clasp the square stems at the nodes and are about 1¼ inches wide. The leaves are almost circular in outline (orbicular), and their edges are crinkled.

Flower: The 6–10 flowers are in whorled clusters in the leaf axils. There are 5 united sepals, ⅛–¼ inch long. Five petals unite to form a 2-lipped corolla, ⅜–⅝ inch long. The lower corolla lip has a middle lobe that is lighter in color, spotted with purple splotches, and deeply cleft at the tip. The upper lip stands erect and hooded at the top and is lined with reddish hairs. The color of the flower is rose-purple and pale rosy-purple with darker markings, usually spots, down in the throat of the corolla tube. There are 4 stamens that grow from deep inside the corolla tube and one 4-lobed pistil. The blooming period lasts from February to May.

Fruit: Inside the 4-lobed ovary are 4 tiny nutlets. The seeds germinate in the fall. The plants then grow lowly and slowly through the winter, blooming early in the spring and dying down with the onset of hot weather.

Range: Henbit grows in nearly all soils. It prefers lawns, cultivated and disturbed places, waste places, and roadsides and can be found generally all over North America.

Remarks: This native of Europe has made itself quite at home in America. Unfortunately, it is considered a weed in lawns and cultivated areas. Because it blooms very early, when the ground is bare from winter, the colorful blossoms show up well. They are too pretty to be dubbed "weeds," but since they prefer groomed lawns, it is understandable that the "groomers" consider

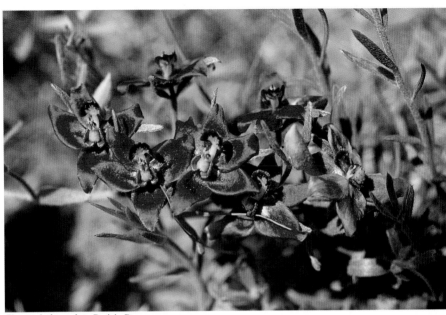

Krameria lanceolata Prairie Bur

Lamium amplexicaule Henbit

Marrubium vulgare Horehound

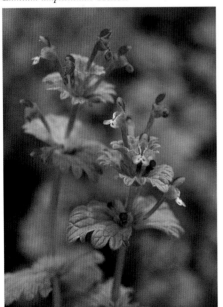

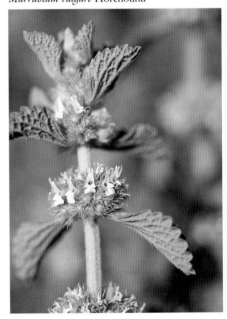

them pests. But if the "groomers" will be patient, after this plant blooms, it dries up and totally disappears.

The plant is also called Dead Nettle because the leaves look like nettle leaves but lack their characteristic "sting."

Marrubium vulgare
Horehound, Common Horehound, Marrubio, White Horehound, Mastranzo

Plant: A perennial plant that grows 2–2½ feet tall, Horehound emerges from a fibrous, spindle-shaped root. It sends up numerous square stems that branch from the base. The entire plant is covered with a fine white wool. The leaves (to 2 inches long) are opposite on the stem, oval, veiny, and wrinkled, with bluntly toothed edges. They are rough on the upper surface and white-woolly underneath. They grow on short (¼–¾ inch) stalks, or petioles.
Flower: The white flowers grow in dense clusters, around the stem, in the axils of the uppermost leaves. The calyx of each individual flower is cylindrical and has 10 teeth. Each corolla is about ¼ inch long and 2-lipped. The upper lip is erect, the lower lip is 3-lobed with the middle lobe broadening out and often having a notch in its tip. There are 4 stamens in 2 pairs of unequal length. The styles are split into 2 lobes at their tips, and the ovary is 4-lobed. The plant blooms off and on from late June through September.
Fruit: Four smooth, oval nutlets about ⅟₁₆ inch long.
Range: This tough, hardy, "weedy" wildflower can be found throughout most of the United States. It is particularly fond of barnyards, fencerows, sandy disturbed ground, neglected areas, dump grounds, and waste places.
Remarks: Horehound was introduced into this country from Eurasia. It is naturalized and quite at home here now and can

be found somewhere in the United States at any given time of the year. Early pioneers, and even people of our grandparents' generation, used the flowering tops and dried leaves as medicine or as a flavoring for candy. It is not as pleasantly aromatic as its cousins the horsemints (*Monarda*); the flavor of the leaves and stems of Horehound is strong and bitter.

An old-timer who was visiting us some years ago became very excited to see a lot of Horehound growing all around. He told me, "My mother would make a cough syrup by boiling those leaves down and straining the juice; then she'd give it to us kids to help us get over winter coughs and colds. Come spring, she would mix some sugar with it, boil it some more, and make hard candy for us." I didn't tell him, but I've tasted Horehound candy and my personal feeling is that it probably makes a better cough syrup. Bitter is surely better for medicine than for candy.

Since it is not used widely today as a cough remedy, it has become a "pest weed" that is cursed by sheep ranchers and others who live in rural areas. The dried stalks of the plant remain erect over the winter and the thousands of calyxes, with their recurved teeth, stand ready to become hopelessly entangled in the wool of sheep (reducing its value), the tails of horses and cattle, or the long hair of the family dog.

Monarda citriodora
Lemon Horsemint, Lemon Beebalm, Plains Horsemint, Horsemint, Purple Horsemint

Plant: Annual, or sometimes biennial, square-stemmed plant growing to 2 feet tall. Several stems usually grow from the base. The entire plant is covered with minute curled hairs. The aromatic leaves are opposite on the stem, 1–3 inches long, up to ½ inch wide, oblong to lance-shaped, and somewhat toothed on their edges. The leaves on the upper portion of the plant are narrower and more linear than those below. The leaf petioles (stalks) are up to 1 inch long.

Flower: Clusters of many small flowers are spaced at intervals up the stem. There can be 1–6 successive clusters (or heads) on a stem, with a whorl of lavender leaflike bracts subtending each cluster. Each individual flower has 5 sepals, united to form a calyx tube ¼–⅓ inch long and filled with bristly hairs. Five united purple petals form a 2-lipped corolla 1 inch long. The 2-lobed upper lip is cupped and arched like a hood. The lower lip is 3-lobed. Two stamens arise from the corolla tube, along with a 4-lobed pistil. This flower is often covered with purple spots. It blooms from April to June.

Fruit: Four nutlets (1 in each lobe), each only 1/16 inch long.

Range: Throughout most of Oklahoma, Texas, eastern New Mexico, and northern Mexico; also from Kansas to South Carolina and down into Florida. It grows well in open pastures, roadside ditches, prairies, meadows, and dry plains.

Remarks: This purple-flowering plant often grows in large colonies and can cover several acres. It is most beautiful, and lemon-scented as a bonus. A large stand of Lemon Horsemint is a good place to find butterflies and bumblebees, as they are strongly attracted to it when it is in full bloom.

The plants in the southeastern portion of its range have white to pale lavender flowers with very visible purple spots on the petals.

An old Native American legend says that young braves, when going to court their favorite maidens, would look for Lemon Horsemint leaves to chew on the way, for it made their breath fresh by the time they arrived.

The Native Americans did actually drink a tea brewed from these leaves.

Citronellol, which has long been used as a perfume and insect repellent, is extracted from the oils of Lemon Horsemint.

Monarda punctata
Spotted Beebalm, Horsemint, Spotted Horsemint, Yellow Horsemint

Plant: Square-stemmed, strongly scented annual, perennial, or biennial 1–2 feet tall. The stems are erect, hairy, growing singly or a few at the base, often in clumps. The leaves are also hairy, oblong-lanceolate, ⅝–3¾ inches long, arranged opposite each other on the stem and sometimes toothed. Short branchlets with tiny leaves are often found in the leaf axils.

Flower: The many flowers are in dense heads clustered up toward the top of the straight stems. There are usually 1–4 of these compact heads on a stem. Each cluster of flowers is subtended by several broad, leaflike bracts of a whitish or yellowish color. The ¾-inch flowers are pale yellow to almost white and spotted with maroon or brown dots. The corolla is tubular at the base, flaring to an obviously 2-lipped blossom. The upper lip is slender, arched forward, and not lobed. It is longer than the 2 stamens that arise from the throat of the flower in an arch just beneath it. The lower lip is broader, bent downward, and 3-lobed. Bloom season is May and early June.

Fruit: Four small nutlets (1/10 inch long) develop in the 4-lobed ovary.

Range: Spotted Beebalm grows in pastures, dry and rocky soils of roadside ditches, and neglected fields in the eastern and midwestern United States, Florida, western Oklahoma, Texas, New Mexico, Arizona, and down into Mexico.

Remarks: This wildflower does not grow as tall as Lemon Horsemint (*M. citriodora*), nor is it as colorful and showy. But, typical of the Mint Family, it is prominently square-stemmed (4-angled), with strongly aromatic leaves. A modern cough syrup ingredient, Thymol, is derived from the oils of this plant (Delena Tull, *A Practical Guide to Edible and Useful Plants*, p. 158).

The arrangement of the compact flower heads up the stem reminds me of miniature topiary trees. Individually, the flowers somewhat resemble a snake with its mouth open.

Not all mints are edible and safe to use for teas. This is one that is not, for this species is bitter and toxic. Do NOT try a tea of Skullcap.

Scutellaria drummondii
Skullcap, Drummond's Skullcap

Plant: Annual herb, from a taproot, branching at the base (somewhat sprawling), 8–12 inches tall. The stems are softly hairy and square (or 4-angled). The plants tend to grow in clumps. The leaves are opposite and arranged close together up the stem. They are ½–¾ inch long, fat oval-shaped, smooth (untoothed) on the edges, prominently veined on the underneath surface, and also softly hairy.
Flower: The numerous bluish-purple flowers (½ inch long or less) grow solitary in the leaf axils of the upper leaves. There are 5 united sepals and 5 united petals that form a 2-lipped blossom. The upper lip is short and hoodlike; the lower lip is broad, flatter, and notched. The 2 side lobes appear to be more a part of the upper lip than the lower. In the center of the blue-purple lower lip, there are 2 small, elongated white spots dotted with purple and covered with a patch of minute shaggy hairs. There are 4 stamens and 1 pistil with a 4-chambered ovary. Skullcap blooms in April and May.
Fruit: The 4-chambered ovary produces 4 tiny black nutlets covered with overlapping plates or scales.
Range: Skullcap can grow in a variety of soils: sandy, rocky, gravelly, clayey, or caliche. It can be found in barren caliche flats, grassy pastures, hillsides, or open prairies throughout southeastern New Mexico, northern Mexico, most of Texas, and western Oklahoma to Kansas.
Remarks: Skullcap is a small, low-growing plant of spring. The flowers are a lovely bluish-purple color and most unusual with their 2 white patches spotted with purple.

Teucrium laciniatum
Cutleaf Germander, Germander

Plant: Perennial 3–6 inches tall from creeping roots. The many square stems are straight, branched at the base, tufted, and minutely hairy. They form clumps as they grow in colonies. The leaves are opposite and deeply pinnately cut (nearly to the midrib), in 2–8 lobes, ½–2 inches long and ⅟₁₆–³⁄₁₆ inch wide.
Flower: The flowers grow crowded at the top of the plant in the axils of the leaves on short ¼-inch stalks. They are greenish-white in color with rather funnel-shaped corollas. There may be purplish veins down in the throat of the corolla, which is ½–¾ inch long, hairy, and 2-lipped. The upper lip is split, allowing the stamens and style to project through it. The lower lip is longer than the upper one and broadly spreading. There are 4 paired stamens. The plant blooms in May.
Fruit: Four oval nutlets, less than ¼ inch long, with lengthwise grooves.
Range: This little plant can grow in hard caliche or in sandy or clay loam, usually by the roadside, in pastures, or on mesas and hillsides of the Western Plains. It can be found in much of Texas, New Mexico, Oklahoma, and Colorado.
Remarks: The blossoms of this short wildflower at first glance do not look like flowers. They appear to be leaves at the top of the plant that have faded to almost white. Closer inspection reveals the unique 2-lipped corolla with the stamens sticking out between the split lobes of the upper lip. There is a faintly sweet and spicy fragrance to the blossoms.

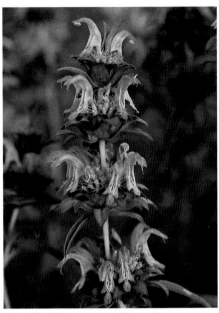

Monarda citriodora Lemon Horsemint

M. punctata Spotted Beebalm

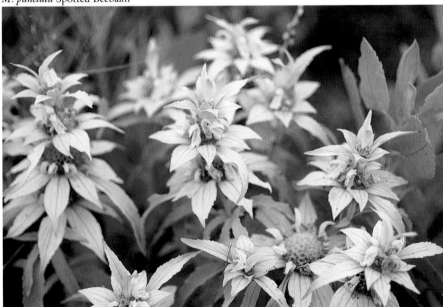

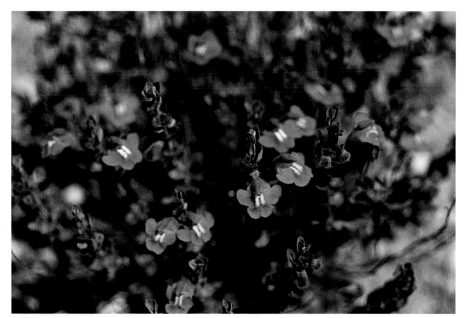

Scutellaria drummondii Skullcap

Teucrium laciniatum Cutleaf Germander

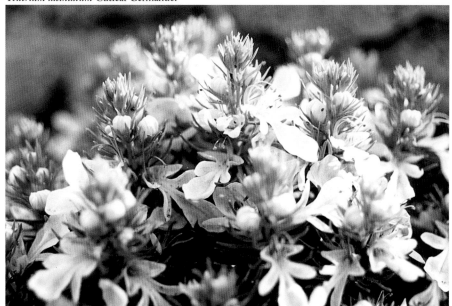

LEGUMINOSAE (Fabaceae) Legume, Bean, or Pea Family

The Legume Family has over 500 genera and more than 10,000 species, including trees, shrubs, vines, and herbs found in every part of the earth.

The main characteristic that unites all members of the family is the fruit. The legume is a 1-chambered fruit that, when mature, looks like a bean or pea pod and usually splits open down 2 sides to reveal the seed or seeds inside.

The Leguminosae fall into 3 subfamilies: Papilionoideae, Caesalpinioideae, and Mimosoideae. These are so distinctive that some authorities elevate each of them to family status.

Members of the subfamily Papilionoideae have leaves that are either simple or pinnately or palmately once compound (never twice compound). Typically, but not always, the calyx is 5 sepals joined to form a cup and there is a 5-petaled, bilaterally symmetrical corolla. One petal (the "banner") usually stands erect above the others, the 2 on the sides look like wings, and the 2 below often are fused along the inside edge, looking like a pouch or boat keel. The stamens and pistil are positioned or enclosed in this lower, pouch-shaped part. The 10 stamens are usually fused at their stalks. One, however, may be free from the fused 9 in some species, while in others, all 10 may be free and not fused together anywhere. This flower is referred to as "papilionaceous," meaning "butterfly-like."

In the subfamily Caesalpinioideae, leaves are pinnately once or twice compound. The flowers are large and showy, with 5 petals almost equal in length; the flowers are only slightly irregular (bilaterally symmetrical).

The Mimosoideae subfamily does not have pealike flowers. Instead, it has regular flowers with numerous stamens, looking like fuzzy balls. The leaves are pinnately twice compound.

Acacia angustissima Whiteball Acacia, Fern Acacia, Shame Weed

Plant: Herbaceous perennial shrub or sub-shrub producing tall, slender unbranched stems, somewhat woody at the base. The stems lack spines and have a brownish cast due to the tiny hairs covering them. They grow to about 40 inches in height, with one to several stems growing from the base, and tend to develop large colonies of fernlike graceful plants. Alternate leaves are twice pinnately compound (usually 7 to many pairs of pinnae), these again divided into 20 or more pairs of crowded linear leaflets on each pinna.

Flower: Small creamy-white flowers grow in clusters on long, slender stalks near the uppermost leaf axils. There are numerous protruding stamens (20–100) on each flower. It blooms from June to September.

Fruit: Flat, sickle-shaped, 1- to several-seeded pod ($5/8$–1 inch long and $1/4$ inch wide). The curved pods are in a cluster, forming a tight ball. They turn dark brown with age, then burst open, dropping the many flat seeds.

Range: Found in grasslands and open roadside ditches, rocky places, and in different types of soils as well as deep sands of disturbed areas from eastern Texas to the Trans Pecos, east-central and southern New Mexico, and into northern Mexico.

Remarks: The foliage of the Whiteball Acacia is fernlike in appearance, and the many fluffy greenish-white flowers are lovely, especially viewed in large colonies. One of its common names, Shame Weed, comes from the small leaflets' ability to fold together when touched. The plant's most outstanding characteristic is the cluster of seedpods tightly wadded in a ball. They look like tiny brown dried bananas gnarled together. At this stage, they make artistic additions to dried flower arrangements.

The plant is a nutritious, palatable browse for livestock and wildlife and is eagerly grazed by them, where available.

Astragalus lindheimeri
Buffalo Clover, Lindheimer's Astragalus, Milk Vetch

Plant: An annual that grows from a slender taproot, Buffalo Clover is an upright to sprawling plant, 6–12 inches tall, usually found growing in large colonies. The leaves are 3/4–2 1/2 inches long and odd-pinnately compound (with 11–21 oblanceolate leaflets). The leaflets are slightly folded down the middle with a small notch on the tip.

Flower: There are 2–6 flowers on stalks emerging from the leaf axils. The petals are bicolored; the 1/2–3/4 inch banner is lilac-margined around a center (or "eye") that is creamy-white with purple veins. The 1/2–3/4-inch wings are white and the 3/8–1/2-inch keel is purple, spotted with white. The keel's broad blades are 1/4–1/2 inch long. Buffalo Clover blooms in April and early May.

Fruit: A pod, thick (3/8–5/8 inch), long (5/8–1 1/8 inch), and curving, containing several hard seeds that are dispersed as the pod dries, becoming brittle, papery, and brownish-black, and finally splits open.

Range: Growing in central and northern Texas, Buffalo Clover has spread up onto the plains and into Oklahoma. *A. lindheimeri* is very similar to *A. nuttallianus,* which is a wide-ranging milk vetch. Buffalo Clover is not so wide-ranging but can be found growing in roadside ditches and covering large areas of pastureland, hills, and mesas in portions of the Western Plains.

Remarks: When this lovely wildflower covers a hill with its beautiful lilac, white, and green, it is a magnificent sight. An added pleasure is its delightful fragrance. When standing amid acres of Buffalo Clover in full bloom, if one inhales deeply, it is like being in a package of grape Kool-Aid. The smell is heavenly and almost intoxicating.

On the Western Plains, this plant is often mistaken for Texas' state flower, the Bluebonnet (*Lupinus texensis*), which in this area is found only infrequently along roadsides, where it has been seeded by the Texas Highway Department. Bluebonnets are primarily blue and white in color, while Buffalo Clover is lilac and white.

There are 5 or 6 species of *Astragalus* that are poisonous to livestock. Many other species are not. In common terminology, the poisonous ones are usually labeled "locoweeds," while the others are called "milk vetches." This sweet-smelling one is not toxic.

Astragalus mollissimus
Woolly Loco, Texas Loco, Purple Locoweed

Plant: Short-lived perennial growing from a taproot, which tends to become woody early in its life cycle. The leafy gray-green stems are much-branched, low (usually less than 1 foot tall) and sprawling on the ground with only the tips of the stems turned up. Stems and leaves are covered with dense, minute silvery hairs. The leaves are up to 10 inches long, alternate, and odd-pinnately compound (paired leaflets plus a single terminal one), with 31 (more or less) rather diamond-shaped leaflets. Each leaflet is 3/8–3/4 inch long.

Flower: The flower spikes emerge from the leaf axils, bearing up to 70 flowers in racemes 2–4 inches long. The pink-purple to dull lavender flowers are papilionaceous (butterfly-like), with a banner, or upper petal, 1/2–1 inch long. The 2 wing petals can be the same length or shorter, with the keel shorter than the wings. The lower petals (wings and keel) have a creamy-white color mixed with the purple, giving the flower an overall pale or dull hue. It blooms in April and May.

Fruit: Pod 3/8–1 inch long and 1/4–5/8 inch in diameter. When ripe, the fleshy halves become dry and papery, and the pod falls to the ground and bursts open, spilling its seeds about.

Range: This plant can be found in Nebraska, Wyoming, Utah, eastern New

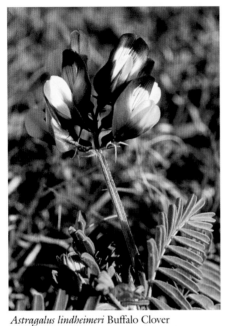

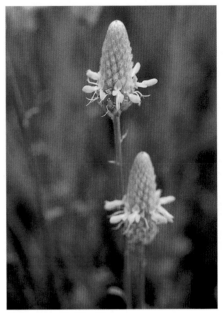

Astragalus lindheimeri Buffalo Clover

Dalea aurea Golden Dalea

A. mollissimus Woolly Loco

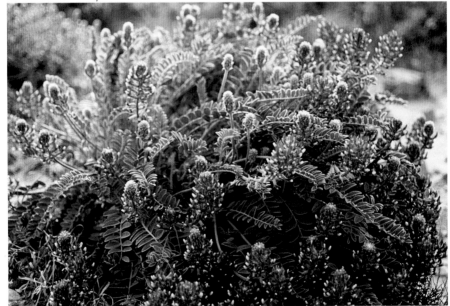

Mexico, and western central Texas. It does well on dry hills and in open range country, preferring gravelly and caliche soils. **Remarks:** Woolly Loco is a pretty wildflower but potentially poisonous to livestock. It is one of several species of *Astragalus* (and closely related *Oxytropis*) that can be fatal to horses, cattle, and sheep. It is, however, fairly unpalatable; therefore livestock will usually eat it only if nothing else is available. When they do ingest large amounts over a long period of time, they become disoriented, stagger around, and act *loco* (Spanish for "crazy").

Dalea candida White Prairie Clover

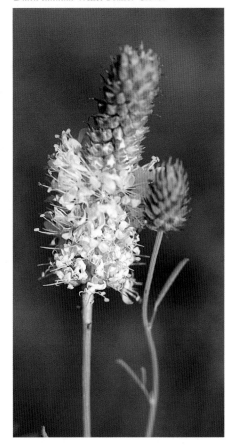

Dalea aurea
Golden Dalea, Silktop Dalea

Plant: Perennial herb with from 1 to several stems 1–1 1/2 feet tall, becoming rather woody at the base. The compound leaves are alternate, gray-green, and hairy, 3/4–2 inches long, pinnately cleft into 5–7 leaflets (1/4–3/4 inch long). The oblong leaflets are minutely hairy on their upper surfaces and dotted with oil-bearing glands beneath. The oil has a pleasant fragrance. The leaves become sparse and smaller toward the top of the stem.
Flower: The flowers grow in a terminal cylindrical spike, 1 to a stem. The spike, or flower head, tapers toward the top and is 1–2 inches long and 1/2–1 inch thick, with silky bracts. The golden yellow flowers, 3/8–1/2 inch long, have 5 petals with tiny stalklike bases called "claws." The banner, or upper petal, is about 1/4 inch long and wide. The 2 wing petals (3/16 inch long) and 2 keel petals (1/4–5/16 inch long) are attached to the filaments of the stamens. The flowers grow in a circle around the spike and open at the base initially, then progress up the spike, making it elongate, as younger ones begin to bloom. Golden Dalea blooms from mid-June into July.
Fruit: Dry, rather flattened 1- or 2-seeded pod, covered with silky hairs.
Range: Prairie habitats, waste places, hillsides, and mesas of the Western Plains; also from South Dakota to Wyoming and south to Mexico.
Remarks: Golden Dalea is easy to locate with its fat, silky golden heads (like thimbles) atop tall erect stems. The flowers need bees and other insects for cross-pollination, and one can often see these busy helpers being accommodating. It is eagerly grazed by livestock, being palatable and nontoxic.

Dalea candida
(= Petalostemum candidum)
White Prairie Clover

Plant: Perennial herb with a rather woody base and several slender stems to heights of 30 inches. The leaves are divided into 5–9 narrow, linear leaflets ($3/8$–1 inch long and $1/16$ inch wide) and are scattered alternately on the lower portion of the stem. They have minute glands dotting the undersides.

Flower: The white flowers grow in clusters on dense spikes. These terminal cylindric spikes are $3/4$–4 inches long and $3/8$–$1/2$ inch thick, elongating as the tiny flowers mature and others begin to bloom. Each flower is subtended by a bract that is longer than the calyx. The individual flowers have 5 petals that are separate and almost equal in length. The banner (upper petal) stands erect above the others and is slightly less than $1/4$ inch long. The other petals are $1/4$ inch long and inserted at the rim of the stamen tube. White Prairie Clover blooms in June and July.

Fruit: A 1- or 2-seeded pod, half-circular in outline. It becomes dry with maturity but does not split open.

Range: From Canada, North Dakota, and Montana southeast to Indiana and Mississippi, and from Texas to Arizona and northern Mexico.

Remarks: White Prairie Clover grows on hillsides, rocky places, and roadsides in scattered stands. When the cylindrical heads, or spikes, are in bloom, they decorate the slender stems with fluffs of white that sway in the breezes of summer. The heads begin to grow in length as the flowers at the base develop seedpods, while the flowers on the uppermost part of the head continue to open and bloom. At this stage, the plant is not as fluffy and white as before, becoming tan mixed with white as the seeds develop.

This plant is also known by the synonym *Petalostemum candidum.*

Dalea formosa
Feather Dalea, Indigo Bush,
Feather Plume

Plant: Shrub 1–$3 1/2$ feet tall. It branches at many angles. The bark on the branches is dark gray to dark brown or almost black. The leaves (less than $1/2$ inch long) are thick, compound, divided into 5–7 (or sometimes 15) segments that are $1/16$–$1/8$ inch long. They are without hairs but are dotted with glands beneath.

Flower: The flowers grow in clusters on short spikes (2–10 flowers in a cluster). The calyx has feathery lobes $1/4$ inch long and grayish-white in color. The corolla is vivid rose-purple with a bright yellow banner petal less than $1/4$ inch long. The stalk-like base of the petal (claw) is almost as long as the petal itself. The wing petals are $1/4$ inch long and the keel petals $3/8$ inch long, with the claws of both about $3/8$ inch long. Feather Dalea blooms as early as April and at different times through August.

Fruit: Flat 1- or 2-seeded pod covered with shaggy hairs and spotted with minute glands.

Range: This shrub prefers rocky hillsides and higher elevations from western Texas through New Mexico to Arizona. It also grows in Colorado, southern Utah, and Mexico. It does well in the dry, shallow soils and semiarid climate often found on the Western Plains.

Remarks: Feather Dalea is a shrub that grows in colonies; usually a hill or mesa is covered with them as opposed to there being only 1 or 2 specimens. They are quite colorful when a large group is in full bloom and delightfully fragrant as they fill the air with a sweet perfume. Each individual blossom is a surprise with its 2 distinct colors and feathery plumes.

Native Americans used the bark and branches to make dyes for coloring their basketry.

The plant is reported to be a palatable browse for sheep, goats, and deer.

Dalea tenuifolia
(= *Petalostemum tenuifolium*)
Pink Prairie Clover

Plant: Perennial herb with slender stems growing erect or slightly curving upward, 6–12 inches tall. The branched stems grow from a woody base. The alternate leaves are 1–1 1/2 inches long with 3–5 narrow, linear leaflets 3/8–3/4 inch long. The leaves are sparsely glandular on their surfaces and grow up toward the top of the stem.

Flower: The flowers grow crowded on cylindrical heads, or spikes, which are 3/4–2 inches long and about 3/8 inch wide. The sepals (calyx) are silky-hairy. The corolla of the tiny flowers is rose-pink or rose-purple, and consists of 5 petals (a banner, or uppermost petal, and 4 others), 5 stamens, and a 1- or 2-celled ovary. It blooms from May to July.

Fruit: Downy 1- or 2-seeded pod enclosed in the calyx.

Range: Indiana to Canada, Kansas to Arkansas, plains of Texas into New Mexico and Arizona. It prefers pastures and open prairies.

Remarks: Pink Prairie Clover, like its cousin, White Prairie Clover (*D. candida*), greatly resembles a decorated thimble when in bloom. The tiny rosy-pink "fluffs" encircle the green heads, or spikes, with delicate color. Having been involved with ballet dancing for many years, I can visualize little ballerinas atop the slender stems with soft rosy-pink skirts or tutus dancing in the sun.

D. *tenuifolia* is also known by a synonym, *Petalostemum tenuifolium*.

Hoffmanseggia glauca
Hog Potato, Mesquite Weed, Rush Pea

Plant: Hog Potato is an herbaceous perennial plant (it has no woody stem above the ground) that grows 6–10 inches tall on the Western Plains. It has several stems, which are branched and covered with short, glandular hairs. The leaves are oddly bipinnate, which means they are twice divided into leaflets (an odd number of primary segments, usually 5–11, each of which is once again divided into 4–11 pairs of leaflets about 1/4 inch long).

Flower: The 5 yellowish-orange petals are about 1/2 inch long. They are covered with tiny hairs that give a brownish tinge to the overall color of the flower. The 10 stamens are shorter than the petals and are hairy also. There are 5–15 flowers in a cluster, called a raceme, borne at the top of the plant. Hog Potato blooms from March to August and often into September.

Fruit: The flat seedpod is shaped like a crescent and is about 1/2–3/4 inch long and less than 1/4 inch wide. There are 4–8 seeds in a pod.

Range: A hardy plant, Hog Potato grows well on hard, dry roadsides. It prefers alkaline soil and can be found from Texas to California, south into Mexico, and north into Kansas.

Remarks: The new leaves of this plant so greatly resemble those of the Mesquite tree, that when they first appear, one thinks a Mesquite is sprouting. Around a farmer's irrigated cotton fields, this can really become a nuisance plant.

The brownish tinge of the flower appears to be enhanced by the tiny hairs that cause dirt to be trapped on their surfaces, adding to the yellow-orange a "dirty" hue.

The common name Hog Potato comes from the fact that deep underground, the root system produces small tubers (thumbnail size) that at some time in the past had value as pig feed.

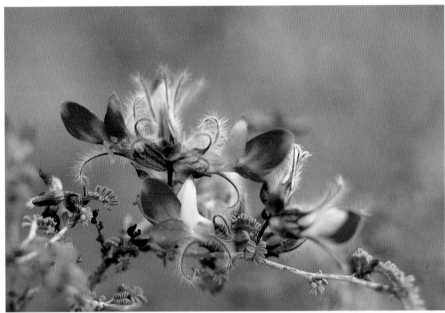

Dalea formosa Feather Dalea

Acacia angustissima Whiteball Acacia

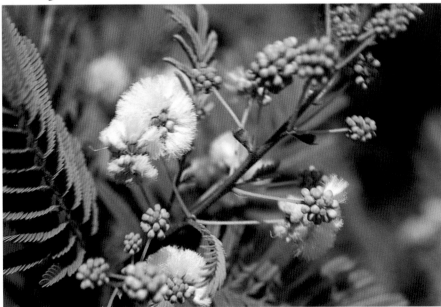

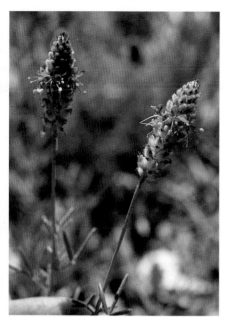

Dalea tenuifolia Pink Prairie Clover

Desmanthus illinoensis seedpod

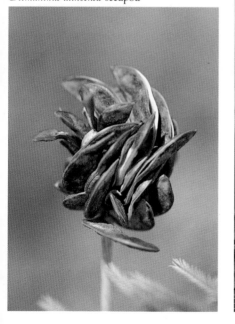

Hoffmanseggia glauca Hog Potato

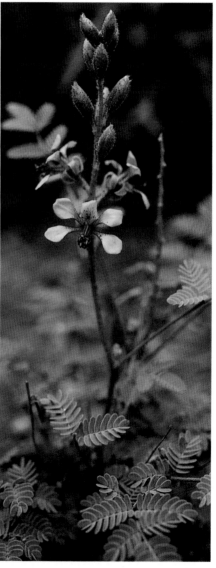

Mimosa borealis
Pink Mimosa, Catclaw, Fragrant Mimosa

Plant: Shrub 3–6 feet tall. The long, slender stems are much-branched, curving or straight. Small thorns, or prickles, which are flat and recurved (like extended claws in a cat's paw), are scattered on the branches. The leaves are bipinnate, or twice compound, with 2–6 pinnae, each with 6–16 small, oval leaflets less than ¼ inch long.
Flower: The soft pink flowers are in dense ball-shaped clusters about ½ inch in diameter. Each tiny flower has 10 stamens that stick out prominently and 5 small petals (each slightly lobed). Pink Mimosa blooms in April and May.
Fruit: Long, linear, shiny, yellowish-tan pod, 1–2 inches long and ¼–⅜ inch wide, bearing 4–7 seeds. The pod has no prickles. As it matures and dries, it becomes constricted, or pinched, between the seeds, revealing the size and shape of each maturing seed inside.
Range: This shrub can grow in grassy pastures or rocky, gravelly slopes of canyon ledges from Oklahoma to Texas, into New Mexico and down into northern Mexico.
Remarks: The delicate, fuzzy pink flowers of Pink Mimosa are fragrant and beautiful. A shrub covered with blooms is delightful, but the "cat claws" that arm the many branches are not so nice. Walking through several of these shrubs is difficult and nearly always painful.

A group of 4-H Club young people saw this flower in my slide presentation and told me they didn't call it Pink Mimosa. They said they called it "Wait a Minute." I certainly understood why.

Oxytropis lambertii
Purple Loco, Crazy Weed, Lambert's Crazy Weed, White Loco

Plant: A perennial, Purple Loco produces several erect, very short, hairy stems from short rhizomes. It can form large colonies of plants 12–18 inches tall. The compound leaves are mostly basal and alternate, with the lower leaves shorter than the upper ones (1½–9 inches long) and silvery-white in color. They are divided into usually more than 11 narrow linear segments ½–1½ inches long and ¹⁄₁₆–⅜ inch wide.
Flower: The flowers are on spikes (10–25 to a spike) to a foot or more in height. Each flower is ½–1 inch long, rosy-lavender, pinkish-purple, or sometimes varying to almost white. As is typical of many legumes, there are 5 petals, the upper petal (banner) ¾–1 inch long, the 2 wings ½–1 inch long, and the 2 keel petals extending into a prominent beak or point. There are 10 stamens, 9 of which are stuck together with the tenth one uppermost and free. It blooms in April and May.
Fruit: Hairy pod, about ⅓–½ inch long, with a long curving tip, which contains several seeds.
Range: Purple Loco is scattered on the higher parts of the Western Plains. It grows from southern Canada down through Arizona, New Mexico, Texas, and the panhandle of Oklahoma, being found in poor, rocky, and shallow soils, in pastures, on hillsides, and in roadside ditches.
Remarks: There are several species of locoweeds, some more poisonous than others. This happens to be one of the most dangerous because it is so eagerly eaten by livestock. Horses are especially fond of it, though it seems to be unpalatable in its early stages of growth. They find it so tasty later on that they can become addicted to it. Its cumulative effects cause the animals to stagger and act crazy, *loco*, often unto

death. It also affects cattle and sheep in the same way.

But for all its unpleasant qualities, it is one of the loveliest of the crazy weeds, or locoweeds. The color of the blossoms is vivid and the fragrance is sweet. The plant is known as White Loco in Arizona.

Prosopis glandulosa
Mesquite, Honey Mesquite

Plant: Deciduous shrub to fairly large tree with stout thorns ½–2 inches long on its branches. The leaves are alternate and pinnately twice compound with 4–30 leaflets each. They are narrow, linear, and soft green in color, ½–1½ inches long. The tree grows from an extremely long taproot, sometimes extending as deep as 60 feet.
Flower: The fragrant flowers grow in cylindrical drooping spikes, 2–3 inches long. They are creamy-white or pale yellow and numerous. The sepals are united and about ¹⁄₁₆ inch long. The 5 petals are united at their base and ¹⁄₁₆–⅛ inch long. The 10 stamens, ¼ inch long, are white but quickly turn yellow with age. There is 1 pistil with its style extending beyond the stamens. Mesquite blooms from late May into June and sometimes July.
Fruit: Leathery several-seeded pod 3–9 inches long. It develops straight and as thick as it is broad. There is a partition between the seeds with a fleshy pulp filling the spaces between them. The seeds mature in August and September.
Range: Open pastures and disturbed grasslands from Kansas through Oklahoma, most of Texas, eastern New Mexico, California, and northern Mexico.
Remarks: On the Western Plains, this is probably the most common legume. Livestock eat the mature beans, or pods, as soon as they begin to be flecked with red spots or stripes. Humans also enjoy syrups, ground meal, and jelly made from the ripe pods.

Mesquite "invades" land that has been plowed, then left fallow, and land that has had the grass cover thinned from overgrazing. Prior to ranching and farming in the plains, Mesquite was found only on steep drainage cuts and bluff edges where there was no grass cover. Farmers and ranchers have, through the years, fought the spread of this hardy plant in their fields and pastures. They believe that the myriad roots rob grass and other beneficial (to livestock) plants of water. Much money is spent yearly to eradicate pastures of Mesquites. They are "killed," or at least set back, temporarily, and only above the ground. In a few short years, this tough, drought-resistant, lacy-leaved plant sprouts again, almost as thick as it ever was. For the cowboy, driving cattle through a Mesquite thicket is unpleasant at best, necessitating sturdy chaps and long-sleeved shirts.

The Native Americans used Mesquite wood (stems and roots) as a fuel, and the ripe beans for grinding into a meal to be used in bread and as dried food to be stored and used during harsh winters. Today it is not widely known nor appreciated as a food source, but the pods are highly nutritious, furnishing protein, carbohydrates, sugars, and minerals, as well as calcium and iron. The flavor of the pods varies from tree to tree, some being sweeter than others, which can be quite bitter. When gathering beans to cook, it is best to break open a ripe pod and taste the pulp to determine its sweetness. Mark the spot where a tasty tree grows in order to find it again another year.

Mesquite continues to grow in popularity as a fuel for barbecue and grilling of steaks. The smoke imparts a flavor to the cooking meat that is becoming more sought after nationwide (elite restaurants in the eastern United States are "importing" Mesquite wood from the western states to use in their specialty cuisine). People from the Western Plains have long known and appreciated this wood for its extremely hot fires in their woodburning fireplaces as well as for the tasty steaks cooked over it. Maybe we should quit cursing and trying to kill this plant and begin to appreciate it more as another profitable crop.

The hard, beautiful reddish-brown wood has been used for years for carving and manufacturing furniture. It is gaining in popularity as an art medium since intricate carvings, bowls, and one-of-a-kind furniture command high prices at today's craft fairs and festivals.

Recipe: MESQUITE BEAN JELLY is quite good and easy to make. When the pods are ripe and beginning to turn mottled with red, gather a gallon of them. Wash the pods and break into pieces. Place in a large pot, cover with water, and boil 5–10 minutes to release the flavor from around the seeds. Pour this liquid through a cheesecloth to strain out the pods, seeds, and stems. Measure 6 cups of liquid; add 1 box of Sure-Jell or other powdered pectin. When this mixture comes to a boil, add 7 cups of granulated sugar. Bring to a hard boil and boil for 3–5 minutes. (Follow the instructions on the Sure-Jell box.) Skim the bubbles or foam from the top and pour into sterilized jars. Seal immediately. Set aside to cool. The color will range from almost colorless to very pale champagne to slightly pink depending on the color and ripeness of the Mesquite beans or pods.

Postscript: You can gather more than 1 gallon of pods. Gather a bushel, if you want. Make the jelly the same way as described above. The more pods used to the same amount of water, the stronger the taste and color. A suggestion would be to start out with a milder jelly and gradually increase to a stronger-tasting one to determine which is your favorite flavor. Have fun and ENJOY.

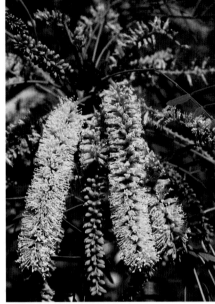

Prosopis glandulosa Mesquite

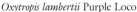

Oxytropis lambertii Purple Loco

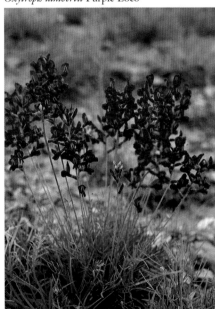

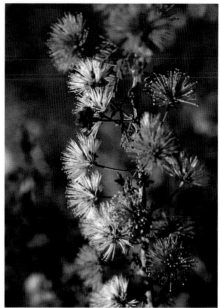

Above and below: *Mimosa borealis* Pink Mimosa

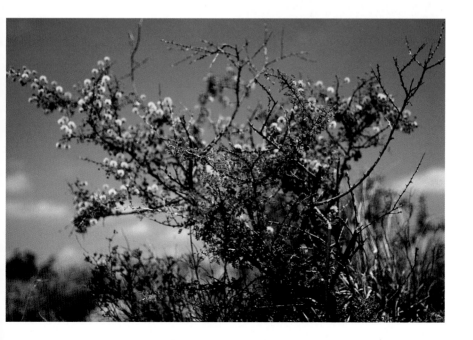

Pediomelum cuspidatum (= *Psoralea cuspidata*)
Scurvy Pea, Scurf Pea, Indian Turnip

Plant: Perennial herb growing from a fat root. The plant is sometimes erect but usually lies on the ground, 10–24 inches long, with the tips of the stems curving upward. The leaves are alternate and palmately 5-lobed. The leaflets are broadly rounded with a pointed tip, ½–¾ inch wide and 1–2 inches long. The leaf has a distinct fold line down the midrib. The stems and leaves have glandular dots covering their surfaces.
Flower: The flowers grow in simple inflorescences (racemes) 1½–3 inches long on the tips of the stems. The bracts, subtending several flowers, have sharp, rigid points on their tips and grow longer with age (¼–½ inch long). There are 5 united sepals. The individual flowers in the raceme are bluish-purple, ½–¾ inch long. These have the "butterfly" appearance; an uppermost petal (banner), 2 wing petals on the sides, and 2 keel petals, united, rounded, and basally attached to the wing petals. There are 10 stamens, 9 of them joined by their filaments, forming a tube, and a tenth one free or sometimes absent. Scurvy Pea blooms in May–June and into July.
Fruit: One-seeded thin, papery, oval pod, enclosed in the calyx and culminating in a small curved beak on the tip. The pod does not split open like an achene; instead it can open by a transverse line around the fruit (somewhat like a lid falling away), or it can rupture irregularly.
Range: Preferring clay and limestone soils, this wildflower grows in open pastures, hillsides, and prairies from Montana and Minnesota south to Arkansas, Oklahoma, and Texas.
Remarks: This weak-stemmed plant sprawls over the ground and is easy to see with its large leaves and colorful flowers. Even though the stems usually hug the ground, the flowers always turn upward. As the flower matures and begins to dry and form seedpods, it fades from a stunning blue-purple to yellow. At first glance, it almost appears to be a yellow flower at this stage.

A cousin of this plant from the northern plains, *Psoralea esculenta*, has such a large edible root that Native Americans used it as a staple part of their diet, calling it "Breadroot."

Schrankia occidentalis
Sensitive Briar, Western Sensitive Briar

Plant: Perennial from a taproot with weak, trailing, sprawling stems, finely hairy and covered with curved-back prickles that harden with age. The stems can extend out 2–4 feet. The leaves are alternate and twice pinnately compound; there are 3–8 pairs of branchlets (pinnae) with 12–16 pairs of small leaflets on each pinna. These little leaflets, ⅛–¼ inch long, fold up when touched.
Flower: The flowers are round, pink spheres, ½–¾ inch in diameter. They grow on peduncles, or stalks, that branch out from the stem ¾–2 inches. There are 8–12 stamens. This plant blooms from May to June.
Fruit: Four-angled pod, 1–4 inches long and ⅛ inch wide, covered with stiff prickles.
Range: Sensitive Briar is found in western Texas, eastern New Mexico, and southeastern Colorado. It grows best in deep sand flats or sandy roadsides.
Remarks: The flowers of this ground-hugging plant resemble fluffy pink balls.

The leaflets are so sensitive, that upon being touched by raindrops or a human finger, they quickly close tightly together. Very few plants do anything fast enough for the eye to see; therefore, when the Sensitive Briar folds up, it is most intriguing.

Senna pumilio (= *Cassia pumilio*)
Dwarf Senna, Pygmy Senna

Plant: Small, tufted perennial herb growing from a branched tuberous root only 3 inches tall or less. It is almost stemless. The leaf is actually a pair of leaflets, often folded or V-shaped, ¾−2 inches long and ⅛ inch wide (appearing grasslike). The leaves are finely hairy.

Flower: The flowers stand up above the foliage on stalks 3 inches tall or less; only 1 flower per stalk. There is a pair of bracts below the flower. The bud droops until it opens out in full bloom. The flowers, about 1 inch across, have 5 sepals, 5 pale yellow petals (3 upper ones and 2 rather cup-shaped lower ones) ⅓−½ inch long, and 10 stamens (the 3 uppermost stamens much shorter than the others). When the petals dry, the veins turn brown and are visible with the naked eye. Dwarf Senna blooms in May and June and often later in the summer after rains.

Fruit: Inflated pod, ¾ inch long and ¼−⅜ inch wide, containing a few seeds.

Range: This little plant grows over the western half of Texas into eastern New Mexico and south into Mexico. It prefers rocky, gravelly, or sandy soils of pastures, hillsides, and roadsides.

Remarks: The *Senna* genus has members that are herbs, shrubs, and even small trees. *S. pumilio* is the smallest of them all, aptly named Dwarf or Pygmy Senna.

An unusual feature of this genus is the ability of the stamen heads to discharge pollen through pores in their tips as opposed to releasing it through a lengthwise split. The seedpod is formed from a single pistil.

A synonym is *Cassia pumilio.*

Sophora nuttalliana
White Loco, Silky Sophora

Plant: A perennial sprouting from underground rhizomes, White Loco forms large colonies with plants 1−1½ feet tall. The stems and leaves are covered with silky-white hairs, giving the plant a grayish color. The leaves (3−3¼ inches long) are alternate and odd-pinnately compound (paired leaflets topped by a terminal one). Each individual leaflet is ¼−⅓ inch long, blunt or sometimes cleft at the tip.

Flower: The pure white flowers are in dense groups (racemes) on stalks that grow from the axils. The large white banner, or upper petal, is about ½ inch long and rounded in shape; the wing petals and keel petals are smaller and white also. There are 10 stamens, all free (not stuck together). Bloom season is April−May.

Fruit: A 1- to several-seeded pod that becomes woody or leathery with age and finally splits open to drop the seeds. The pod is as thick as it is broad and is constricted between the seeds.

Range: This is a plant of the Western Plains and higher country. It grows from the High Plains of Texas throughout most of New Mexico, into Arizona and north to South Dakota.

Remarks: A large colony of this wildflower is showy in its snow-white and gray-green array. *S. nuttalliana* is the only herbaceous *Sophora*; the other species on the Western Plains are small to medium-size shrubs. Most of the shrub varieties are poisonous to different degrees. The seeds of *S. nuttalliana* are the most poisonous parts, but are only dangerous if eaten in large quantities. Cattle seem to be the most susceptible.

This plant is often mistaken for an *Astragalus*, since many of the characteristics are similar. It is excluded from that genus because of the stamens being free or separate. (*Astragalus* has 10 stamens with only 1 free, while 9 adhere to each other.)

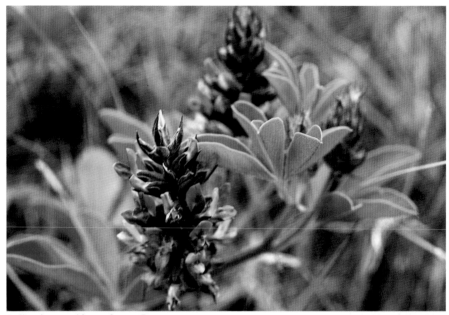

Pediomelum cuspidatum Scurvy Pea

Opposite: *Sophora nuttalliana* White Loco

Schrankia occidentalis Sensitive Briar

Senna pumilio Dwarf Senna

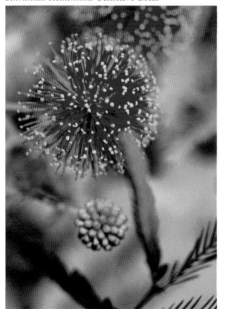

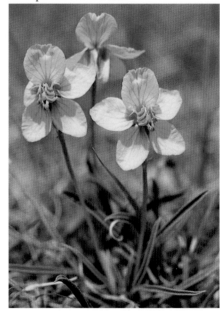

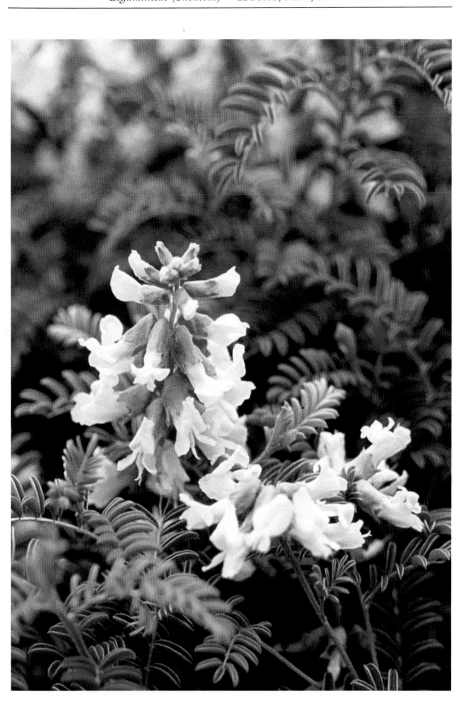

LILIACEAE
Lily Family

The Lily Family is a large and familiar one that includes many favorite garden flowers as well as the wild ones. Some of the most commonly recognized domesticated species are onions, garlic, lilies, and asparagus. Their wild cousins are yuccas, wild onions, and bear grass.

General characteristics of this family are their 6 perianth parts arranged in 2 circles of 3 segments each. There are 3, 6, or more stamens. The ovary is superior, with a stigma that is usually 3-lobed. The fruit is a pod that dries and splits open when ripe, revealing 3 seed-filled compartments. There are no branches; the leaves grow up from an underground bulb, corm, or tuber. The leaves are usually fleshy but sometimes have toothed margins. Veins on the leaves run from the base to the tip.

Liliaceae and Amaryllidaceae closely resemble each other in that each family has flowers with 6 perianth parts, sometimes uniting to form a tube, and 6 stamens. The leaves are generally the same, being linear and sometimes hollow. The plants in both families grow from a bulb or corm. The most distinguishing difference between the two families is the position of the ovary. In Liliaceae, it is superior and easy to locate in the midst of the stamens. In Amaryllidaceae, the ovary is inferior, embedded in the flower stalk below the flower, creating a bulge there.

Recently some authors have taken certain members from the Liliaceae and Amaryllidaceae and created a new family called Agavaceae. It is possible that future publications will include this family. However, for this book, I have retained the older classifications, since there were so few members to include.

Allium drummondii
Wild Onion, Drummond Onion, Prairie Onion, Cebolleta

Plant: Stemless, herbaceous perennial that grows from an ovoid bulb covered by a brown fibrous coating. The bulbs are commonly found in pairs. The 3 (or more) rich green leaves are basal, linear, hollow, 4–9 inches long, and ⅛ inch wide. When crushed, the leaves emit an onion odor. The bulb also has an onion odor.

Flower: Each bulb produces a solitary hollow scape that equals the height of the leaves. On the tip of the scape is an umbel of 10–25 flowers (generally only 10–15) subtended by 2 or 3 paperlike 1-nerved bracts. Each flower has 6 stamens, united into a cup at their base, 1 pistil with 3 chambers, and 6 spreading petallike perianth parts (pointed on the tip and about ¼ inch long). Flowers grow on unequal (¼–1 inch) stalks in the cluster. They range in color from white to pale pink to a deeper rosy-pink. Wild Onion blooms April–June.

Fruit: Ovoid capsule that becomes papery and splits open when ripe, exposing 3 chambers filled with shiny black seeds.

Range: This odorous plant appears quite early in the spring, flourishing in sunny, barren, open ground, on hillsides as well as flat plains areas. It grows from Mexico into Arizona and New Mexico, Colorado, western Nebraska, Kansas, Oklahoma, and Texas.

Allium drummondii Wild Onion

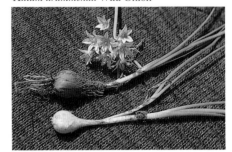

Remarks: Because this Wild Onion is an early spring bloomer, dairy owners curse it. Their cows love it and eat it as fast as they can, thereby imparting a strong onion flavor and odor to the resulting milk and butter. Wherever it grows, it does so in large stands of many small clusters of plants. Growing fast, it is tender and juicy, and it is easy to understand why cattle would eagerly consume this delicacy after a long winter.

History tells us that the early explorers sometimes existed almost entirely on Wild Onions as they forged through the wilderness that became the United States. Native Americans have long used this plant for food and medicine. Today, the many "eating from the wild" cookbooks usually include recipes and uses for this little herb.

I must emphasize very strongly that if you are inclined to sample this plant, you must BE ABSOLUTELY SURE the plant you are about to eat is truly Wild Onion and not the similar, very poisonous Crow-poison (*Nothoscordum bivalve*).

Nothoscordum bivalve
Crow-poison, False Garlic

Plant: Small perennial herb, stemless and odorless, growing from a membranous-coated bulb ⅓–¾ inch long. The leaves (all basal) are grasslike, narrow (less than ⅜ inch), and linear, reaching a height of 4–15 inches. All parts of the plant die down to the ground at the end of its growing season.

Flower: From the center of the plant rises a scape, or naked stalk, less than 12 inches tall. On its tip, a loose umbel bearing 6–12 flowers develops. Subtending this umbel are 2 thin, dry, almost translucent bracts. Each flower is on a pedicel 2 inches or more in length. There are 6 petallike perianth parts that are white, with a prominent central greenish vein, and narrowly oblong, ¼–½ inch long. The 6 stamens have filaments shorter than the petallike parts. There is one 3-chambered pistil. Crow-poison blooms from April to July.

Fruit: Capsule (inversely ovate, attached at the narrow end) about ³⁄₁₆ inch long and slightly 3-angled. It differs from *Allium* in that there are more than 6 ovules in the ovary. These ovules later become flat black seeds.

Range: This plant grows in open neglected grasslands and disturbed and overgrazed soils from Florida to Texas and Mexico, Virginia to Nebraska.

Remarks: This is an attractive early spring-blooming bulb that appears with the Wild Onion (*Allium drummondii*) in the same areas and at the same time of year. This also is the very plant that should not be mistaken for the Wild Onion and eaten, for IT IS POISONOUS. Crow-poison does not have the typical onion odor; thus one can tell that it is not a Wild Onion and should not be tasted or eaten.

Yucca angustifolia
Bear Grass, Soapweed, Yucca

Plant: This evergreen plant can have a stem or be stemless. In the areas where it can be found growing on the Western Plains, it tends to be without a noticeable trunk or stem, with the leaves growing at or near ground level. Forming large groups of spiky clumps, each individual plant has a cluster of many narrow, flexible, sharp-tipped leaves, 1–2 feet long and ¼–⅜ inch wide. These leaves are rather flat on the upper surface and convex on the underside, pale green in color with narrow white margins, which are smooth and untoothed. Toward the base of the leaves there are marginal fibers that separate from the edges and impart a shaggy look to the center part of the clump.

Flower: A leafless naked scape rises from the center of the plant to a height of 1–2 feet, from which a flowering inflorescence

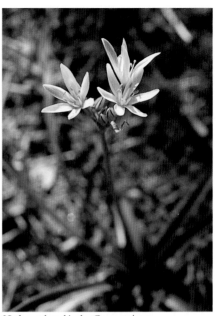

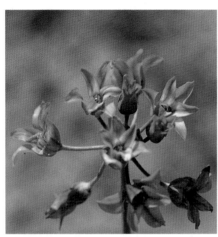

Allium drummondii Wild Onion;
pink variety above

Nothoscordum bivalve Crow-poison
Opposite and below: *Yucca angustifolia*

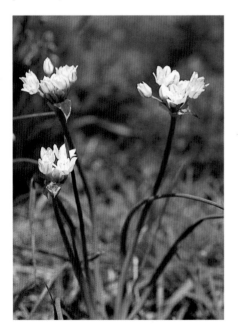

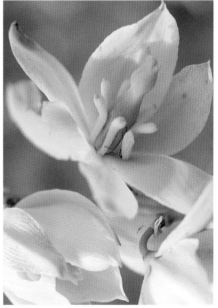

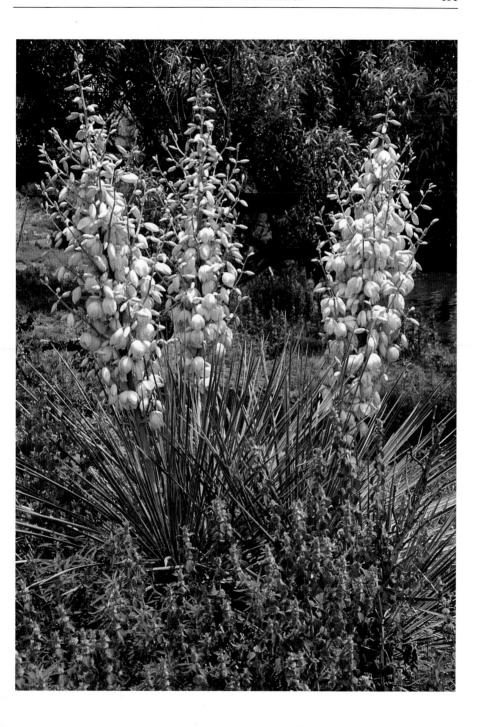

extends another 2–3 feet. The bell-shaped flowers have 6 petallike perianth parts that are greenish-white, thick, brittle, broad, and pointed at the tip. The sepals are 1½–2 inches long and 1–1¼ inches wide. The petals are about 2 inches long and 1–1½ inches wide. There are 6 stamens, ¾–1⅛ inches long, and a pistil with 3 green stigmas. Blooms appear in May and June.

Fruit: Capsule about 2 inches long and 1½ inches in diameter, oblong-cylindrical in shape, green when first forming, then gradually drying to become brown when mature, and finally gray with age. The fruit is dehiscent, which means it splits open at maturity. Each locule of the 3-chambered fruit has 2 compartments filled with thin, smooth, black seeds (¼–⅜ inch in diameter) stacked on top of one another. Each seed has a rather broad wing on one edge.

Range: Growing on grassland plains and in pastures of well-drained rocky soils, Bear Grass is found in parts of New Mexico, the Texas panhandle, Oklahoma panhandle, Colorado, Kansas, Missouri, Nebraska, South Dakota, and Wyoming.

Remarks: There are many species of *Yucca*, usually associated with the Southwest but actually found over a much larger portion of the United States. They hybridize with each other, making positive identification difficult. Native Americans have for centuries used different parts of this plant for food, drink, clothing, baskets, fiber, and even soap.

Cattle love the tender blossoms and green stalks. I have friends who gather the petals and use them in salads. Beautiful baskets and mats are being woven today by Native Americans in Arizona, New Mexico, and Mexico utilizing the long, slender leaves.

A most extraordinary fact about *Yucca* is its remarkable relationship with a small white moth (*Pronuba yuccasella*); this Yucca Moth and the plant depend upon each other exclusively for the perpetuation of their species. The structure of the *Yucca*

flower is such that self-pollination is impossible, making outside pollination by some other agent necessary. That agent is the Yucca Moth. The female moth enters flower after flower gathering pollen and putting it behind her head. She then lays an egg deep in the flower ovary and deposits a ball of pollen on the surface of the stigma. This insures pollination and development of seeds to be used as food for the growing larva that hatches from the egg. (She pollinates the flower sufficiently to produce a multitude of seeds, of which the tiny larva eats only a few.) As it develops, the larva eats its way out of the capsule, boring a hole and dropping to the ground by a silken thread to burrow a few inches underground near the plant. Here it develops, emerging as a full-grown moth when the plant is again in bloom the next spring or summer.

I have observed that Bear Grass blooms every other year. Since it grows in clumps of many plants, there are always plenty in bloom even if others are not blooming that year.

LINACEAE
Flax Family

Members of the Flax Family can be herbs or shrubs. The leaves are simple, opposite, or whorled around the stem. The flowers have a calyx that has 4 or 5 parts, as does the corolla. The petals are separate, only rarely being united at their base. Usually there are as many stamens as petals; the stamens are united at their base. The ovary is superior, and there is 1 pistil. The ovary consists of 2–5 compartments (carpels), and there are 2 seeds per carpel. The seeds are small, flat, and oily.

On the Western Plains the Linaceae are represented by only 1 genus, *Linum,* which is Latin for "flax." It is the root from which we have derived our words "linen" and "linseed." Flax has had value down through the ages for its many uses, such as for thread, fabric, oil, paper money, and cigarette papers.

Linum pratense
Blue Flax, Prairie Flax, Meadow Flax

Plant: Annual with slender sprawling stems 3–15 inches tall. Several stems branch from the base. It is a thin and delicate plant with small lance-shaped alternate leaves (3/8–3/4 inch long), numerous on the lower part of the plant and more sparse on the upper. Their margins are untoothed. Both stems and leaves are without hairs.
Flower: The 5-petaled flowers (3/4 inch across) are blue, or a faded bluish-white, with veins of a darker blue. Several flowers bloom on a stem, starting at the lower portion then advancing toward the top. It is not unusual to see seeds maturing and flowers blooming on the same stem. There are 5 sepals, 5 stamens, united at the base, and 5 separate styles. Blue Flax blooms from April to June.
Fruit: Rounded 5-celled capsule growing on short, down-curved stems. The seeds are flat, shiny, and oily.
Range: This wildflower prefers sandy open places, pastures, grasslands, prairies, and roadsides. It grows over the western United States from Canada into northern Mexico.
Remarks: Blue Flax, like its cousin, Yellow Flax (*Linum rigidum*), has a most fragile and delicate blossom. The petals will fall off in extremely hot weather or at the slightest disturbance. It is not unusual to observe the petals of many plants littering the ground when the days become hotter. Sometimes the petals are still joined, with the hole in the middle where the stamens were, while the stamens remain on the plant.

Linum rigidum
Yellow Flax, Stiff-stem Flax

Plant: Annual erect plant 6–16 inches
tall (usually less than 10 inches). The stems
are stiff and branching near the top. The
leaves are linear (⅜–1¼ inches long), very
narrow (¹⁄₁₀ inch wide), and alternate on
the stem.

Flower: The yellowish-orange flowers,
½–¾ inch across, are terminal on the
branches (blooming at the tip). There are 5
petals united near the base. Each petal has
orange veins extending from the center out
to ½–⅔ its length. The color fades to a
pale green down in the throat of the corolla. The 5 sepals, beneath the petals, are
glandular and toothed. There are 5 stamens
and 1 pistil with 5 segments. Yellow Flax
blooms in May and June.

Fruit: Ovoid 5-celled capsule containing
10 (or fewer) seeds. They are ¹⁄₁₆–⅛ inch
long, round, and oily.

Range: This is a prairie-loving plant,
growing from Canada down to Georgia,
westward through Oklahoma, Texas, and
eastern New Mexico. It inhabits grasslands,
pastures, and open areas with sandy or
gravelly soils.

Remarks: Yellow Flax is a delicate-looking plant that appears in the spring. It must
be appreciated up close, for if one is speed-
ing along the highway, where this wildflower is growing by the roadside, one will
completely miss the lovely pale green center
and orange veins of the fragile petals. After
1 or 2 days, the petals quickly fall.

From days gone by up to the present,
linseed oil has been extracted from the
seeds of many flax species and linen thread
has been spun from the fibers of the stem.

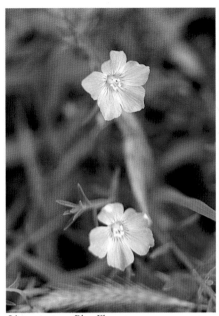

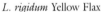
Linum pratense Blue Flax

L. rigidum Yellow Flax

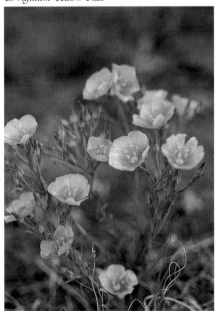

LOASACEAE
Stick-leaf Family

Members of the Stick-leaf Family can be perennial or annual. They have barbed and sometimes stinging hairs on their leaf surfaces. The leaves can be either alternate or opposite with smooth or lobed margins. The flowers have regular symmetry and both male and female parts. The sepals remain on the plant. Petals are free (or separate) in some species and united in others. Some have petallike sterile stamens that alternate with the petals themselves. There can be 5 stamens to many, but there is always 1 style and an inferior ovary. The fruit can be a many-seeded capsule or a 1-seeded achene.

Mentzelia nuda
Stick-leaf, Sand Lily

Plant: Tall (1–3 feet), coarse herbaceous perennial with rough whitish stems, sparsely branched in the upper portion. The leaves form a basal rosette on the ground and are up to 6 inches long. The alternate stem leaves are shorter (1–2 inches long), lance-shaped, and irregularly dentate with minute barbs on both surfaces.
Flower: The white flowers, which open late in the afternoon, bloom all night, and close in the morning, are single at the tips of the branches. The 5 sepals are united to form a cylindrical tube. There are 10 white petals about 1–1¾ inches long, narrow, and oblanceolate. The numerous stamens (10–150) are fertile with very narrow filaments. They range in length from ¼ to ¾ inch and are arranged in bundles opposite the petals. There is 1 pistil, with the ovary inferior. The blooming period is from June to October.
Fruit: Dry cylindrical capsule, about 1 inch long, bearing many oval flattened seeds, each with a wing less than 1/16 inch wide.

Range: Found in caliche and gravelly and sandy soils, east of the Rocky Mountains from Montana and South Dakota into New Mexico and from the panhandle of Texas to the Rio Grande Valley.
Remarks: This is a tall, spindly, gray-white plant with clinging leaves, not worthy of much attention until it blooms. But when it blooms, it appears more graceful and is truly magnificent. The large white flowers are showy, with their lance-shaped petals softened by the multitude of graceful tiny yellow-tipped stamens. The leaves, with their thousands of barbed hairs, give it the common name Stick-leaf and its bad reputation. They tenaciously adhere to any fabric brushing against them, becoming almost impossible to remove, especially from cotton knits. Sheep ranchers curse the plant openly because it sticks so permanently in the wool of their sheep, lowering its value.

Like the other *Mentzelias*, this one has leaves that cling to clothing readily. During our school's Outdoor Education Day each spring, the Middle School children (at different scheduled times during the day) spend an hour with me on a "Wildflower Walk." They find any Stick-leaf, white or yellow, one of the easiest flowers to remember when they experience firsthand the clinging nature of what I have dubbed "Nature's Velcro."

Mentzelia oligosperma
Stick-leaf, Chicken-thief, Pegajosa

Plant: Semiwoody, bushy perennial that grows only about 10–18 inches tall from a tough root. The stems are many-branched and spreading, giving the plant a rounded silhouette. The alternate leaves are rough on both surfaces, being covered with barbed hairs. They are ½–2 inches long, ovate, and trilobed, their margins rather jagged or irregularly toothed.
Flower: The flowers grow singly near the tip of the stem. The many flowers on a

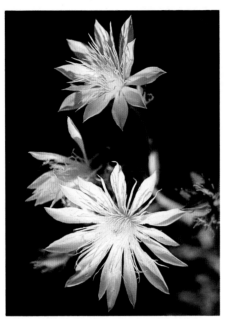

Above and below: *Mentzelia nuda* Stick-leaf

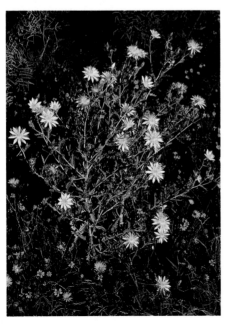

plant open in the early morning. They are a deep yellow, yellow-orange, or salmon color with 5 ovate petals, ¼–⅓ inch long, and 5 sepals, united below to form a tube. The 25–35 stamens are ¼–½ inch long, with threadlike filaments. The stamens are united at their bases, thereby forming a ring in the center of the flower. There is 1 pistil with the ovary inferior. The blooming period is from June to August.

Fruit: Woody, cylindrical capsule containing 1–4 seeds. The seeds are oblong, 3-sided, and tough (woody).

Range: This plant can be found clinging to bluffs and canyon walls in caliche, limestone, sand, and clay soils from Wyoming to Illinois, North and South Dakota, south to Missouri, Arkansas, Louisiana, Texas, New Mexico, Colorado, and Mexico.

Remarks: This Stick-leaf differs from the taller species in its bushier growth and also its habit of opening early with the morning sun and slowly closing as the heat of the day increases. It has only 5 petals instead of 10. One wants to draw near and examine the bright flowers, but one soon discovers that the leaves stick tightly to clothing if brushed too closely.

Mentzelia reverchonii
Yellow Stick-leaf, Stick-leaf

Plant: Perennial with several stout stems from a semiwoody taproot. The gray-green stems branch somewhat toward the upper third of the plant, which can grow as tall as 36 inches. The darker gray-green leaves are oval to lance-shaped with shallow lobes around the edges, growing to 4 inches long and about ½–1 inch wide. The leaves in the upper portion of the plant are shorter and broader at the base and slightly clasp the stem. Both surfaces of the leaves are covered with microscopic, crystal-clear, barbed hairs.

Flower: The clear yellow flowers bloom at the tips of the branches. The calyx lobes,

⁷⁄₁₆ inch long, open out in starburst fashion
and stay that way as they dry and mature
but do not fall off. The 10 petals are shaped
like pointed spatulas with very narrow
bases. They are ½–1 inch long. There are
numerous fertile stamens on threadlike filaments with some staminodes present; the
length of the stamens ranges from ³⁄₁₆ to ¾
inch. A single style rises in the center,
⅜–⅝ inch long. The flowers open near
sunset, staying open only during the night.
They bloom from May to September.

Fruit: Cylindrical capsule, ⅝–1¼ inches
long, filled with flat, oval, winged tan seeds
about ⅛ inch wide, including the wings.

Range: Gravel-filled and caliche soils in
open pastures, on dry sandy and gravelly
creek banks, and sometimes even dry, barren, rocky hillsides in southwestern Oklahoma, southeast Colorado, eastern New
Mexico, Texas, and Mexico.

Remarks: Yellow Stick-leaf has a flower
that looks almost identical to that of the
Sand Lily, *M. nuda*, except that it is yellow
instead of white and smaller. The plant is
not attractive until the flowers open, and
they wait until late in the day to do that.
Only night people and insects get to enjoy
their loveliness, for they close tightly as the
sun approaches.

The microscopic barbed hairs cover all
surfaces of the leaves, but on the edges of
the lobes the barbs are tipped with perfect
5-pointed stars. Under a strong microscope
they look like crystal tree trunks with tiny
stars placed on the tops. This gives the
leaves the ability to stick tightly to clothing.

The seed-bearing capsules dry out as they
mature, spilling the seeds to the ground;
the empty capsules remain on the branches,
becoming still drier. In the fall when
ranchers gather cattle for branding, they
often ride horseback through areas where
these plants remain standing. When touched
by vehicle, horse, or rider, the seedpods
and leaves rattle, sounding almost exactly
like a rattlesnake. Our cowboys call the
plant "Rattlesnake Bush."

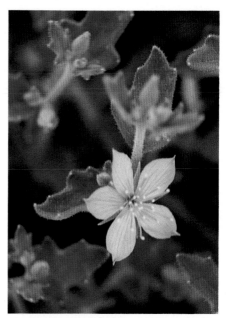

M. oligosperma Stick-leaf

M. reverchonii Yellow stick-leaf

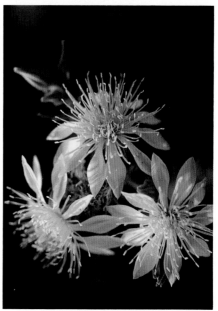

MALVACEAE
Mallow Family

Plants of the Mallow Family are usually herbaceous or shrubby and slightly hairy. Under a microscope, the hairs are star-shaped (stellate) on the tips. The leaves are borne singly, veined palmately, and, in many genera, cleft, lobed, or parted palmately. They have 5 sepals and 5 petals, and some genera have a circle of bracts just beneath the sepals.

A distinctive feature of this family is the uniting of the numerous stamen stalks to form a tube around the pistil that resembles a tree trunk with the anthers and nonfused filaments as the "branches and leaves." This "stamen tree" sticking up in the center of the flower is almost a "never-fail" characteristic for recognizing members of this family. The anthers are 1-celled with large pollen grains. The fruit is in capsule form in some, but in others, the segments separate or split into a number of nutlike parts.

Some members of this family are cotton, okra, hibiscus, hollyhock, and a European cousin, *Althaea officinalis*, called Marsh Mallow, from whose root the flavoring for the sweet and popular confection marshmallow is derived.

Callirhoë involucrata
Wine Cup, Poppy Mallow

Plant: A low-growing (1–2 feet) perennial plant with hairy stems that are vinelike and spreading, this Wine Cup grows from a turnip-shaped root. Its leaves are 1–2 inches long, palmately lobed, with the lobes cleft or lobed again into 5 or 7 narrow segments.

Flower: This particular species is readily identified by the 3 linear, 1-inch-long bracts that grow beneath each flower. The corolla consists of 5 separate cherry-red, reddish-purple, or wine-colored petals which are a

lighter color (almost white) at their base. The flowers are borne on long stalks growing from the leaf axils and are 1½–2½ inches across and cupping (hence the common name Wine Cup). Numerous stamens, united at the base, form a whitish or yellowish column. Five threadlike stigmas emerge from this column of stamens. Wine Cup blooms in May and June.

Fruit: Flattened disklike capsule (¼–⅜ inch across) that breaks apart into 1-seeded segments at maturity. (Visualize the seeds as tiny spokes in a wagon wheel.)

Range: Wine Cups prefer deep sands of grasslands and dry stream beds. They grow from North Dakota to Wyoming and Utah and in Missouri, Oklahoma, and Texas (except the far western part).

Remarks: This species is widespread. Bees are the main, and much-needed, pollinators of the pretty plant. Because the anthers discharge pollen before the style branches emerge from the stamen column, cross-pollination must occur for fruit to develop. Bees busily extract nectar, getting pollen on them from the newly opened flowers, then transfer it as they push past the widely spread styles of the older flowers.

Rhynchosida physocalyx
(= *Sida physocalyx*)
Bladderpod Sida, Sida

Plant: Perennial with spreading stems that lie on the ground, 14–16 inches long, and a somewhat woody taproot. The leaves and stems are covered with microscopic star-shaped (stellate) hairs. The alternate leaves are deep green, succulent-looking, roundish to oblong, with a rounded tip and heart-shaped base, growing up to 2¼ inches long and 1¾ inches wide. They are coarsely toothed, or serrate, around their edges. The leaves have petioles 1 inch long.

Flower: The flowers are solitary, growing from leaf axils on short stalks (pedicels).

The calyx lobes are heart-shaped and grow as long as and sometimes longer than the 5 soft-yellow or yellowish-white petals, almost to 1 inch. The petals are united at the base to the column, or stamen tree, which is very prominent in the center of the flower. There are numerous stamens with 1-celled anthers. The plant blooms from May to September or October.

Fruit: The calyx, in this species, enlarges after the flower has bloomed and becomes a thin papery covering that envelops the fruit, consisting of 10–15 black carpels, flat and oval, with beaklike tips.

Range: Clay and limestone soils, sandy, rocky, and gravelly washes, prairies, roadsides, and canyon ledges from Arizona to western Texas.

Remarks: Bladderpod Sida is an unusual member of the *Rhynchosida* genus. It is the only one that has calyx lobes that enlarge and turn into a structure that greatly resembles a Japanese paper lantern or a bladderlike 5-angled covering for the seeds.

As in other members of the Mallow Family, the stamen tree is clearly visible and should help in identification.

This plant is also known by its synonym, *Sida physocalyx*.

Sphaeralcea angustifolia
Copper Mallow, Narrowleaf Globe Mallow

Plant: A tall stately plant, with several erect stout stems that grow to 5 feet in height from a thick woody root. A yellowish or ashy-gray down on the leaves and stems is composed of star-tipped hairs. The leaves are narrow and 2–4 inches long, sometimes as long as 6 inches on the lower part of the plant. They look folded down the midrib, have small indistinct lobes or teeth near the base, and are slightly scalloped or crinkly on the edges.

Flower: The flowers (1½ inches across) grow here and there at random up and down the tall stem. They grow from the leaf axils in terminal racemes. There are 5 bright orange petals (½–¾ inch long) and 5 partially united sepals. The numerous purple-tipped stamens, with united filaments, form a tube around the styles. Bloom season is from April to August and sometimes on into October.

Fruit: Ten to 15 carpels arranged like the spokes in a wheel.

Range: Found in sandy or rocky soils, waste places, and roadsides, this plant grows in Kansas, Colorado, southern Nevada, Arizona, Mexico, and western Texas. It is less common as one goes eastward.

Remarks: Copper Mallow is a tall, erect plant greatly resembling a hollyhock (to which it is related), only in miniature.

Sphaeralcea coccinea var. *coccinea*
Scarlet Globe Mallow, Red Globe Mallow, Red False Mallow, Caliche Globe Mallow

Plant: Perennial rarely more than 1 foot tall. Its slender stems, growing from a stout taproot, are erect and/or spreading, often prostrate at the base. Sometimes it can be found growing in clumps. The leaves are arranged alternately on the stem and are divided into several lobes, which are parted or divided again to form many 3-, 5-, and 7-fingered leaves. The leaves are ¾–1 inch long and about the same width.

Flower: Many orange flowers clasp the upper half of the stem in a dense cluster. This particular species lacks the 3 bracts under the calyx that are common to other mallows. The 5 petals are ⅓–½ inch long. The stamens are numerous, uniting into a column around the styles. Scarlet Globe Mallow blooms from March through July and often into autumn.

Fruit: The pistil has 5 or more carpels, arranged like orange segments, that mature as 1-seeded compartments and split apart when fully ripe.

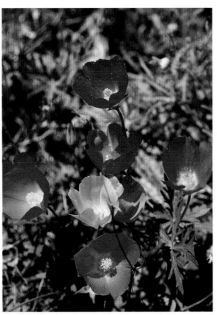

Range: Dry grassy plains and hills, caliche outcrops and gravelly places, and sandy-clay soils over most of Texas, New Mexico, and Arizona. Found also in Canada, it ranges southward to Iowa.

Remarks: From New Mexico folklore we learn that the crushed leaves can be made into a poultice to be used for topical application to skin irritations. The same crushed leaves can also be used as a soothing shoe liner for blistered feet. The Pima and Hopi tribes of Native Americans called it "Sore-eye Poppy," reputedly using it for curing or relieving some eye maladies.

Scientists have found this plant to be rich in Vitamin A and are researching its value as a nutritive herb for wildlife, especially those animals lacking Vitamin A in their diet.

Callirhoë involucrata Wine Cup

Rhynchosida physocalyx Bladderpod Sida

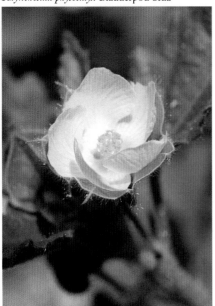

Sphaeralcea angustifolia Copper Mallow

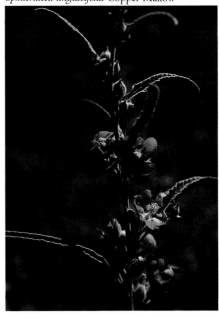

Sphaeralcea hastulata
Orange Globe Mallow,
Yerba de la Negrita

Plant: Another perennial of the Mallow Family, this is a small plant growing from a small crown or from root-shoots below the surface of the soil. The stems can be up to 12 inches tall but are usually shorter. The leaves are bright green and not as hairy as those of other mallows. There are star-tipped hairs on the surfaces of the leaves, but they are rather sparsely distributed. The leaf is shallowly lobed at the basal end with a much longer midlobe (from ¾ inch to 2½ inches long). The leaf edges are crinkly.

Flower: The flowers are rose-orange, or grenadine, and there is usually only 1 blossom at each node and no more than 8 per stem. On the Western Plains there are commonly 3 or 4 per stem. There are 5 sepals and 5 petals, ⅖–⅘ inch long. The stamens form a column through which the 5, or sometimes more, styles emerge with their purple stigmas. They begin to bloom in April or May, continuing through October, depending on the amount of summer moisture.

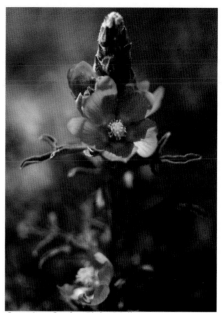

S. coccinea Scarlet Globe Mallow

S. hastulata Orange Globe Mallow

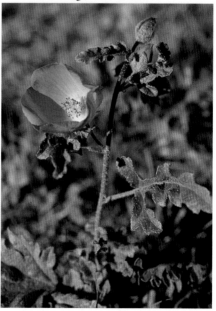

Fruit: The fruit splits into 10 or 12 nut-like parts; these are separate segments of the ovary, which, in cross section, look like the segments of an orange.

Range: This plant is common in gravelly places, sandy or rocky soils, and especially roadsides in western and central Texas, including the plains, and northeastern Mexico.

Remarks: Being short, this little mallow is not noticed until it blooms. The flowers are a bright, splashy red-orange and, low as they are, command attention.

The stems of the species have been known to be chewed like chewing gum. A tea was made from dried leaves, then used by Native Americans as a hair rinse, after shampooing, to give dark hair an even darker luster. A very strong tea rinse will curl hair if it is not rinsed out.

MARTYNIACEAE
Unicorn Plant Family

The Unicorn Plant Family includes annual and perennial herbs with coarse, branched stems. All parts of the plant have a strong, unpleasant odor when crushed. The simple leaves are alternate on the stems in some species and opposite in others. The stems, leaves, and fruits are densely covered with tiny gland-tipped hairs. The flowers of this family have a calyx that is 2-lipped, composed of 5 irregular sepals, and a corolla that is deeply 2-lipped, also 5-lobed. The lower lip of the corolla is larger and has 3 lobes. In the center of this lip, there is a bearded area (usually a different color from the rest of the corolla) that extends internally the length of the tube. There are 4 stamens of 2 sizes and 1 pistil. The fruit is a curved, tapering capsule that bears 4 to many seeds. The fruit in all species terminates in a very prominent 2-horned, incurved beak. As the fruit matures and dries, the capsule splits open and the incurved beak becomes 2 claws or hooks.

Proboscidea louisianica
Devil's Claw, Unicorn Plant, Ram's Horn

Plant: Annual 1–3 feet tall with stout, coarse branches that are opposite on the stem, sometimes prostrate on the ground, and often zigzag. The leaves are large (up to 5 inches across and 3–12 inches long), smooth to wavy on the edges, and slightly heart-shaped or rounded-triangular. A clammy-feeling plant, it has minute hairs that cover the stems, leaves, and flowers. It is also ill-smelling.

Flower: The inflorescence is a raceme of 1–20 soft pink to off-white flowers. They open 1 or 2 at a time. The calyx is 2-lipped and irregularly 5-lobed. There are 5 petals united to form a 2-lipped corolla 1–2¼

inches long. The bottom lip is deeply 3-lobed and mottled, or spotted, down toward the throat of the corolla tube. The central lobe is bearded and often yellow in color, with the coloring extending down into the center of the tube. There are 4 stamens of 2 sizes and 1 pistil. Devil's Claw blooms from June to July or August.

Fruit: Curved, tapering capsule up to 5 inches long. At first it is thick, green, and fleshy, but as it matures and dries out, it becomes dark, woody, stiff, and hard. It splits in half lengthwise, releasing 4 or more seeds. The incurved ends of the pod become 2 stout, hooklike tips or claws ("devil's claws").

Range: This plant grows in waste places, around the edges of playa lakes and stock ponds, and in the low-lying portions of pastures, preferring moist, sandy soils. It is distributed from Maine to Iowa, south into Georgia and west through Texas and western Oklahoma. Another species, *P. parviflora*, grows in eastern New Mexico.

Remarks: This sticky, hairy, bad-smelling plant often appears dirty, as the minute hairs that cover it catch and trap sand and dirt. But when in bloom, the large, funnel-shaped flowers are exotic-looking.

The seedpods are interesting in the manner in which they dry and split open, forming a pair of hooks or claws that easily become entangled in the tails or around the hooves of livestock. They just as easily can get caught in the fur of wild animals to be transported to distant areas, dispersing seeds along the way.

These strange seedpods have long been collected for making interesting craft items. The green pods have been pickled for table fare, and the seeds are reportedly gathered and eaten in some areas of Mexico.

I once watched a Pima basket weaver, from Arizona, using the dark blackish-brown bark (from the dried claw of this plant) in a basket she was constructing. She told me she prized it so highly that she saved seeds to plant each year, cultivating for use in her baskets.

NYCTAGINACEAE
Four-o'clock Family

Members of the Four-o'clock Family can be annual, biennial, or perennial herbs, shrubs, or trees. The ones found on the Western Plains are generally herbaceous annuals or perennials. The leaves are usually opposite with untoothed margins but sometimes are lobed. Flowers of this family have no petals; instead they have bracts that mimic sepals and sepals (often colorful) that mimic petals. The sepals join to form a tube with 3, 4, or 5 lobes on the flared edges. There are 1 to many stamens with filaments united at the base. The 1-celled ovary in the perianth tube appears to be inferior but is not. The fruit is a small, nutlike achene with a tough outer skin and 1 seed inside. The skin forms wings on the achenes of some species.

Abronia fragrans
Sand Verbena, Heart's Delight, Sweet Sand Verbena, Snowball

Plant: Spreading perennial herb from a long woody root with numerous many-branched stems, 8–36 inches long, which are gray-white in color because of the microscopic sticky hairs covering them. The leaves are opposite, variable in shape but mostly triangular to oblong, rounded at the base and rounded or pointed at the tip, ¾–3½ inches long, and rather thick. The surface is also sticky.

Flower: The fragrant flowers grow in large globular clusters, 2–3 inches across, with 30–40 flowers in each many-bracted involucre. There are no petals, but the calyx is petallike (consisting of 5 sepals that form a long funnel shape with 5 deeply cut lobes around the edge) and ranges in color from a pinkish white to a rosy pink. Each flower in the cluster is ½–1¼ inches long and subtended by 5 thin, dry bracts. The ovary is superior, with 5 stamens of varying lengths. This plant blooms from April to August and sometimes into the fall.

Fruit: Achene about ⅓ inch long, narrowly 5-winged, dark brown, and wrinkled.

Range: Preferring deep sand, this lovely plant can be found often in large stands covering dunes or hillsides along stream beds and roadsides. It grows from Idaho, Montana, and South Dakota to Arizona, New Mexico, Texas, and into Mexico.

Remarks: Sand Verbena has a misleading common name, since it is not related to the true verbenas. It grows best in sandy locations and could be mistaken for a large verbena (hence its name) but is truly a four-o'clock, blooming late in the afternoon and through the night, filling the evening air with a sweet perfume. The umbellike or ball-shaped flower clusters are easily visible and worth a trek through deep sand to find.

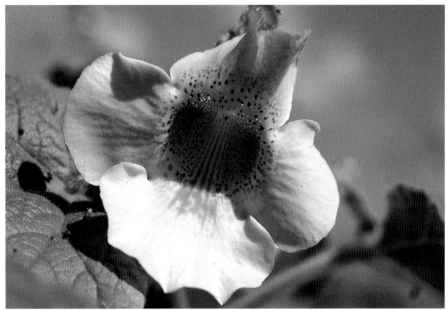

Proboscidea louisianica Devil's Claw: flower above, fruit below

Opposite: *Abronia fragrans* Sand Verbena

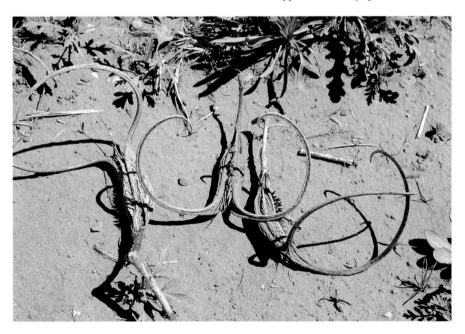

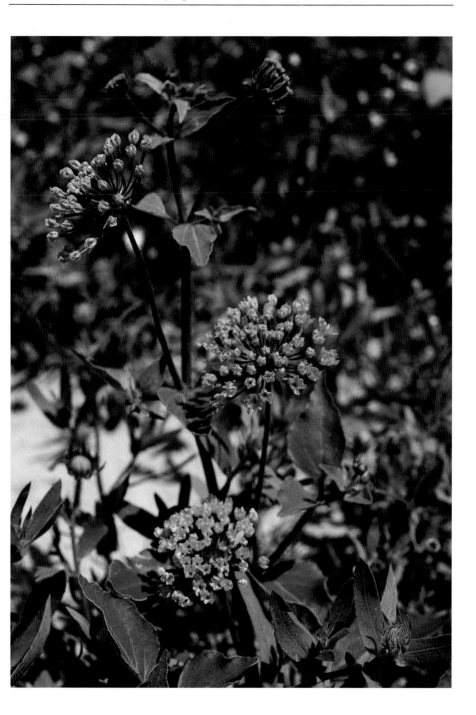

Acleisanthes longiflora
Angel Trumpets

Plant: Perennial herb from a woody root.
It is vinelike, with many branching stems,
and tends to form low clumps. The gray-
green leaves are somewhat succulent, opposite but of unequal lengths, triangular-
lanceolate in shape, ½–1½ inches long,
with untoothed and often wavy margins.
Flower: Solitary white flowers, subtended by small bracts, grow from the leaf
axils. Lacking petals, the perianth unites to
form a slender pinkish-green tube that at-
tains a length of 3–6 inches above the
ovary. It then flares out (trumpetlike) in a
white 5-lobed rim 1 inch across. The 2–5
long stamens and the style extend beyond
the opening of the tube. The superior ovary
is positioned below the elongated tube. Angel Trumpets bloom best after rains from
spring to fall.
Fruit: Narrow, oblong 5-ribbed achene,
¼–⅜ inch long.
Range: Sandy or clay loams, dry alkaline
to rocky soils, in pastures, hillsides, roadsides, and dry riverbeds from Texas to California and into Mexico.
Remarks: These fragrant wildflowers are
some of the longest to be found on the
Western Plains. One does not need a vivid
imagination to agree that they really do
look like "angel trumpets" in miniature.
The only drawback to appreciating them is
that they are nocturnal. They bloom at
dusk, staying open all night to be polli-
nated by night-flying moths, only to close
when the sun appears. For this reason, they
are most difficult to photograph. During
the day, Angel Trumpets are hardly distin-
guishable among the other green pasture
plants. But on a moonlit night, those previously unnoticed vinelike clumps come alive
with a silvery shimmering grace as they re-
act to the night in the same way neighboring wildflowers do to the day.

Allionia incarnata
Trailing Four-o'clock, Trailing Allionia, Umbrellawort, Hierba de la Hormiga

Plant: Perennial vine, low and sprawling
along the ground with many branched
stems at the base. It has a woody root and
produces stems 1–3 feet long, making an
individual plant often 9–10 feet across. The
entire plant is covered by sticky, glandular
hairs. The leaves, unequal in size, are opposite, ½–1½ inches long, oval to oblong,
with tips that can be rounded or pointed
and edges that are smooth to wavy.
Flower: The rosy-pink to purplish
flowers grow on peduncles (stalks) in the
leaf axils in clusters of 3, each with its
petallike perianth forming a short 4- or
5-lobed tube or funnel, ¼–½ inch long.
The 3 flowers together, appearing as
one, measure about 1 inch across. Each
individual flower in the cluster has 4–7
stamens and a superior ovary and is subtended by 3 bracts. It blooms from late
May to July.
Fruit: Achene, ⅛–³⁄₁₆ inch long, enclosed by the 3 bracts that subtended the
flowers. The fruit has prominent curved lateral wings with 3 teeth on each side.
Range: This plant prefers full sun and
flat pasturelands that are sandy or gravelly.
Dry climate does not seem to deter it. It
grows in southeastern California, Nevada,
southern Utah, southern Colorado, Texas,
New Mexico, and central Mexico.
Remarks: This is a small American
genus with only 2 species, *A. incarnata* and
A. choisyi.

Because it is covered with sticky hairs,
this ground-hugging plant with its colorful
flowers is often found with sand and dirt
clinging to it. Many members of this family
are noted for opening late in the day and
closing early the next day, but Trailing
Four-o'clock seems to like the bright sun
and usually does not close its flowers by
noon.

Mirabilis linearis
Umbrellawort, Four-o'clock

Plant: Perennial from a woody taproot to heights of 1–3 feet. It is erect at first but later trails on the ground, as it grows taller. The plant has forked branches which are gray-white in color and without hairs. There are few to many linear leaves, often crowded, opposite, also gray-white, 1–4 inches long and only about ¼ inch wide. The margins are smooth (only rarely toothed).

Flower: The flowers grow from the leaf axils usually in a 3-flowered cyme. The fused perianth (there are no petals) is ½ inch long, pink to pinkish-white in color, flaring out into 5 deeply incised lobes. There are 3–6 stamens of unequal lengths and a superior ovary positioned below the tube. Umbrellawort blooms from June to September and sometimes into October.

Fruit: The 5-pointed involucre of this flower enlarges and becomes papery with age, resembling a flower itself. It loosely envelops the 3–6 seeds, with their bristly-hairy surfaces, gradually opening out flat with the rounded ⅛-inch seeds in the center. They are easily dislodged from this flat "perch" and fall to the ground.

Range: Dry sandy plains and rocky places from South Dakota, Montana, Missouri, Texas to Arizona, and down into Mexico, rarely extending eastward.

Remarks: This is a scraggly plant, pale in color, with few features to draw one's attention to it. The most noticeable thing is its fruiting structure, which looks like a flat 5-pointed, star-shaped flower with a few small fuzzy balls stuck in the center. The flower, which blooms earlier, is delicate in color and very pretty, but it only blooms for a short time (usually early in the morning) and then withers to begin developing the seeds and enlarging the involucre.

Common names are often given to wildflowers because they resemble some ordinary item that anyone would recognize.

One definition of "wort" is, "a plant; herb; vegetable; now chiefly in composition, as in *liverwort* or *figwort*." The common name Umbrellawort surely comes from the fact that this papery involucre looks like a miniature umbrella growing on a plant—thus "umbrella-plant."

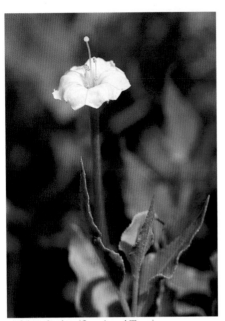

Acleisanthes longiflora Angel Trumpets

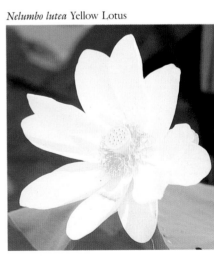

Allionia incarnata Trailing Four-o'clock

Mirabilis linearis Umbrellawort

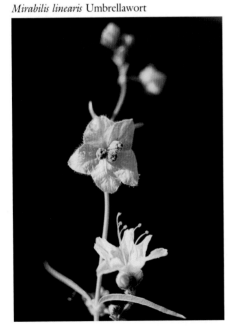

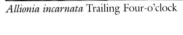
Nelumbo lutea Yellow Lotus

NYMPHAEACEAE
Water Lily Family

The Water Lily Family consists of aquatic perennial herbs with stems (rhizomes) that grow in the soil underwater and leaves and flowers, on stalks, that either stick up above or float on the surface. Large round or oval leaf blades usually float, and the stems bearing the showy flower heads usually project above the surface. The flowers grow singly on the tips of stalks. They have both stamens and pistils. There are 3–6 sepals, 3 to many petals (large and showy), 3 to many stamens, and 1 to several pistils. The fruit is a many-seeded nut or a 1–3-seeded small nut or berry that does not split open at maturity.

On the Western Plains, members of this family are rare indeed. The semiarid climate, winters with ice and snow, and deep canyons make the plains a place where water lilies find it difficult to grow. But occasionally, in a playa lake or city park, a colony of water lilies gets started and, in spite of the harsh conditions, flourishes and reproduces. How the seeds get here is merely a guess, but one theory is that migratory birds drop them.

Nelumbo lutea
Yellow Lotus, Water Chinquapin, Pond Nut, American Lotus, Yellow Water Lily, Sacred Bean

Plant: Aquatic plant with underwater rhizomes deep in the mud. The stems are submerged in the water, with the leaves and flowers extending above the surface. The leaves are circular or shield-shaped, with the stalk attached on the underneath side near the center. They are large and can reach 2 feet in diameter (usually less, on the Western Plains). The center of each leaf is cup-shaped or somewhat depressed.
Flower: Each pale yellow flower is borne singly on the tip of a stem and is 6–10 inches across. There are 20 or more sepals and petals, with no sharp distinction between them. Numerous stamens closely surround several pistils in a strange-looking inverted cone in the center of the flower. Yellow Lotus blooms in July and August.
Fruit: The fruiting receptacle is an inverted cone in the middle of the flower. It is thick and large, 3–4 inches across. There are several holes on the surface of this receptacle with a pistil in each hole. One large (3/8–1/2 inch across) single-seeded nut forms in each hole. As the petals fall off, the seedpod (or receptacle) dries, turning brown and hard. The holes widen and the stalk shrivels, allowing the heavy pod to fall to the water to float and decay, or turn upside down—either way, depositing the heavy seeds to the mud to begin a new plant.
Range: Preferring the quiet water of ponds and slow-moving rivers, this aquatic plant grows in great numbers from eastern Canada through New England, down into Florida, then westward into Texas, with only occasional specimens on the Western Plains.
Remarks: This distant cousin to the Sacred Lotus of the eastern tropics has spectacular blooms, unusual seedpods, and large, waxy leaves. If one is spotted in a lake, stream, or pasture stock pond, it is an impressive sight. The mystery of how it gets started on the Western Plains, an area so inhospitable to water lilies, only adds to its mystique.

Yellow Lotus is considered by many to be a noxious water weed, for it can quickly choke small ponds and waterways, making navigation impossible.

The dried seedpods are an exotic addition to flower arrangements and decorations needing dried materials. They can be found packaged in many floral supply houses with an expensive price tag.

The tubers along the rhizome are farinaceous storage tubers and are edible, as are the seeds. As with many underground and underwater rhizomes, a mealy starch is stored in them.

ONAGRACEAE
Evening Primrose Family

The plants commonly called evening primroses are not related to the true primroses, which belong to the Primulaceae. Many of the Onagraceae open in the morning and stay open all day, but others open late in the day and bloom at night, closing before noon the next day.

A significant feature of this family is the normally regular flower, which nearly always has 4 sepals, 4 petals, 4 or 8 stamens, and a 4-chambered ovary. There is a genus, however, that has 2 sepals and 2 petals and

Oenothera albicaulis
(Prairie Evening Primrose)

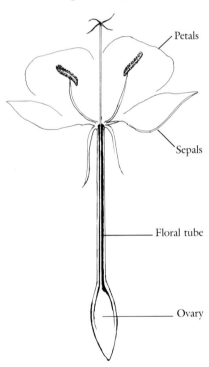

Petals

Sepals

Floral tube

Ovary

another with irregular flowers. Usually the plants tend to be somewhat woody near the ground, and the leaves are varied in shape as well as in how they grow on the stem. The ovary is always inferior and swollen at its base. There is often a tube from the top of the ovary to the attachment of the sepals and petals. The flowers vary in size, but most are lovely and showy. The color of the corolla ranges from white to pale pink or yellow. The fruit is usually in a capsule or nutlike structure.

Nearly all yellow Onagraceae have been called buttercups because of their color. (They are not related to the true buttercups of the Ranunculaceae.) Since there are many yellow ones, lumping them all together by a common name is confusing. There are differences, and they are interesting to note: for instance there are heart-shaped petals as opposed to plain-edged ones; cross-shaped stigma tips (in the genus *Oenothera*) or shield-shaped tips (in the genus *Calylophus*); those that grow seemingly stemless out of the ground and those with long stems; seedpods that are almost buried at ground level or capsules on the stems.

Oil of evening primrose is said to be the world's richest source of natural unsaturated fatty acids, helpful in cases of obesity, mental illness, heart disease, and arthritis. It is advertised widely in natural-food publications.

Many of our plants today were brought to this country by the colonists long ago. But the evening primroses (Onagraceae) have a different history. They were already here when the colonists arrived and eventually were transported back to Europe, where they still flourish today.

Calylophus hartwegii
Hartweg Evening Primrose, Western Primrose

Plant: An almost shrubby perennial 4–18 inches tall. The stems are stout, rather hairy, and many-branched from the ground. The leaves, 1 to 2 inches long, are narrow, lanceolate, about 5/16 inch wide, and smooth to slightly toothed.

Flower: The sepals are streaked with red while in the bud stage, but upon opening, the petals are a bright yellow as they bloom singly from the leaf axils. The 4 petals are ½–1 inch long and diamond-shaped. There are 8 stamens, and the stigma is shaped like a shield (peltate). It is flat, with the stalk attached to the undersurface instead of at the base or on the margin. The blooming period is from April to June.

Fruit: From the inferior ovary, a cylindrical capsule forms well below the floral tube or corolla. The tiny seeds are in 2 rows in each locule.

Range: Hartweg Evening Primrose grows in rocky places and on dry stony hills from Texas through much of New Mexico and Arizona, then north to Kansas and Colorado.

Remarks: This yellow evening primrose grows on a much-branched plant making it look like a bouquet. The flowers are not as large and showy as other evening primroses, but they are as pretty and bright yellow as the other yellow ones.

Gaura suffulta var. *suffulta*
Bee Blossom, Wild Honeysuckle, Kisses

Plant: Annual, with many branches growing from the ground, 1–3 feet high. It has a stout taproot and is rather softly hairy on the lower parts. The lance-shaped leaves are narrow (less than 1 inch wide) and ½–3½ inches long. The leaf margins are somewhat smooth to slightly toothed or wavy.

Flower: The flowers grow on tall spikes blooming from the lower portions up toward the tip. The color can vary from white to pinkish-purple to red. As they mature, they turn a darker pink or red. The flowers are bilaterally symmetrical with 4 petals (approximately ⅓ inch long) all arranged at the top of the blossom. The 8 stamens point downward and have burgundy-red tips. The stigma is delicately cross-shaped at the tip. The blooming period is from April almost through June.

Fruit: An inferior ovary is at the base of a very short floral tube. It begins to swell as the blossoms shrivel and fall off and the seeds begin to mature. The seedpod is a solid oval shape bulging almost to points in the middle. There are 4 prominent wings on the four corners of the tough pod.

Range: Bee Blossom is fairly common on the Western Plains, being very widespread by the roadsides, as it prefers sandy, weedy ground. It grows in Oklahoma, Texas, and south into Mexico.

Remarks: Studied for the beauty of the blossoms, this is a marvelous plant with its graceful flower-covered spikes. Its fragrance is delicate but strong enough to attract honeybees, which love the pollen of this flower.

There are several other *Gauras* that grow well on the Western Plains. Some of them are shorter and shrubbier; others are much taller and straggly-looking. The flowers, generally, all resemble each other with the 4 upswept petals at the top of the blossom and the 8 downswept stamens hanging below them, their colored anthers being very distinctive features.

Oenothera albicaulis
Prairie Evening Primrose

Plant: Annual with stems up to 20 inches long spreading horizontally in a circle from the root. The leaves are oblanceolate, ½–3 inches long and ¼–¾ inch wide. They are pinnately cleft into narrow lobes that do not reach to the midrib. The margins of these cleft leaves are very wavy.

Flower: The heart-shaped white petals are about ¾–1½ inches long. The mature buds droop until they open; then the flower straightens up as it faces upward. The flowers open near sunset but remain open several days. There are 4 sepals, ⅝–1 inch long, 4 petals, and 8 stamens. The tip of the stigma is threadlike and cross-shaped. It blooms from April to May.

Fruit: Cylinder-shaped capsule, ¾–1¼ inches long, with indistinct ribs. The tiny seeds develop in 2 rows inside each locule of the capsule.

Range: Prairie Evening Primrose prefers sandy spots, grassy plains, and disturbed soil. It grows from northern Mexico through Texas, New Mexico, and Arizona, northward to South Dakota and Montana.

Remarks: Most information about evening primroses states that they open late in the day and close the next day. Recently I noticed one growing in our pasture. Not being sure just when the blossoms opened, I went one evening after sunset, but before darkness, to observe this particular specimen. As I approached, I saw a bud open and the white petals unfurl. Unaccustomed as I am to seeing flowers actually "move," I didn't believe that it had happened. So I sat down, waited, and watched until another bud burst the delicate bonds of the calyx and, ever so elegantly, slowly opened to the night. For the duration of its blooming period (which was nearly 3 weeks) this plant produced many lovely snow-white blossoms.

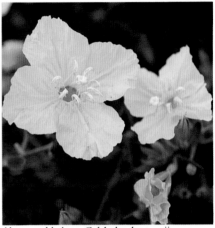

Above and below: *Calylophus hartwegii* Hartweg Evening Primrose

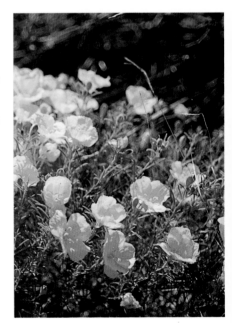

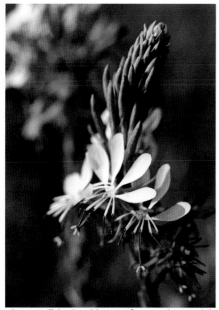

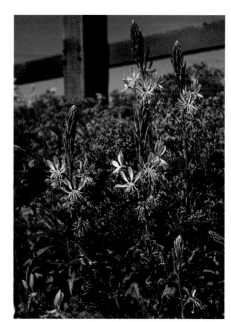

Gaura suffulta Bee Blossom flower; plant at right

Oenothera albicaulis Prairie Evening Primrose

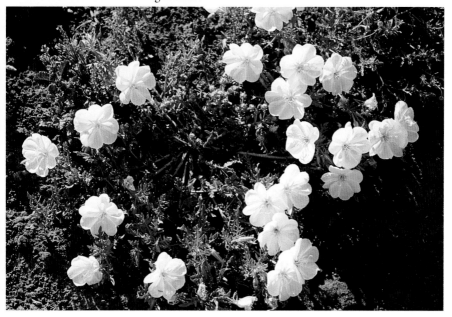

Oenothera missouriensis (= *Oe. macrocarpa*)
Missouri Primrose, Fluttermill, Sundrop, Ozark Sundrop, Yellow Evening Primrose

Plant: Perennial, with reddish stems that can either sprawl on the ground or be upright and up to 12 inches tall. The many stems are branched, with alternate leaves, narrowly to broadly lance-shaped (lanceolate). The edges are smooth to wavy to somewhat toothed, 2–8 inches long and ⅙–1 inch wide.

Flower: The flower buds droop at first, then become erect as they open near sunset and close between midmorning and noon on the following day. The large buttery-yellow flowers can measure 3–4 inches across and are found at the end of a 4–8-inch green tube. There are 4 sepals (which turn down when the petals open), 4 petals, 8 stamens, and a cross-shaped stigma tip. The flowers grow from the upper leaf axils. They bloom from May to July.

Fruit: Large capsule ¾–2½ inches long, with 4 wings about ½ inch wide. The seeds grow in 1 row in each locule.

Range: Missouri Primrose seems to prefer caliche hills and harsh conditions, for it grows in places where nothing else will, such as rocky roadcuts. It is found from western Missouri and Arkansas to Nebraska, Kansas, Oklahoma, and Texas.

Remarks: This plant produces a large, spectacular flower, but one must get out early in order to appreciate it. The morning heat makes it close up tightly, droop, and turn orange; thus by noon it is gone. The seedpods are large and tough, forming a cluster at ground level. They are tan-colored, often with red streaks, and can be used in dried arrangements.

Some taxonomists use the synonym *Oe. macrocarpa* for Missouri Primroses appearing in the panhandle of Texas.

Oenothera rhombipetala
Four-point Evening Primrose, Diamond-petal Evening Primrose

Plant: Tall winter annual or biennial unbranched plant 2–4 feet high, growing from a fleshy taproot. It is heavily leafed from the ground up to the flowers, which are clustered near the top. The leaves are narrowly oblanceolate, slightly broader at the tip, 3–5 inches long (decreasing in length as they grow up the stem) and ⅜–¾ inch wide, with wavy, untoothed margins.

Flower: The 4 petals are bright yellow, diamond- or rhomboid-shaped. There are numerous flowers, 2–2½ inches across, growing in spikes, which terminate in a cluster at the top of the stem. The flowers spread outward, forming long-stemmed groups of translucent sunshine-yellow bouquets. They open near sunset and stay open the following day, blooming from May to September.

Fruit: Slightly curved cylindrical capsule, ½–⅔ inch long, with seeds arranged in 2 rows in each locule.

Range: This tall evening primrose prefers sandy soil and waste or disturbed ground. It grows on prairies in western Oklahoma, as well as from Indiana to Wisconsin and Minnesota, and from Minnesota south to Texas from the plains to East Texas and into Louisiana. It is found occasionally over to the Atlantic Coast.

Remarks: Easily visible from the highways, the Four-point Evening Primrose is an elegant-looking member of this family.

Oenothera triloba
Texas Buttercup, Evening Buttercup, Stemless Evening Primrose

Plant: A winter annual or biennial, 6–7 inches tall. The leaves are more than twice as long as they are broad and shaped like an oblong lance (oblanceolate). They are irregularly cleft into narrow lobes and are 2–8 inches long and ¼–1½ inches wide. This plant has scarcely any stem above ground; the leaves appear to be "bunched up" in a basal rosette.

Flower: The large yellow flowers nestle among the bunched leaves. There are 4 petals nearly 1 inch long, making this flower a spectacular one. The mature buds stand erect, not drooping, until the blossoms open late in the day, near sunset. There are 8 stamens, and the stigma is tipped with 4 threadlike branches, rather cross-shaped or X-shaped. The inferior ovary is down among the leaves nearly at ground level. Texas Buttercup blooms from April to June.

Fruit: The seedpod is a capsule shaped like an upside-down pyramid with 4 wings about ¼ inch wide near the top. The seeds are arranged in 2 rows in each locule. They have tiny wings on them too, and are about 1⁄16 inch long. The plant forms a cluster of these pods that becomes very hard as it matures and dries out.

Range: Texas Buttercup prefers prairies and pastures but does well in disturbed soils as well as on grassy slopes and hills. It has been observed from Kansas to Kentucky, Tennessee, and northern Alabama, and is found over most of Texas.

Remarks: The large size of these lovely flowers is an important feature, but even more distinctive is the cluster of seedpods that remains tightly clinging to the ground after the leaves have withered and gone. One could compare this cluster to a pine cone, since it is almost the size of a fist, dark brown, hard, and woody in texture. I think it looks like a round barnacle-covered object. The seedpods are open after the seeds have been dispersed, and they can puncture and cut just like barnacles. These pods can be used in dried arrangements and as unusual "found" objects on a coffee table for guaranteed conversation pieces.

Oenothera speciosa
Pink Evening Primrose, Showy Primrose, Amapola del Campo

Plant: Perennial growing from underground rhizomes to a height of about 1 foot. The leaves are alternate, oblong-lanceolate, ¾–3½ inches long, and ¼–1 inch wide, with wavy, toothed margins.

Flower: The flowers are solitary in the leaf axils, with buds that droop until time to open, then rise to an erect position and display white to pink petals 1–1¾ inches long. There are 8 stamens and 1 pistil with a cross-shaped tip. Pink or red veins in the petals run toward the yellow center of the flower. This showy plant blooms from May to August.

Fruit: A tough, narrow, ribbed capsule 3⁄8–¾ inch long and tapering downward. The tiny pink seeds are arranged in several indistinct rows in each locule.

Range: One can find this lovely flower beside the highways as well as in prairies and open pastures. It also grows throughout the southeast and in Kansas, Missouri, Oklahoma, throughout Texas, and into Mexico.

Remarks: In the northern and western areas of the Western Plains, this species usually is white-flowered and more upright than elsewhere. In the remainder of its range, it is more often pink. The flowers are largest in the spring, dwindling in the summer heat. These plants form colonies, in the areas where they flourish, especially if there is plenty of room for them to spread. The blossoms usually open in the morning and stay open all day.

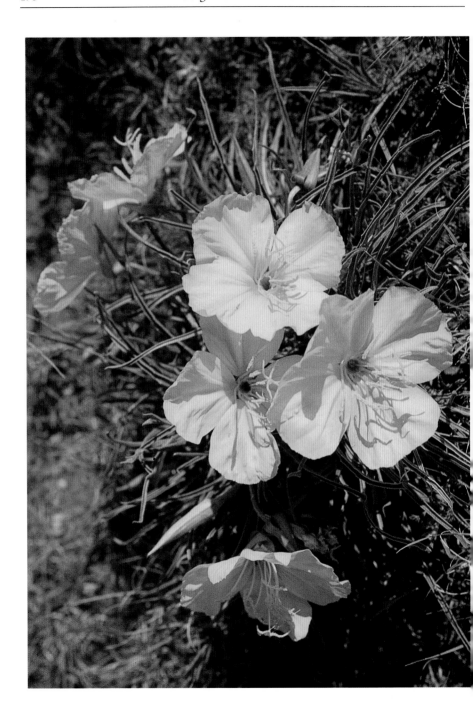

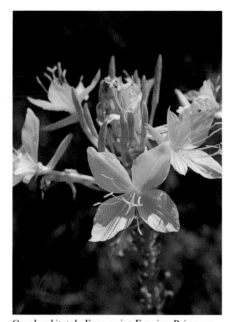

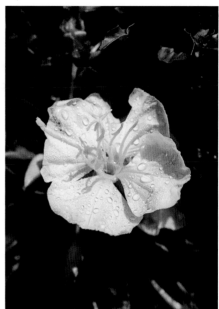

Oe. rhombipetala Four-point Evening Primrose   *Oe. triloba* Texas Buttercup
Opposite: *Oenothera missouriensis* Missouri Primrose
Oe. speciosa Pink Evening Primrose

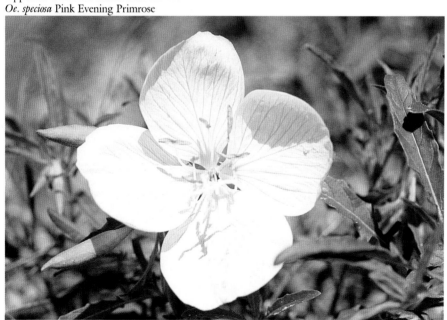

ORCHIDACEAE
Orchid Family

Orchids are truly the most elegant of all flowering plants. In the tropics, where they abound, they grow on the branches of trees. On the Western Plains, they grow on the ground from underground rhizomes.

All the different species of orchids share certain peculiar, yet easy-to-observe characteristics. There are 3 sepals and 3 petals, but the symmetry is definitely bilateral. One petal, usually the lower one (called the lip), differs from the others (called "lateral petals") in size, shape, or color, or all three. The lateral petals are often the same color and shape as the sepals. The stamens and pistil are not separate; instead the style, stigma, and stamen (or stamens) are all fused to form a column that often looks like a petal. An inferior ovary is situated deep in the end of the stem just beneath the flowering parts. The flowers in this family range from small and inconspicuous to large and very showy.

The Orchidaceae are the largest family of flowering plants in the world with the greatest number of species flourishing in the jungles of both hemispheres. There are over 15,000 species of orchids in several hundred genera.

Epipactis gigantea
Stream Orchid, Giant Helleborine

Plant: Aptly named, this lovely orchid can grow up to 5 feet high. From a short underground rhizome develops a simple tall stem with clasping leaves, broadly elliptic to linear-lanceolate in shape, 2–8 inches long and 1–2½ inches wide.

Flower: The flowers grow up the stem, and there can be as few as 2 or 3 or as many as 20 individual blossoms on a single stem. The small flowers are greenish-red and about 1 inch long. The lateral petals are marked with deep reddish veins. The lip is maroon or purple and spurless. The plant blooms from April to July.

Fruit: Dry, elliptically shaped pendant. It opens by pores, or slits, to discharge the seeds.

Range: Found on wet, seeping slopes, bluffs, or ledges, Stream Orchid is scattered from Montana to Colorado, South Dakota, Oklahoma, Texas, California, and Mexico.

Remarks: Orchids are favorites of many flower lovers. Their family has been called the "royal family of flowers." In tropical regions, it is often the largest family (the one with the most different kinds or species). On the Western Plains, it is one of the smallest.

After 10 years of searching, I finally found this wild orchid in bloom. It possesses a fragile beauty, being small, delicate, and rather inconspicuous. Since it is not large and showy, one can only hope that unthinking flower pickers will not notice it and, therefore, will pass it by. If so, it will continue to flourish in its grottolike habitat safe from extinction.

OXALIDACEAE
Wood Sorrel Family

The Wood Sorrel Family consists of herbs (either annual or perennial), shrubs, and a few trees. They all have a very sour sap containing oxalic acid. All of the species found on the Western Plains belong to 1 genus, *Oxalis*. They are small plants with leaf blades divided into 3 heart-shaped segments. The flowers are 5-merous (5 sepals, 5 petals, 10 stamens, and a pistil with 5 styles). The flowers are borne on the tip of a stalk, either solitary or in clusters. The colors of the several species of *Oxalis* are either yellow or pinkish-purple. The seedpods split open, often rather explosively, scattering the many tiny seeds some distance from the plant.

The botanical name *Oxalis* is the source of the chemical name "oxalic acid" for the substance that gives the plants a tart taste. In large amounts, oxalic acid would be poisonous, but the leaves have been found to be quite harmless and have been used as a garnish in salads and soups for many generations.

Oxalis corniculata
Yellow Wood Sorrel,
Creeping Lady's Sorrel, Agrito

Plant: Perennial low, branching plant growing in a compact mass up to 6 inches tall. It has several stems that grow creeping from a main taproot. The stems are covered with straight, whitish, microscopic hairs. The bright green leaves are trifoliate (divided into 3 heart-shaped segments) and ½ inch wide. The leaf segments, or leaflets, have no teeth on their margins and are folded down the middle.

Flower: Two or 3 yellow flowers, ⅜ inch wide, rise on stalks in umbrella fashion (umbrellike structure). There are 5 sepals, 5 delicate petals of equal size and shape, barely joined at their base, 10 stamens, and a pistil with 5 styles. The blossoms are fragile and fall away after a day or two of blooming. They close up at night, as do the leaves. This plant can be found blooming somewhere on the Western Plains from April until frost (October or November).

Fruit: A 4-angled capsule that looks like a miniature okra pod. It is about ½ inch long, green, juicy, covered with tiny hairs, and contains the seeds, which turn brown as they dry and mature. The little seeds have white markings on their ridges. When in fruit, the pods stick straight up on stems that are bent down.

Range: This plant can grow almost anywhere, in dry, sandy, gravelly, or clay soils. It is found in pastures, canyons, gardens, disturbed places, and on limestone banks. It is native to North America and found throughout the country.

Remarks: This plant contains oxalic acid. Livestock grazing on it for several weeks have been known to be poisoned by ingesting large amounts of the acid.

It is true that large dosages are harmful, but small portions (such as those used in salads and soups) have been used, with no ill effects, and enjoyed by people from the ancient Native Americans up to present-day gourmet cooks. Yellow Wood Sorrel is high in vitamin C. The leaves and tender green fruit pods add a tart taste to salads and vegetable dishes. The fresh yellow flowers are a tasty and colorful addition to a salad.

In "manicured" flower beds, this wildflower is considered a pest weed. I think, however, that it might be interesting when I take this plant out of my garden next time to eat it instead of throwing it away.

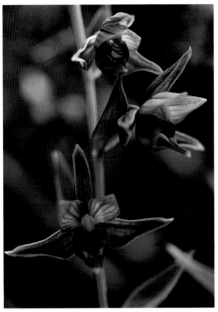

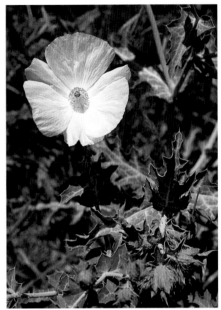

Epipactis gigantea Stream Orchid

Argemone polyanthemos White Prickly Poppy

Oxalis corniculata Yellow Wood Sorrel

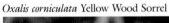

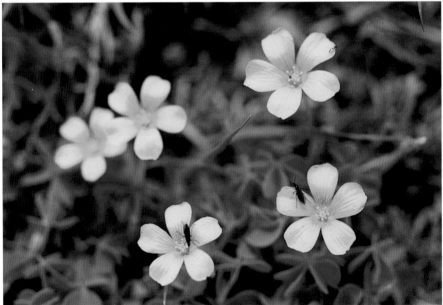

PAPAVERACEAE
Poppy Family

The plants in the Poppy Family are characterized by the colored sap they contain: red, orange, yellow, or sometimes white. The leaves are borne singly, usually alternate on the stems and clasping them. They are wavy along the margins and blue-green in color. The flowers are solitary or clustered on the stems, subtended by a bract or leaf. There are 2–3 sepals, which fall off as the petals open out. The 4–6 petals are large, showy, fragile-looking, and arranged in 2 rows. There are many stamens and a 1-celled ovary. The fruit is a capsule inside which many dark brown or black seeds develop in 2 or more vertical rows.

One of the most notorious members of this large family is the Opium Poppy, *Papaver somniferum*, known for its poisonous sap, which is the basis for opium, morphine, and heroin.

Poppies are abundant over the western portions of North America. The family includes approximately 200 species in 26 genera growing mostly in the temperate regions of North and South America.

Argemone polyanthemos
White Prickly Poppy, Texas Prickly Poppy, Thistle Poppy, Chicalote

Plant: Annual or biennial growing from a deep taproot. The stems (1–5) are branched and 1–3½ feet tall. The blue-green succulent leaves (3–8 inches long) are spine-tipped and wavy on the edges. The upper leaves are shallowly lobed and clasping the stem. The larger leaves, toward the base of the plant, are more deeply, pinnately lobed and less clasping. Each leaf is prickly on the underside and smooth on the top, with the spines, or prickles, on the margins of the leaves. All parts of the plant exude a sticky, bright yellow latex sap.

Flower: The flower buds are 3-horned and well barbed. These are the 3 sepals with horns (about ⅓ inch long), which fall as the petals open. The flowers are 2½–4 inches across, pure white, with usually 6 papery petals subtended by 1 or 2 bracts. Very rarely the petals can be lavender or yellow, but white is the most common color. The petals are in 2 rows, with the outer ones somewhat roundish in shape while the inner ones are more ovate, with the smaller end attached to the flower head. There are 150 or more stamens, equal in length, with bright yellow filaments and anthers. A 3–5-lobed purple stigma sticks up almost ¼ inch tall. The blooming period is from late April through June.

Fruit: Spine-covered, football-shaped capsule, or pod, filled with many dark brown or black seeds about ¹⁄₁₆ inch long. The seeds are sown by the wind as the sides of the mature fruit pod open and curl back. The surface of the little seeds has a netlike or sculptured appearance.

Range: This wildflower grows well in sandy or gravelly soils on hillsides, pastures, prairies, mesas, fields, and roadsides especially through the northern half of Texas and on to the Western Plains, growing from South Dakota to eastern Wyoming, down through New Mexico, Arizona, and northern Mexico.

Remarks: The white petals of this wild poppy are some of the purest white and most delicate and fragile-looking (almost onionskin thin) of all the white wildflowers. Because it is sometimes 4 inches across, it is a showy plant, especially in large stands. Livestock leave it alone because of its spines and the acrid-tasting sap. Up close, the lemon-yellow stamens and vivid purple stigma in the center of the petals look like a miniature "pom-pom" in the middle of a delicate white bowl.

The seeds of the *Argemone* species have been used as food in the past, but they are so difficult to extract that it hardly seems worth it. The juice has reportedly been effective in the elimination of warts.

PLANTAGINACEAE
Plantain Family

The Plantaginaceae are a family of annual or perennial herbs with or without stems. The leaves are nearly always basal and usually linear and narrow. The flowers are always in spikes; the spikes are of varying lengths, but the flowers are consistently very small (best viewed and appreciated with the aid of a microscope). The flowers have conspicuous bracts and can be either perfect (having both pistils and stamens) or unisexual. The calyx and corolla are 4-lobed, and there are 2 or 4 stamens deep in the corolla tube. The fruit is a capsule that develops from a superior 2–4-celled ovary, there being 1 or more seeds to a cell at maturity.

Plantago helleri
Indian Wheat, Heller's Plantain, Ribbon Grass, White Man's Foot

Plant: Annual stemless herb growing from a slender taproot. The numerous 3-veined leaves are linear, basal, erect, or bending outward. They can be from 1 to 8 inches long and are only about ¼ inch wide. A solitary scape (or several) grows up from the center of the plant, usually shorter but sometimes taller than the surrounding leaves. The entire plant is somewhat "shaggy," being covered with minute hairs.
Flower: On the tip of the scape (leafless peduncle, or stalk, rising from the ground) an oblong-cylindrical dense-bracted spike (1–1½ inches long) bears many tiny greenish-white flowers, each growing in the axil of a bract. The calyx and corolla are 4-lobed, with 2–4 stamens and 4 sepals. The calyx lobes are only ³⁄₁₆ inch long and oval. The corolla lobes are slightly smaller than the calyx lobes and are roundish, spreading, and often bent down. Indian Wheat blooms in April–June.

Fruit: From a superior 2–4-celled ovary, the fruit (a capsule) develops. Thus each tiny flower on the pencil-shaped spike turns into tiny seeds clinging to the greenish-brown surface. The capsules are oblong, ⅛ inch long, with 1 or 2 brown oblong seeds, about ¹⁄₁₆ inch long and ¹⁄₃₂ inch wide.
Range: This plant grows in sand, gravel, or limestone soils, in moist waste places, dry open ground, roadsides, hillsides, vacant lots, and even cracks in sidewalks. There are 19 species of *Plantago*, with only small differences between them, that can be found over the United States from Canada to Mexico.
Remarks: This little wildflower is definitely not showy or eye-catching at first glance. But if one will be aware of small round pencillike spikes rising from bunches of straight narrow leaves and then examine a spike under a hand microscope or loupe, the delicate beauty encountered there will be a pleasant surprise.

The common name Indian Wheat comes from the resemblance of the seeds to wheat. Some species were introduced by the colonists from the Old World, and the common name White Man's Foot comes from the Native Americans' recognition that these plants, different from the native species, grew wherever the white colonists had been.

The seeds and leaves have long been used for medicinal purposes by Native Americans, early colonists, present-day naturalists, and manufacturers of modern cosmetics. A tea was made from the seeds and used as a bulk laxative and also as a fever reducer. The leaves were either wet or crushed, made into pastes or dried, and used as poultices, bindings for wounds and snake, insect, or spider bites. They were also used as bandages for blisters and other abrasions, to prevent infection. The dried roots were ground into a powder by Native Americans to be used for easing the pain of toothaches.

I feel that this is one of those interesting plants that is worth searching out and appreciating for its other features, not its beauty.

POLEMONIACEAE
Phlox Family

Members of the Phlox Family can be perennials, biennials, annuals, and sometimes, but only rarely, subshrubs. The plants vary from straight and leafy to rather mosslike. The leaves can be opposite, alternate, or both (one changing to the other as they progress up the stem); they can be divided or not, broad or thin, threadlike or prickly. Usually the flowers are in a type of terminal cluster called a "cyme," but some are borne singly. There are 5 sepals and 5 petals joined to form a bell-shaped or tubular corolla with 5 lobes. There is often an "eye," a spot of different color, in the throat of the corolla. The closed corolla is "twisted" at the mature bud stage (like a wrung-out washcloth). The pistil has 1 ovary with 3 chambers. The style is terminated by a 3-lobed stigma. The fruit is a 3-chambered capsule with 1 to many seeds in each chamber.

Gilia rigidula
Blue Gilia, Prickleleaf Gilia, Stiffleaf Gilia, Needleleaf Gilia

Plant: This compact perennial, from wandering roots, has a rather woody base and grows only about 4 inches tall. It is several-branched, with alternate leaves, pinnately cleft into 3–7 segments (¾–1 inch long), that are stiff and almost pine-needle-like. The leaves are usually borne below the midstem point. (In very dry conditions, the leaves may be sparse.)

Flower: The flowers are a bright lavender-blue with a yellow center. They are on stalks ¼–1 inch long. The corolla is funnel-shaped, with scarcely any tube, having 5 oval lobes spreading at right angles to the corolla. The flower head is ½–¾ inch across. The stamens project up above the spreading lobes. This little plant blooms from late March to July. With any extra summer rains, it can bloom again in the early fall.

Fruit: A 3-celled capsule with 1 to many seeds in each cell. The cells burst open independently to disperse the minute seeds, which become sticky when wet.

Range: Blue Gilia grows on the dry plains from western Nebraska, Kansas, across northwestern Texas, into New Mexico, Arizona, and Mexico. It does well in shallow, dry, gravelly, and caliche soils.

Remarks: To be so small, Blue Gilia is stunning, with its vivid violet-blue "face" and golden "eye." It opens late in the morning. This is another drought-resistant plant that likes barren soils in rocky, harsh places, pastures, and prairies.

POLYGALACEAE
Milkwort Family

Of the Milkwort Family only 1 genus, *Polygala*, is found on the Western Plains. The family contains only 12 genera worldwide, including several in South America.

In general, the family has members that are annual or perennial. The leaves can be alternate, opposite, or whorled. The flowers are usually in terminal racemes but can be in axillary racemes. Their structure is intricate and unusual, for there are 5 sepals, the 3 outer ones looking like sepals but the 2 inner ones much larger, colored, and looking like petals (petaloid). They are called "wings" because they are positioned like wings, on either side. Typically there are 3 petals, united at their base and to the stamens. The lowest petal forms a "keel," which is clawed or sometimes 3-lobed or fringed. There are 8 stamens with the filaments united nearly to the tips. The ovary is 2-celled. The fruit is a 2-celled capsule with the cells splitting open at maturity (dehiscent). The seeds are round to cone-shaped and softly hairy.

Polygala alba
White Milkwort

Plant: Common perennial herb with many erect stems growing from a fairly woody base, 8–15 inches tall. The stems are usually unbranched (simple) but can be sparsely branched, with the alternate linear leaves more numerous and smaller at the bottom than at the top (¼–⅜ inch long and ¹⁄₁₆ inch wide near the base; ½–1 inch long and ¹⁄₁₆ inch wide or less as they grow up the stem).
Flower: The numerous white flowers with green centers grow in dense, spikelike racemes, 1–4 inches long and ¼ inch in diameter, on the tips of the stems. There are 5 sepals (2 large, petallike, and extending out like wings, while the other 3 are typical sepallike) and 3 rounded white petals (1 forming a purplish keel). The petals are only about ¹⁄₁₀–⅛ inch long and the keel is ⅛ inch long. Eight joined stamens form a ring or collar around a single pistil. The plant blooms from April to July but can continue blooming into the fall, September and October.
Fruit: Oblong-elliptic capsule bearing 1 shaggy, hairy seed.
Range: This hardy wildflower grows on dry plains, disturbed ground, eroded places, rocky hillsides, and canyon edges. Its distribution includes states from Louisiana west to Arizona, north to North Dakota and Washington. White Milkwort also grows in Oklahoma and Kansas as well as in Mexico.
Remarks: White Milkwort, with its dense spikes of flowers, greatly resembles some clovers. It is a delicate-looking plant bearing very small but intricate flowers, unusual in their makeup, with sepals and petals becoming wings and keels.

Milkworts, which do *not* exude a milky juice, are not to be confused with milkweeds (*Asclepias*), which do ooze white sticky liquid from broken stems and leaves. Milkwort derives its name from the ancient belief that nursing mothers, human or animal, would increase their milk output after eating the plant, although I found no evidence it is used for that purpose today. *Polygala* translates from Greek into "much" (*poly*) "milk" (*gala*).

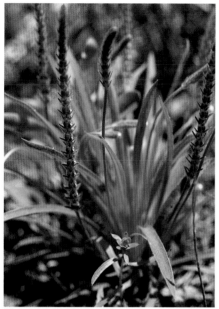

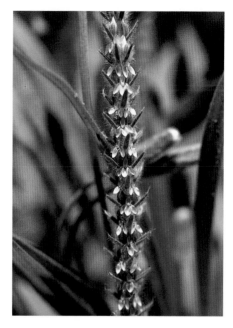

Plantago helleri Indian Wheat; close-up at right

Gilia rigidula Blue Gilia

Polygala alba White Milkwort

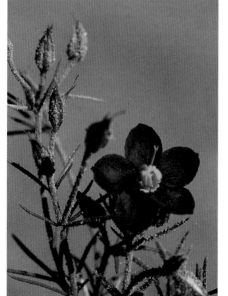

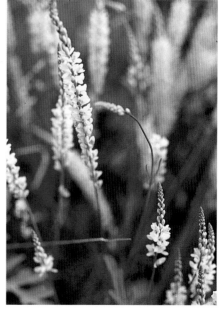

POLYGONACEAE
Knotweed or Smartweed Family

The Knotweed Family includes 35–45 genera. Generally, the plants have leaves that are alternate; rarely they are opposite or whorled. Most species have joined stipules that sheath the stem at the leaf nodes. The leaf edges are usually smooth, rarely lobed or toothed. The flowers are nearly always small, growing in spikes, heads, or umbels, unisexual or perfect (having both stamens and pistils). They have no petals, but the sepals of some species are colored. There are 3–6 sepals, 2–9 stamens, and a 1-celled ovary with 2 or 3 styles. The fruit is a 1-seeded achene with 2 or 3 angles or sections.

Many species of this family are unlovely enough to be called just "weeds" (plants growing where you do not want them to), but the ones described here have some redeeming features other than beauty and are therefore included.

Eriogonum annuum
Wild Buckwheat

Plant: Tall biennial or late-flowering annual, 18–36 inches high, a delicate plant with a white stem, unbranched until toward the top. The leaves are generally on the lower portion of the plant. They are alternate, oblong, 1–3 inches long and, like the stem, covered with soft, silky, matted, grayish hairs. The hairy covering is thicker on the undersides of the leaves than the upper. Sometimes the leaves are undulate or wavy.
Flower: The numerous flowers are in loose, flat-topped, or umbrella-like inflorescences. The bracts are joined to form a cup from which emerge several small white flowers, and there are hundreds of these at the top of a plant. There are no petals, only 6 petallike sepals in 2 rows, the inner row white, narrow, and only ⅛ inch long or

less; the outer row inversely ovate and almost ¼ inch long. There are 9 stamens and a 1-celled ovary with 3 styles. Bloom season is June to October.
Fruit: A 3-angled achene, reddish-brown, ⅛ inch long with a slightly winged beak.
Range: This plant is common on the Western Plains, in sandy soils of neglected fields, roadsides, and overgrazed pastures. It can be found in dry climates in Nebraska, Oklahoma, Texas, New Mexico, and Mexico. It grows northward to South Dakota and Montana.
Remarks: A tall, lacy-looking plant, Wild Buckwheat does not show up well unless it is growing in a large colony. Even when in full bloom, it is nothing to brag about (livestock will hardly graze it), but in the late fall, it dries and turns a striking red-brown or terra cotta color. When gathered and used in dried arrangements, it is wonderful. By spring, however, it should be thrown away, as the tiny dried flowers shatter easily. If you use preservatives when drying the stems, it will last much longer.

Polygonum pensylvanicum
(= *Persicaria pensylvanica*, *Persicaria bicornis*)
Smartweed, Pink Smartweed, Pennsylvania Smartweed

Plant: Erect, bushy annual growing from a taproot to heights of 6 inches to 3 feet. The stems are many-branched and red at the nodes, turning almost entirely red with age. The new growth is green, with less color at the nodes. The lance-shaped leaves are 2–6 inches long and ⅜–1½ inches wide. Where they are attached to the stem, there is a sheath around the stem derived from the leaf stipules.
Flower: The many small pink to rose-colored flowers are borne in racemes that resemble spikes. The ½-inch-thick racemes stand erect and are terminal and lateral on

the stems. There are no petals, but the calyx is 5-parted and pinkish (or sometimes whitish). Usually only 1 or 2 flowers are open at the same time on the crowded flower head. Smartweed blooms June–September.

Fruit: Shiny black or dark brown achene with 1 strongly convex side. It is a round lens-shape, $\frac{1}{8}$–$\frac{3}{16}$ inch in diameter.

Range: Found in moist waste places, fields, poorly drained ditches, shores, and around the edges of playa lakes, throughout North America.

Remarks: Smartweeds grow in large colonies, often covering entire playa lakes with their soft pink or rose blossoms and red-tinged stems. The seeds provide food for songbirds, gamebirds, and waterfowl.

I always thought the plant was named Smartweed because it seemed smart enough to find wet places in which to grow, when other plants were suffering for lack of water. Further research revealed that it contains an acrid juice that causes "smarting" when it gets on the skin.

It is also known by the synonyms *Persicaria bicornis* and *P. pensylvanica*.

Rumex hymenosepalus
Dock, Canaigre, Wild Rhubarb, Curly Dock, Common Dock, Sour Dock, Spinach Dock

Plant: Perennial 1–3 feet tall from clusters of tuberous roots rich in tannin. A basal rosette of leaves sprouts in the fall, then is followed in the spring by the tall stem, which is erect, usually unbranched, stout, fleshy, and often red or red-brown in color. The leaves are alternate, oblong to narrowly lance-shaped, 4–15 inches long, with somewhat wavy margins. These leaves are thick, fleshy, and sometimes tinged with red. The leaf stalk, or petiole, clasps the stem, almost forming a sheath around it.

Flower: The leafy flower stalks become many-branched near the top third of the plant, where they bear many clusters of pinkish-green flowers. There are 6 sepals that make up the flowers, with the inner 3 developing wings which eventually surround the small seeds. The outer 3 sepals are smaller than the inner 3. There are 6 stamens and 3 styles. This plant blooms from March to May.

Fruit: A 3-angled achene encased in a 3-angled russet-brown papery "wing," or calyx, approximately $\frac{1}{4}$ inch long. As the achenes mature, they turn much darker in color.

Range: This plant prefers sandy soil and disturbed but neglected areas. It grows in roadside ditches, around the edges of playa lakes, and dry stream beds from Mexico north through western Texas, as well as in New Mexico, Arizona, California, Nevada, Utah, Colorado, and Wyoming.

Remarks: Dock does not look like a wildflower at all. It is easily mistaken for maize. It has fruits that are much more attractive than its inconspicuous blossoms. The flowers that bloom first are nondescript and hardly colorful. But as the plant matures, the flowers begin to turn a wonderful rich red-brown as the fruit develops with its fragile wings. (At this point it truly looks like maize with crowded heads of ripening seeds.) Birds enjoy the seeds, and people gather them for their bird feeders. After frost, the entire plant turns a dark reddish-brown.

The tender young leaves are great as a potherb (being high in vitamins A and C). It is best to use the leaves before the flowering stalk appears and prepare them as you would your favorite greens. If they are old enough to taste bitter, pouring off the first boiling water and replacing with fresh boiling water might remedy this.

The roots of this plant contain enough tannic acid to make it a potential commercial source of tannins, which are used in tanning hides for leather.

Some Native Americans in Arizona still use the roots for treating colds and sore throats.

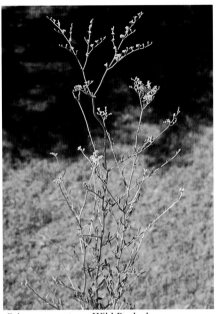

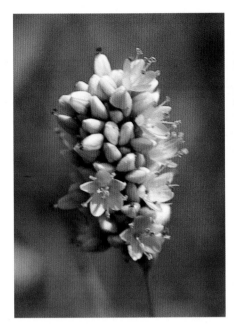

Eriogonum annuum Wild Buckwheat

Opposite: *Rumex hymenosepalus* Dock

Below and above right: *Polygonum pensylvanicum* Smartweed

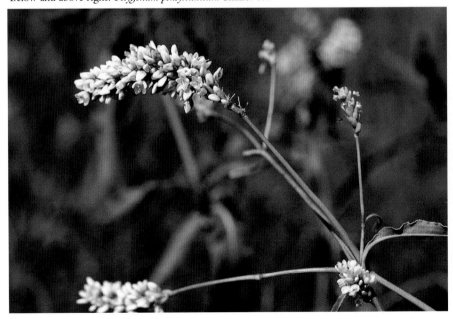

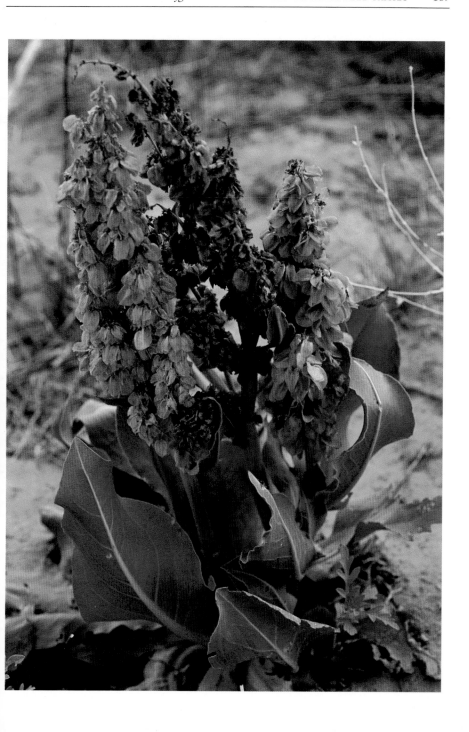

PORTULACACEAE
Purslane Family

The Purslane Family consists of somewhat succulent annual or perennial herbs. The leaves can be alternate, opposite, or in rosettes at the base of the stems. They are smooth-edged and fleshy, or succulent. The flowers can be solitary, in racemes (elongate inflorescences of flowers with pedicels—like grapes), panicles (compound racemes), or cymes (inflorescences characterized by flowers blooming from the center out or from the tip down). The flowers can bloom at the tip of the stem or in the axils of the leaves. Each flower has both stamens and pistil and radial symmetry; usually it has 2 sepals and 4 or 5 petals; the color can be yellow, orange, pink, red, white, or lavender. The stamens (at least as many as there are petals and sometimes more) grow attached to the petals at their bases. Usually the ovary is 1-celled and superior except in *Portulaca*, where it is partially or sometimes totally inferior. The fruits of this family are capsules bearing 1 to many round, flat, lens-shaped seeds. The capsules either split open to dispense the seeds or empty their seeds by means of a lid that opens when seeds are ripe.

Portulaca oleracea
Purslane, Verdolaga, Pussley, Purslance, Low Pigweed

Plant: Semisucculent annual that grows sprawling on the ground with several jointed, reddish-green, branching stems spreading out to lengths of 2½–12 inches. The alternate leaves are spatula-shaped, ¼–1 inch long and ⅛–½ inch wide, flat, and somewhat succulent. They can be either in pairs or single on the stem. There are minute tufts of hairs in the leaf axils. This plant often forms dense mats of the dark green flat leaves which carpet the ground.

Flower: The yellow flowers are borne terminally in clusters or singly in the axils of the leaves, where they are subtended by a whorl of up to 10 leaves. The flowers are small and inconspicuous with notched petals ⅛–¼ inch long and ¹⁄₁₆–³⁄₁₆ inch wide. There are 2 sepals, 6–10 stamens, and a partially inferior ovary with 4–6 style lobes. Purslane blooms in June–August.

Fruit: Capsule, ¼–⅜ inch long, bearing hundreds of tiny black, flat, kidney-shaped seeds with bumpy surfaces. The capsule has a "lid" that opens, dries, then drops away to allow the seeds to be dispersed. This peculiar structure of the capsule is termed "circumscissile."

Range: Widely distributed over the world, this plant is common throughout the United States from Canada to Mexico, preferring lawns, gardens, waste places, and roadsides.

Remarks: An interesting plant, Purslane is a native of Persia and India. After its spread to Europe, it came with the early settlers to the United States and was readily used by the Native Americans as well as the colonists. The plant's uses included medicinal remedies and culinary delights, which is why it used to be sown in garden plots. Today it is treated as a troublesome weed and usually hoed out of the garden.

The stems, leaves, and seeds are virtual storehouses of vitamins and minerals. The U.S. Department of Agriculture has found this lowly plant to contain vitamins A and C, riboflavin, and iron.

The tiny black seeds (more than 50,000 per plant) have been steeped for teas and historically used for relaxation, to treat burns, as a diuretic, and for relief from headaches, intestinal problems, gout, and gonorrhea. The seeds were also crushed for use as a flour in breads and were used instead of poppy seeds on bread and other baked goods.

RANUNCULACEAE
Buttercup or Crowfoot Family

Members of the Buttercup Family can be either herbaceous or woody. The leaves are usually basal, but can be alternate, opposite, or whorled. In some genera, however, they grow in pairs of threes or singly up the stem. The leaf blades may be divided into segments on one stalk and sometimes can vary in shape on the same stem. Flowers are radially symmetrical (regular) or bilaterally symmetrical (irregular). Sepals are present; petals can be present or absent. There are numerous stamens, 1 to many pistils (usually more than 1) with 1 to many ovules. The fruit is either a berry, an achene, or a follicle.

Some species in this family are poisonous to varying degrees, while others are used in medicines.

Anemone heterophylla
(= *A. decapetala*)
Windflower, Anemone,
Tenpetal Anemone

Plant: Erect perennial herb up to 1 foot tall but usually much shorter (4–8 inches). It grows from a small corm or tuberous root. The basal leaves are divided into 3 broad segments, each wedge-shaped and somewhat lobed (shallowly cleft), ½–1½ inches long. More leaves grow about midway up the stem, but these are deeply palmately cleft, with narrow, linear segments (almost fingerlike and very unlike the basal leaves).

Flower: A single smooth stem arising from the center of the plant bears a solitary white or pink flower. There are no petals but 10–20 greenish-white sepals that resemble petals, each about ½ inch long, narrow, and lance-shaped with rounded tips. Many stamens encircle a thick, elongate (¾ inch long), cylindrical green column in the center. This column consists of numer-

ous spirally arranged pistils. Windflower blooms very early, February to March or April.

Fruit: Elongate compact head, or spike, of flattened achenes. These many 1-seeded achenes are almost entirely hidden in a thick wool at maturity.

Range: Preferring limestone clays or sandy clay soils of prairies and pastures, this early wildflower grows from Florida and Alabama through Arkansas, Oklahoma, and Texas to Mexico and into Central America.

Remarks: Often one of the very earliest flowers to bloom on the Western Plains, Windflower is always a welcome surprise in the early spring when pastures and hillsides are still clothed in their winter colors of dry yellow grasses and bare brown stalks, remnants of last summer's plants.

This species is often listed by a synonym, *A. decapetala*, meaning "ten petals" (which are actually sepals).

Clematis drummondii
Old Man's Beard, Clematis,
Virgin's Bower, Barbas de Chivato

Plant: Perennial vine that climbs on any nearby shrub, tree, or fence. If it cannot find something to climb upon, it forms semiupright clumps. The stems can grow to more than 6 feet long. The stalks of the leaves twine and grasp the neighboring plants. The entire plant is covered with a grayish soft down. Its leaves are opposite with 5–7 leaflets (pinnately divided) that are 3-cleft. The leaflets are ½–1⅜ inches long.

Flower: One to 3 peduncles (stalks) bearing terminal flowers grow from the leaf axils. A pair of leafy bracts is at the base of the petalless flower. The 4 sepals look like petals and are creamy-white tinged with pale yellow, thin, and narrow. They are ½ inch long with a silky surface and crinkled edges. There are many narrow, threadlike stamens, as long as the sepals, on the male

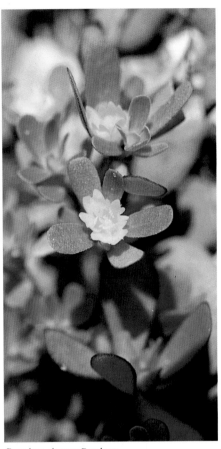

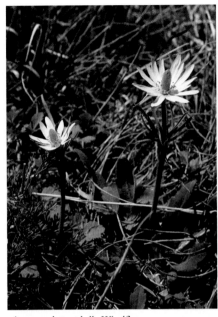

Anemone heterophylla Windflower

Clematis drummondii Old Man's Beard

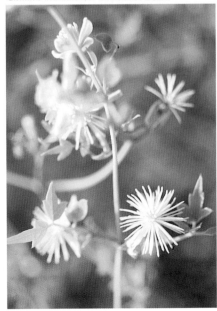

Portulaca oleracea Purslane

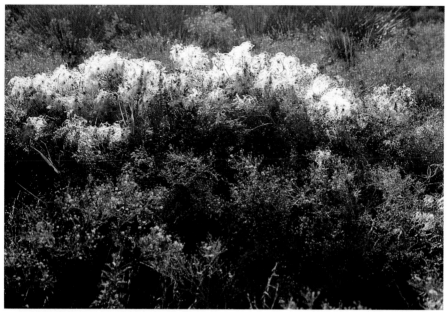

Above and below: *C. drummondii* seed plumes

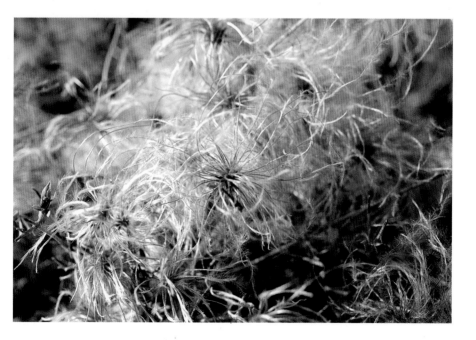

flowers and many long-styled pistils on the female flowers; these male and female flowers grow on separate plants. Old Man's Beard blooms August–September.

Fruit: Achene, or seed, ⅛ inch long. Several grow in a tight ball with each seed developing a long, slender, silky, plumelike "tail" up to 3 inches long.

Range: Old Man's Beard grows along fences by the roadsides. It finds weeds and shrubs to cling to in disturbed soils, dry washes, and open pastures. It can be found from Texas and New Mexico to Arizona and Mexico at altitudes of 3,000–5,000 feet.

Remarks: The flowers of Old Man's Beard are hardly noticeable, but when in fruit, it is hard to miss. Often a plant sprawled over a weed or small shrub will be literally covered with white "fluffs." When the sunlight catches them just right, there is a shimmering golden iridescence to the mass of plumes.

Reportedly, it is used today as a treatment for migraine headaches by brewing a tea of the leaves and stems.

Delphinium carolinianum (= *D. virescens*)
Prairie Larkspur, White Larkspur, Plains Larkspur

Plant: Tall perennial herb growing from long, rather woody roots. The slender stems are unbranched, straight, and erect, 12–18 inches tall. The leaves are basal and alternate on the lower parts of the stems. They are palmately divided into narrow linear segments.

Flower: The several white flowers grow above the foliage in a terminal spike or raceme 6–20 inches long. Each has 5 white petallike sepals, the uppermost elongated into a backward-curving spur nearly ¾ inch long, and 4 white petals, 2 of them noticeably split, or cleft, and bearded, the other 2 extending back into smaller spurlike projec-

tions. There are many stamens, ⅝ inch long and ¼ inch wide, and 3 pistils, each with many ovules. Bloom season is April–June.

Fruit: Follicle, ⅝ inch long, erect, and oblong in shape. The seeds inside are brown to gray and wedge-shaped. Terminal pores open on the follicle to disperse the many seeds.

Range: This prairie plant grows in dry grassy plains, pastures, fields, and roadsides from Colorado through eastern New Mexico, parts of Arizona, and the panhandle and South Plains of Texas, through the panhandle of Oklahoma, up to Kansas, Nebraska, and into Wisconsin and Illinois.

Remarks: Prairie Larkspur is a tall, graceful plant, lovely when in bloom with its spike of white, spurred, bearded flowers. They are not a pure white but rather a dingy or faintly blue white. The younger, newly opened flowers prominently display the stamens with their pollen-covered tips; the older flowers display the pistils more prominently. Bees, seeking nectar, help in cross-pollination by walking through the pollen-laden stamens, then accidentally depositing the pollen on the pistils, as they move to the older flowers.

The plant and its seeds are known to be poisonous to livestock, but cattle and horses usually have sense enough not to eat it, especially if there is anything else green to graze upon instead.

It has been used to kill body lice on humans. NEVER TAKEN INTERNALLY, different parts of the plant have been made into tinctures for topical applications to remove the offending vermin.

This plant has been known for a long time by the Latin name *D. virescens*. Very recently authorities have agreed that it should be combined with *D. carolinianum* and have changed its Latin name accordingly.

ROSACEAE
Rose Family

The Rose Family consists of trees, shrubs, and some herbs. The leaves are alternate on the stems, either simple (having no leaflets) or compound (having 2 or more leaflets). Each leaf has a conspicuous pair of appendages (stipules) where it is attached to the stem. Thorns are sometimes present. The flowers have few to numerous stamens and 1 or more pistils, regular symmetry (the floral cup a fusion of the sepals, petals, and stamens). There are usually 5 sepals and the same number of petals. The fruit can be a small pod (follicle), a drupe (as in a plum or peach), a pome (applelike fruit), a seedlike achene (as on a strawberry), or an achene.

Everyone is familiar with our garden variety of rose as well as its many cousins the wild roses, but other members of this large family include wild plum, strawberry, blackberry, cherry, and many others. The Rose Family contains a variety of cultivated fruits eaten by humans: almonds, pears, apples, peaches, apricots, raspberries, plums, strawberries, cherries, and blackberries. Domestic and wild life also find useful food and forage in this family.

Prunus angustifolia
Wild Plum, Chickasaw Plum

Plant: Shrub or small tree to a height of 10–12 feet, forming thickets. The many branches, growing in almost zigzag fashion, are a reddish color and have some small thorns. The leaves are a sharply tipped oblong lance shape with a fold down the middle, ¾–2½ inches long, about ¾ inch wide, and slightly toothed around the edges.

Flower: The flowers (¾ inch across) are in clusters of 2–4; several clusters may occur close together. Each flower has 5 white petals and numerous stamens that turn pink with age. The blooms appear in late March or early April, well before the leaves emerge.

Fruit: A 1-seeded drupe, or a small hard seed covered by fleshy pulp, encased in a thin skin, either yellow-orange or red upon ripening, which occurs around mid-July. The shape is ellipsoid (¾–⅞ inch long and ½–¾ inch across). On the Western Plains, there are trees that bear red fruit and other trees that bear a larger, yellowish-orange fruit. The yellow-orange fruit is sweeter to use in preserves and wine.

Range: These small trees form dense thickets in sandy soil, mostly along dry river and stream banks; they also do well along old sandy fencerows. They are found in Maryland and Delaware, south to Florida, west through Arkansas and Texas. A similar species, *P. americana*, grows in Oklahoma.

Remarks: Wild Plum blossoms appear very early in the spring and fill the air with a delightful fragrance. On the Western Plains, they often bloom before the last freeze has occurred; therefore, in many seasons the trees do not produce fruit. When they do, it is well worth the pain (of the dense branches and thorns) and effort (100-plus degrees of heat in mid-July) to gather the ripe plums, which can then be canned, frozen, dried, or preserved. Delicious wine, jelly, or preserves can be made from this fruit. The Native Americans dried the small plums on hot rocks and stored them for future use. Today, naturalists string the pitted fruits on long strings and air-dry them.

Recipe: My family's all-time-favorite wild food delicacy is WILD PLUM BUTTER.

Gather about a gallon of ripe wild plums. Wash them and put in a large deep pot. Barely cover with water and boil 5–10 minutes to cook the fruit. Mash through a colander, saving the juice and mashed pulp and throwing the seeds, stems, and skins away.

Measure 6 cups of thick juice (juice and pulp). Add 1 box of Sure-Jell or other powdered pectin. Bring this mixture to a hard, rolling boil. Add 7–8 cups sugar and again bring to a boil, boiling for 3 minutes. Remove from heat, skim off any foam on top, and quickly pour into hot sterile jars to within ¼–⅛ inch of the tops. Cover with hot lids and screw the bands on tightly. They should vacuum seal in a few minutes. The preserve should "set up" (or get firmer) after several days on the shelf.

Cook small batches at a time. The preserves turn dark after several months on the shelf. Instead of cooking up all the fruit at once, wash the plums and freeze them in plastic bags until needed. They always taste fresh when handled in this way.

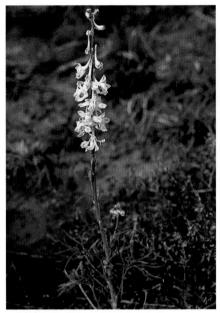

Delphinium carolinianum Prairie Larkspur

Prunus angustifolia Wild Plum

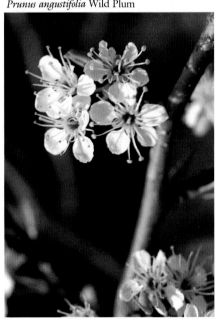

RUBIACEAE
Coffee, Bluet, or Madder Family

Sometimes called the Coffee Family (because the popular beverage, *Coffea arabica*, is one of the species included), the Rubiaceae include trees, shrubs, and herbs. The leaves are paired, being joined by their stipules. They are undivided, untoothed, and unlobed. The small flowers are perfect (having both pistils and stamens) or unisexual. They usually have 4 sepals, 4 petals, and 4 stamens, but some are 3- or 5-merous. The flowers are in cymes, solitary, or grouped into heads. The corolla varies from funnel-shaped to tubelike (a corolla that flares out abruptly at a right angle) to wheel-shaped. The calyx tube is joined with an inferior ovary, which has 2 or 4 compartments. There can be 1 to several seeds in each compartment.

Hedyotis humifusa Bluets

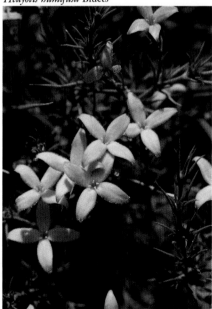

Hedyotis humifusa (= *Houstonia humifusa*)
Bluets, Quaker Ladies

Plant: Small erect or spreading annual growing only 1½–4 inches tall. The fine stems are much branched from a slender taproot. The small leaves are opposite, linear, ⅜–⅝ inch long and 1/16–3/16 inch wide. There is a rosette of larger leaves at the base of the plant.

Flower: The small flowers emerge from the leaf axils on short stalks. They are white to pale pink and only rarely very pale blue. There are 4 sepals and 4 petals, 1 slender style, 2 stigmas, and a 2-celled ovary. The united petals become the funnelform corolla, ¼–⅜ inch long, with 4 lobes curving out toward their tips. Bluets bloom in April.

Fruit: Capsule, ⅛ inch in diameter, bearing a few to 20 seeds. Under a microscope, the capsule is covered with minute conical projections (papillose).

Range: This little Bluet grows in western Oklahoma, western Texas, New Mexico, Arizona, and southward into Mexico. It is commonly found in waste places, disturbed areas, roadside ditches, and open pastures. It can often be observed in large colonies in roadside ditches.

Remarks: When in full bloom, Bluets look like miniature bouquets of soft, pinkish-white blossoms, each with its face turned up to the sky. Every feature of this flower is simple and delicate—its size, color, and shape—which may be why it received the common name Quaker Ladies.

The genera *Houstonia* and *Hedyotis* are often used to identify the same flowers, depending upon the book and its author.

SCROPHULARIACEAE
Snapdragon Family

The Snapdragon Family is made up of mostly herbaceous plants; occasionally shrubs and trees. The leaves can be in a variety of shapes and sizes (alternate, opposite, or whorled). The flowers have both stamens (2–5 but most often 4) and pistil and 5 petals that are joined to form a blossom with 2 "lips." In some species, the lower lip forms a raised or humplike part that closes the opening between the lips. This part is called the "palate." There are 4 or 5 sepals and a single style with a stigma that can be undivided or 2-lobed. A 2-celled capsule contains many seeds.

There are more than 3,000 species in this family.

Penstemon sp.

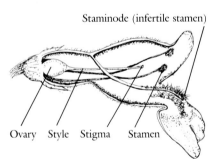

Staminode (infertile stamen)

Ovary   Style   Stigma   Stamen

Castilleja sessiliflora
Pink Paintbrush, Plains Paintbrush, Downy Paintbrush

Plant: Perennial herb that grows 4–12 inches high in clusters. The stems are covered with shaggy hairs. The alternate upper leaves are laterally lobed and very narrow; the lower leaves are unlobed, narrow, ¾–1½ inches long, and also covered with fine hairs. These shaggy hairs give the plant an almost woolly look.

Flower: The flower is subtended by 3- to 5-lobed floral bracts, which are broader and shorter than the leaves. The greenish bracts, tinged with pink or red, are covered with fine hairs. The flowers are in dense spikes standing out from the bracts. The calyx has long, linear lobed parts. The corolla can be soft pink to purple, pinkish-green, or yellowish-green in color, 1¼–2¼ inches long, and curved or sickle-shaped. The lower lip is ¼ inch long with flaring lobes, while the upper lip is helmet-shaped. There are 4 stamens. Blooms open in April and May.

Fruit: Oval-shaped capsule containing many tiny seeds.

Range: Dry rocky hills and open prairies as well as sandy terrain from southern Canada and Montana to Illinois, southeastern Arizona, most of New Mexico, and western Texas.

Remarks: This clumpy, fuzzy plant has flowers that truly do not look much like flowers from a distance; they resemble colored leaves instead. The colorful rosy-pink bracts are the prettiest parts of the plant. But up close the flowers become more interesting with their hooded, helmetlike upper lip and shorter lower lip sticking out. The color is always soft and muted, mixed with green; never vivid.

Penstemon albidus
Beard-tongue, Wild Foxglove

Plant: Erect, herbaceous perennial 12–16 inches tall from a stout, woody root. The stems and leaves are "sandpapery" to the touch because of the tiny, rough hairs on their surfaces. The leaves are lanceolate (lance-shaped) and slightly toothed. Toward the lower portion of the plant, the leaves are 1½–3 inches long and ½–¾ inch wide, growing smaller higher up.

Flower: The flowers, white to pale lavender, are ½–¾ inch long and shaped like a narrow funnel at the throat. The 5 petals are joined to form the narrow corolla, then flaring and cleft into 2 lobes at the top (slightly reflexed or bent back) and 3 lobes at the bottom (projecting). The flower is somewhat 2-lipped but not as prominently so as other species. The lower inner surface of the corolla (throat) has easy-to-see purple lines. The inflorescence is densely glandular and sticky. Inside the tube, or funnel, are the 4 stamens plus 1 sterile stamen (staminode), enlarged and covered with yellow hairs (source of the name Beard-tongue). Blooms appear in April and May.

Fruit: A 4-valved capsule (½–⅝ inch long) containing many angular black seeds.

Range: Growing quite well in gravelly or sandy prairies and pasturelands and on hills and slopes, Beard-tongue can be found from Canada southward to the panhandle of Oklahoma, the plains of Texas, and eastern New Mexico.

Remarks: The flower of this erect plant has an interesting "face" with its wide open "mouth" and petals (2 at the top and 3 at the bottom) appearing to be almost folded in place. When one peers into the throat of the flower, the hairy tongue is easy to see. "Beard-tongue" is a humorous name, but one that is understandable after becoming acquainted with the flower. The purple lines in the throat are visual "roads" that help guide bees and other nectar-gatherers to the sweet treasure deep inside.

Penstemon ambiguus
Pink Plains Penstemon

Plant: Showy perennial shrub up to 18 or 20 inches tall with many rather woody stems, which usually branch out into a large bushy shape, with several blossoms at their tips. The opposite leaves are linear, ½–1 inch long and only 3/16 inch wide, with margins that are untoothed, or smooth. The leaves and stems are minutely hairy.

Flower: There are few to several flowers in terminal clusters on the many stems. These flowers have a white corolla with a pink-tinged throat and are ¾–1⅛ inches long. The unusually shaped corolla is tubular with the narrow curved tube being ⅔ the length of the flower. Abruptly the tip of the corolla expands into 5 lobes of equal size. These lobes turn back and become 2-lipped, 2 lobes forming the upper lip and 3 forming the lower. There are 4 stamens plus an extra sterile one (staminode), which is not "bearded." Bloom season is May to July or August.

Fruit: Capsule, ¼ inch long, containing many tiny seeds.

Range: This bushy wildflower definitely prefers sandy soils of roadsides, stream banks, and pastures from Kansas through Oklahoma, the panhandle of Texas, New Mexico, and northern Arizona, to Mexico.

Remarks: Pink Plains Penstemon is one of those roadside plants that is so outstanding one feels compelled to stop the car and photograph it or at least look at it closer. From a distance it appears to be a large bouquet of white, but when you get nearer, the delicate pink, which is such a beautiful part of it, is a subtle surprise.

Botanists consider *P. ambiguus* unusual in shape partly because the 5 lobes flare back so abruptly and are positioned on the slender corolla tube at an angle. Interestingly enough, it is a "Beard-tongue" that does not have a "beard," since the staminode, unlike those of other "Beard-tongues," is smooth.

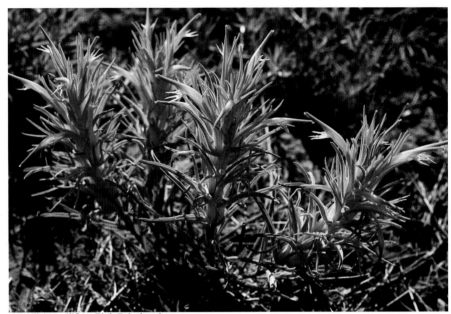

Castilleja sessiliflora Pink Paintbrush

Penstemon albidus Beard-tongue

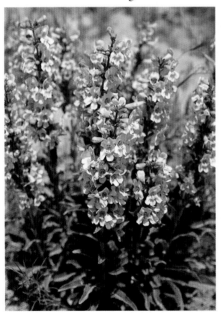

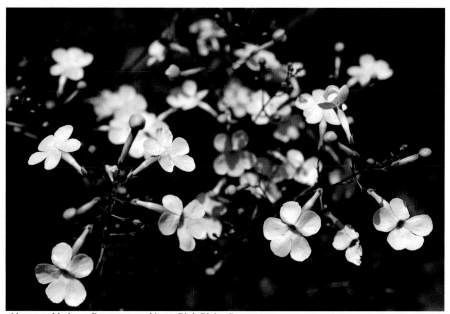

Above and below: *Penstemon ambiguus* Pink Plains Penstemon

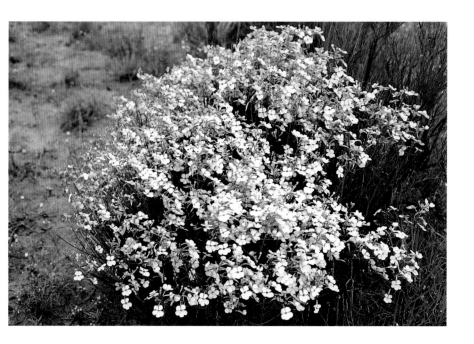

Penstemon buckleyi
Buckley's Penstemon, Buckley Beard-tongue

Plant: Perennial herb 16–24 inches tall on smooth, erect stems. The stem and leaves have an almost waxy bloom. The leaves are opposite, untoothed, thick, and hairless, 1–3 inches long and ⅜–1 inch wide, from the lower part of the stem to about midstem. These lower leaves are broad above the middle, then taper to a petiole, or stalk. The upper leaves are thinner and more oval in shape.

Flower: The pale blue to lavender flowers are borne on a dense, leafy inflorescence, or spikelike cluster. Each flower is nestled in the axil of a floral bract, making the clusters seem crowded or bunched. The corolla is irregularly funnel-shaped, ½–¾ inch long, with the lower inner surface (throat) marked with prominent purple lines. It is typically 2-lipped, with spreading lobes, 2 on the upper lip and 3 on the lower. There are 4 stamens and a sterile staminode bearded with golden hairs. It blooms in April and May.

Fruit: Many-seeded capsule, the seeds only ⅛ inch long.

Range: Sandy places, open pastures, hillsides, roadsides, and even sand dunes in western Kansas, Oklahoma, western Texas, central, southern, and eastern New Mexico.

Remarks: This is another tall, stately plant that commands attention when in full bloom. The flowers are stunning, and the darker lines in the throat of the corolla are interesting, their main purpose being to advertise, "This way to the sweets."

I do not advocate large-scale cutting, pulling up, or transplanting of native wildflowers, but gathering some seeds is an acceptable way to try to get them to grow in a yard or garden. The seeds of this plant are easy to collect by breaking a few of the dried capsules off and scattering their contents. But please leave plenty on the stems for next season's crop.

Penstemon fendleri
Purple Foxglove

Plant: Purple Foxglove grows 12–18 inches tall, slender and erect. The stem and leaves are smooth. The opposite leaves are undivided and thick, ¾–2 inches long and ½–1¼ inches wide. They have a whitish look, making the plant appear pale or gray-green.

Flower: The inflorescence, or arrangement of flowers, is sometimes more than half the height of the plant, with the soft lavender-violet flowers growing in loose clusters of 2–3 flowers up the stem. The petals are joined, forming a slightly curving corolla, ½–¾ inch long, which flares at the end and has a 2-lobed upper lip and 3-lobed lower lip. The lower lobes spread apart more than the upper. The lower inner surface, or floor, of the tube is lighter in color, nearly white, and bears dark purple lines. There are 4 stamens and a staminode covered with short yellow hairs on its tip. Purple Foxglove blooms April–June and sometimes into August.

Fruit: Capsule that splits into 4-valved segments. There are many brown seeds, to ³⁄₁₆ inch long.

Range: Sandy or rocky hillsides of western Kansas, Oklahoma, the plains of Texas, eastern New Mexico, and eastern Arizona.

Remarks: An elegant plant with softly colored smooth stems and leaves, Purple Foxglove surprises you when you encounter a few plants (usually growing in hard, rather barren ground) and amazes you when you are fortunate enough to find a large stand of hundreds of plants.

I have gathered the dried black stems, with capsules attached (after they have split open and dropped their seeds), and used them as package decorations with brightly colored ribbons or yarns. They also add strong bold color to dried arrangements. If you do this, shake any remaining seeds out of the capsules before taking the stems home.

SOLANACEAE
Potato or Nightshade Family

The Potato or Nightshade Family includes herbs, shrubs, and trees. The leaves can be opposite, alternate, or clustered, and untoothed to toothed, pinnately lobed, or divided. The flowers can be solitary or in many-flowered cymes or panicles. They are 4- to 6-merous, but the parts, generally, are in 5's, the calyx being 5-toothed or cleft, the corolla usually radially symmetrical and 5-lobed with 5 stamens. The calyx and corolla, in most of the species, are either bell-shaped (campanulate), wheel-shaped (rotate), or hollow cylinder-shaped (tubular). In other species, the corolla is funnel-shaped. The superior 2-chambered ovary becomes a berry or capsule (pod).

Strangely enough, this family is notable both for its edible members and for the many poisons provided by several of its species. Atropine (belladonna) and scopolamine are two alkaloids which can be deadly in large amounts. However, eye doctors today use atropine, in very exact small doses, as an effective dilator when examining the eyes.

Some of the better-known members of this family are potatoes, tomatoes, peppers, tobacco, and petunias.

Quincula lobata
(Purple Ground Cherry)

Chamaesaracha coniodes
Ground Saracha, False Nightshade, Prostrate Ground Cherry

Plant: Low, prostrate perennial herb with branching stems 8–10 inches long. The roots are woody. The stems and leaves are covered with hairs, some of them sticky and gland-tipped. The alternate leaves are broad lance-shaped (lanceolate) to somewhat diamond-shaped (rhombic), 1–2¼ inches long and ⅜–¾ inch wide. The leaf margins are deeply cleft into narrow lobes.

Flower: The flowers grow either solitary or in pairs in the leaf axils on pedicels ¾–1 inch long. The ½-inch-wide corolla has 5 short, broad lobes, creamy greenish-white in color and somewhat star-shaped, with a slightly deeper-colored star design radiating out from the center. There are 5 yellow-tipped stamens alternating with small tufts of hairs. The single pistil is in the center, its style projecting beyond the stamens. There are blooms from spring to fall.

Fruit: The calyx is somewhat enlarged in fruit, but not bladdery and inflated, as it envelops the round berry, which contains many flattened seeds.

Range: This plant thrives in dry, compact, clay soils of plains and slopes from

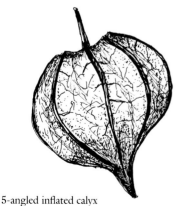

5-angled inflated calyx

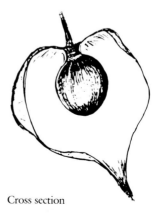

Cross section

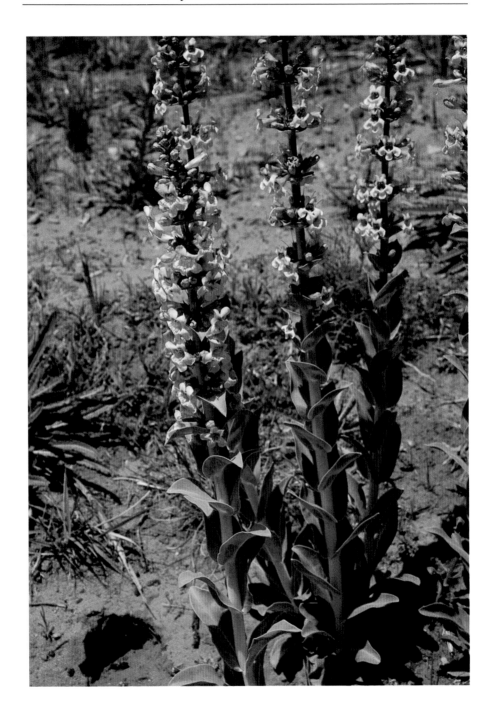

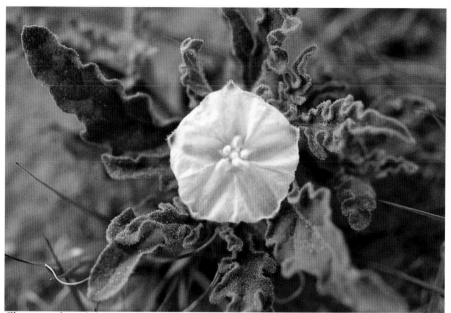

Chamaesaracha coniodes Ground Saracha

Opposite: *Penstemon buckleyi* Buckley's Penstemon

Below and right: *Penstemon fendleri* Purple Foxglove

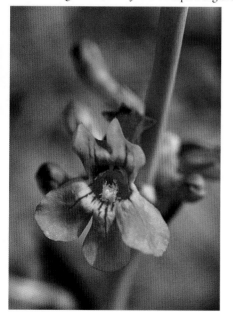

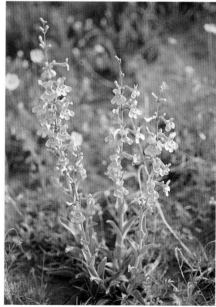

Kansas and Colorado to Oklahoma, western Texas, across New Mexico, into Arizona and Mexico.

Remarks: Ground Saracha is a lowly, inconspicuous plant that is usually noticeably "dirty." The gland-tipped hairs trap and hold dirt and sand. The flowers turn face up to the sun and are a pretty shape with the slightly darker star "embossed" on the surface of the petals. With the naked eye, it is fun to discover the tufts of hairs between the stamens.

The several species of *Chamaesaracha* resemble those of *Physalis* but should not be confused with them. *Chamaesaracha* does not have the inflated "Chinese lantern" covering around the fruit. The calyx does envelop the berry, but closely. Also, the flowers are flatter, with more spreading corolla lobes, in *Chamaesaracha* and not bell-shaped as in *Physalis*.

Nicotiana trigonophylla
Wild Tobacco, Desert Tobacco, Tabaquillo

Plant: Perennial or biennial, stout and tall (to 3 feet), covered with sticky-downy hairs, not much branched. The alternate leaves are without teeth or lobes, lanceolate to oval. The lower ones are on stalks, the upper ones having a pair of basal lobes, projecting like "ears" on either side, and clasping the stem. The larger leaves can be up to 8 inches long but usually are 3–6 inches and up to 2¼ inches wide.

Flower: The flowers are borne at the top of the plant, appearing to be a spikelike inflorescence bearing flowers on short stalks, or pedicels (raceme). In reality, the inflorescence contains loosely branched flower clusters whose central flowers bloom first, followed by the flowers subtending the terminal one (cyme). The corolla is a tubular funnel shape, greenish-white in color, with the 5 petal lobes flaring out abruptly at the edge. The flared-out surface is softly wavy,

somewhat 5-pointed, and ⅜ inch in diameter. The 5 dark green calyx lobes extend to about halfway up the softly hairy corolla tube, which is ½–1 inch long. The 5 stamens are inserted in the corolla tube. The plant blooms from April to October.

Fruit: A 2-celled oval capsule (⅜–½ inch long) that splits apart in 4-valved sections. Inside are many tiny brown seeds, shiny, yet pitted with a network of fine veins on their surfaces.

Range: Wild Tobacco is a tall, sticky plant that grows from western Texas to California, clinging to canyon walls, rocky ledges, mesas, and sandy, gravelly washes along the way. A favorite place that it grows is along the seeping water line of rocky walls and ledges.

Remarks: This is not a typical roadside wildflower. It inhabits the hard-to-find, out-of-the-way places, high up on canyon walls and at the base of large boulders. The flowers are greenish-white, not bright and easy to see.

This plant is rather strong-smelling and is one of the species smoked by Native Americans in their ceremonial pipes on special occasions. The tobacco smoked today in commercial cigarettes is a hybrid cousin to this species.

Physalis viscosa var. *cinerascens*
Yellow Ground Cherry, Starry-hair Ground Cherry

Plant: Perennial with several stems 12 inches long or longer; they are not erect but rather lying on the ground with just the tips turned upward. The stems and leaves are covered with microscopic star-shaped (stellate) hairs. The alternate leaves are almost round to broadly ovate in shape and on petioles ½–1½ inches long. The leaves can be 1½–3 inches long, bluntly toothed, with wavy or smooth edges.

Flower: The flowers grow solitary in the axils on drooping peduncles 1–2 inches long. The 5 sepals are united to form a thin, papery, bell-shaped covering. The 5 yellow petals are united at their bases, flaring out to ½ inch across. At the base of each petal is a dark purple (almost black) spot or blotch. There are 5 stamens joined where the petals are fused together. They have bright yellow or slightly purplish anthers. The single pistil is 2-celled. This plant blooms from April to September or October.

Fruit: The 5 united sepals that enlarge and form the inflated bell-shaped covering eventually enclose the fruit, which is a yellow berry, ⅓–½ inch across. The berry only half fills the bell-shaped covering.

Range: This wildflower seems to prefer hard, dry, rocky ground but does quite well in cultivated fields also. It grows from Arkansas to Kansas, Oklahoma, western Texas, eastern New Mexico, and northern Mexico.

Remarks: Yellow Ground Cherry is somewhat of a "camouflage expert." Because the flower stalks (peduncles) droop and the calyx lobes enlarge and enfold, the flower turns its bright face down to the ground. A casual passerby would probably never notice this slumped-over plant with its down-facing flowers in bloom. But a serious lover of wildflowers who is alert will observe the drooping calyx lobes, reach down, and turn up the bright yellow flower with the surprising dark spots in its center. If you miss the flower in bloom, remember that one of the identifying characteristics of the genera *Physalis* and *Quincula* is the 5-angled Chinese or Japanese lantern appearance of the inflated calyx coverings, or "bladders," around the berries, called "ground cherries."

Quincula lobata (= *Physalis lobata*)
Purple Ground Cherry, Chinese Lantern of the Plains

Plant: Low-growing, almost prostrate perennial, much branched in a zigzag fashion. It grows in a round, low mound rarely 6 inches tall, with stems less than 12 inches long. The stems and leaves are sparsely covered with microscopic bladders, or bubbles, that have a crystalline look and texture. To the naked eye, this appears to be a rather rough, mealy, or granulose surface. The alternate leaves (1½–4 inches long and ¼–1 inch wide) are oval lance-shaped to linear lance-shaped, narrowing at the stem and having a winged petiole, or stalk. The leaves are sometimes deeply toothed or pinnatifid (cleft into narrow lobes but not to the midrib) with rounded, shallow lobes.

Flower: The corollas of the flowers, which grow from the leaf axils, are deep purple to blue-purple, flat wheel-shaped (rotate), and ½–¾ inch across. There are 5 united sepals that form a bell-shaped calyx. The 5 stamens have yellow anthers atop purple filaments. A single pistil is 2-chambered. Purple Ground Cherry blooms from April to September.

Fruit: The bell-shaped calyx enlarges with maturity and eventually encloses the fruit, which is a yellowish or greenish, slightly oval berry, ¼ inch in diameter. The 5-angled, papery, inflated-looking calyx is ⅝–¾ inch in diameter when it is fully mature and enveloping the berry.

Range: Western Oklahoma, western Texas, eastern New Mexico, western Kansas, eastern Colorado, and northern Mexico, preferring dry, barren places, roadsides, hillsides, and compact ground; seemingly drought-resistant.

Remarks: Purple Ground Cherry is a lowly little plant never noticed until it blooms, and then, what a remarkable flower it has. The flat, purple, wheel-shaped corolla has a perfect 5-pointed star, of deeper purple, "embossed" on its velvety

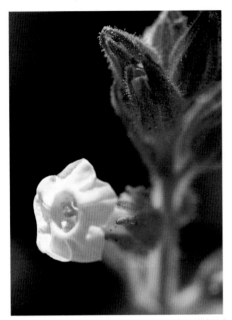

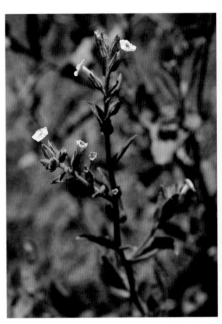

Above and right: *Nicotiana trigonophylla* Wild Tobacco

Physalis viscosa Yellow Ground Cherry   *Quincula lobata* Purple Ground Cherry

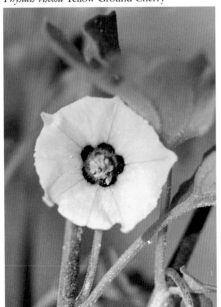

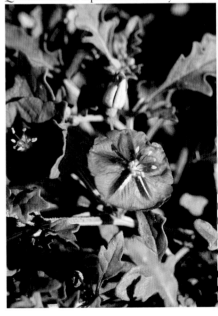

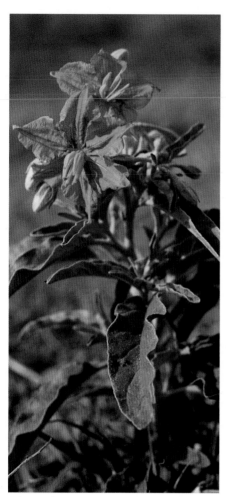

Solanum elaeagnifolium Silver-leaf Nightshade

surface. The bright yellow stamens form a vivid contrast in the center.

This is another wildflower that seems to pay no attention to the rain gauge. At the end of a long, unbearably hot, dry summer, on the hardest, barest ground (often in the tire tracks of pasture roads), this intense purple flower continues to thrive in the sun and ignore the heat.

The difference between the genera *Physalis* and *Quincula* is that *Physalis* has yellow flowers that "droop" or hang down, while *Quincula* has purple flowers that face up. They both have the interesting 5-paneled "Chinese lanterns" that enclose the seedpods.

Quincula is a monotypic genus. Some authors have included it with *Physalis*, but recent publications retain it as a distinct genus.

Solanum elaeagnifolium
Silver-leaf Nightshade, Trompillo, Bull-nettle, White Horse-nettle

Plant: Rather tall (12–28 inches), much-branched perennial with silvery, star-shaped (stellate) hairs covering the stem and leaves, giving it a gray-green or pale silvery-green color. Sharp prickles are interspersed over the stem and undersides of the leaves. The leaves are alternate, untoothed but wavy on the edges, oblong lance-shaped, 1–5 inches long and ⅜–1 inch wide.

Flower: The pale purple or violet (rarely white) flowers grow from the leaf axils in few-flowered cymes or clusters. Each star-shaped flower is shallowly 5-lobed, ¾–1 inch wide, with triangular-oval lobes. There are 5 prominent bright yellow anthers (at the stamen tips) standing erect in the center of the corolla. Bloom season is April to October.

Fruit: Round berry, almost ½ inch in diameter. The tough outer covering of the berry is yellow, turning golden with age. The berries remain on the plant for several months, finally shriveling and becoming dark.

Range: This hardy plant grows well in dry, caliche waste places, disturbed soils of roadsides, neglected or abandoned fields, and open pastures in Missouri, Kansas, Louisiana, Texas, Oklahoma, New Mexico, Arizona, and into Mexico.

Remarks: Usually associated with disturbed or cultivated land, this plant is not much loved by farmers, who fight it in their fields continually. They cannot find kind things to say about it. Because it is prickly, it is unpleasant to touch. But the star shape and the color of many flowers blooming together in a large stand make Silver-leaf Nightshade a wildflower worth knowing. In late July and August, when the heat of summer has sizzled other green plants, this hardy wildflower simply thrives.

The prominent long yellow anthers that stick out from the center of the flower are a common characteristic of all the *Solanums*, as is the star-shaped flower. Sometimes the petals bend backward, resembling a "shooting star."

Economically, some important food plants of the *Solanum* genus are eggplant and potato.

Solanum rostratum
Buffalo Bur, Kansas Thistle, Mala Mujer

Plant: Annual, much-branched plant forming a low, sprawling, rounded mound, 8–24 inches high. The stems and leaves are covered with microscopic star-shaped (stellate) hairs. Strong, slender, sharp yellowish prickles arm the stems and veins of the leaves. The alternate leaves, 2–5 inches long, are oval, deeply cleft into irregular lobes or divided pinnately into leaflets.

Flower: The flowers grow in racemes toward the top of the plant. Each bright golden star-shaped flower, 1 inch across, has 5 petals united at the base, flaring to 5 spreading lobes at the rim. The 5 stamens, with their erect yellow anthers, stand erect in the center of the flower; one anther is longer, larger, and apart from the others. These stamens surround the single 2-chambered pistil. The plant blooms from June to October.

Fruit: Berry, enclosed by a prickly calyx, about ½ inch wide. There are many black seeds inside.

Range: This plant is found on dry, rocky soils of disturbed ground, flats, and waste areas, especially overgrazed pastures and lots. It grows from Nebraska to Oklahoma, across Texas, into eastern New Mexico and south into Mexico. It also is found in Mississippi, South Dakota, and Tennessee.

Remarks: The golden yellow star-shaped flowers with their interesting elongated anthers must be appreciated from a respectable distance, since the sharp stickers, or prickles, covering all parts of the plant except the flower are extremely painful to touch.

The spine-covered berries easily become entangled in the bushy tails of cattle to be transported to other places before falling out to germinate there the next year. Buffaloes of long ago, in their wallowing, accomplished the same thing when the burs stuck in their woolly hair.

This is another drought-resistant plant that seems to love dry, barren places and hot, dry weather.

TAMARICACEAE
Tamarisk Family

A family of shrubs or small trees, the Tamarisk Family has small leaves that are alternate, scalelike, and overlapping. The flowers, with both stamens and pistils, have radial symmetry and grow in racemes. The many racemes are collected to form a panicle of either pink or white blossoms. There are 4 or 5 sepals that overlap and 4 or 5 petals, also somewhat overlapping. Each tiny individual flower has 5 or 10 lobes with 4–10 stamens. The superior ovary is 1-celled with 2–5 stigmas. The fruit is a capsule bearing seeds with tufts of hairs on their tips.

Tamarix gallica
Salt Cedar, Tamarisk, Tamarisco, Rompevientos

Plant: Deciduous shrub with many widely spreading stems growing from the ground to heights of 8–12 feet. The slender, straight stems are covered with a smooth bark that varies in color from blackish-brown to deep purple to dark red-orange. Small alternating branchlets bear feathery, soft-green leaves that are rather sheathing and overlapping. These branchlets, with their leaves, drop off in the autumn.

Flower: The numerous soft pink flowers grow on the green branches (new growth) in racemes ¾–2 inches long. Many racemes are collected to form a panicle. Each tiny individual flower has 5 petals that are only about 1/16 inch long and elliptic to ovate-elliptic in shape. These petals are inserted under the disk and tend to fall off prematurely. Bloom season is March–July.

Fruit: Capsule that bursts open into 3–5 valves, from which many hair-tipped seeds are dispersed.

Range: This native of the Old World grows wild in those areas of the Western Plains that have salinity in the groundwater, along stream banks (if the water is saline), and in and around salt flats or waste places that tend to hold water. It has become naturalized in western Texas, much of New Mexico (below 6,000 feet), and the southwestern United States.

Remarks: A native of Europe, this plant has found a home along the salty stream banks of many of the waterways on the Western Plains. It was originally planted to deter erosion in sandy soils and for use as windbreaks. But the plant has a tendency to spread and "take over" large areas; therefore it is not much loved by landowners. Apparently unpalatable, it is not grazed by livestock.

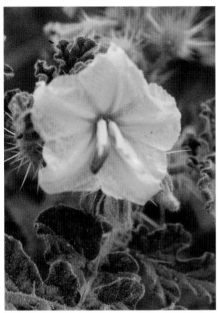
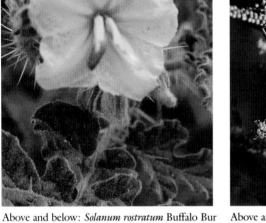

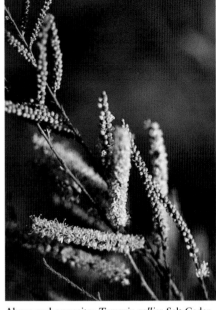

Above and below: *Solanum rostratum* Buffalo Bur   Above and opposite: *Tamarix gallica* Salt Cedar

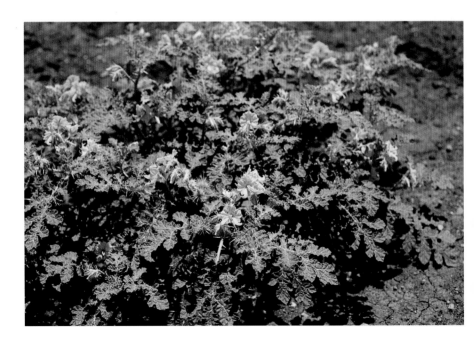

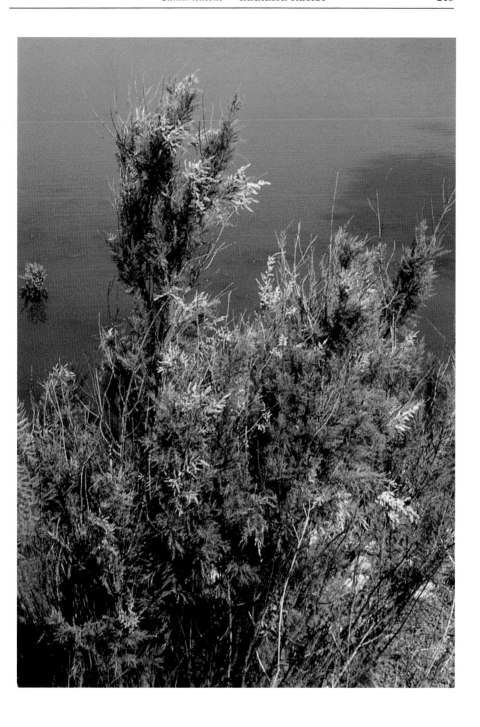

VERBENACEAE
Vervain Family

The Vervain Family has both woody and herbaceous species; shrubs, herbs, vines, and trees. The stems and branchlets are mostly square or 4-angled. The leaves are usually simple, with the edges smooth or variously toothed or cleft and opposite on the stem. The inflorescences can be in clusters of 2 or 3, single in the axils on short stalks, or terminal; also in spikes or racemes. The flowers can be large or small, having both stamens and pistil (perfect) or having only one or the other (unisexual). They are usually slightly irregular in symmetry, bell-shaped, tubular, or tubular with a flaring outer edge. The flowers are mostly 5-lobed, and the corolla can be minimally 2-lipped. (The individual flowers have been described as resembling a gingerbread man with the single larger lobe as the head and the other 4 as the arms and legs.) There are generally 4 stamens inserted in the corolla tube, with sterile stamens (staminodes) sometimes present. The superior ovary is compound. The fruit is a lobed fruit with many 1-seeded cells.

The only places this family is not represented worldwide are in the Arctic and Antarctic.

Phyla nodiflora
Frog Fruit, Fog Fruit, Cape Weed, Turkey Tangle, Mat Grass

Plant: Perennial herb with low stems that creep along the ground, root at the swollen nodes or joints, and form dense mats. They can reach a length of 1–3 feet but only grow 3–5 inches tall. The opposite leaves are spatulate (shaped like a spatula) or oblong lance-shaped; they are thick and have sharply pointed, toothed edges from the middle of the leaf toward the tip and smooth edges toward the base. They are ½–3 inches long and ¼–1 inch wide.

Flower: The small flower heads grow on 3–4-inch-long peduncles from the leaf axils. The compact heads of flowers are ball-shaped at first but gradually elongate and become cylindrical, ½–1 inch long and ¼–⅜ inch thick. Only a few flowers open at a time, usually on the tip, forming a circle or crown of tiny white flowers with yellow throats. There are 4 united sepals. The 4 petals are also united to form a trumpet-shaped corolla, ¹⁄₃₂–¹⁄₁₆ inch long. It flares out on the end to about ⅛ inch across. There are 4 stamens attached at about the middle of the corolla tube. The 1 pistil has a 2-celled ovary. This creeping ground cover blooms May–August.

Fruit: The fruit is encased by the calyx until maturity, when it divides into a pair of 1-seeded nutlets.

Range: Preferring moist, low-lying places, Frog Fruit is a native of South America that has successfully escaped cultivation. It grows well in lawns, fields, ditches, open pastures, and sandy, dry stream banks, as well as around the edges of playa lakes and open stock ponds, in Colorado, New Mexico, Arizona, southern California, Texas, Oklahoma, and northern Mexico.

Remarks: I love this dainty flower because it is small and beautiful and for its funny common name. Since it grows close to the ground with only the flower heads sticking up, I believe it got the name Frog Fruit because it is just about "eyelash high to a frog."

To give some idea of their small size, a thimble would make a nice vase for a bouquet of Frog Fruit flowers.

Verbena bipinnatifida
Prairie Verbena, Small-flowered Verbena, Dakota Vervain

Plant: Low (often nearly prostrate), much-branched, and rather hairy perennial up to 12 inches tall; the branched stems creeping on the ground are 6–18 inches long. It often roots at the nodes, toward the base of the plant, where it lies on the ground. The stems are square or 4-angled. The opposite leaves grow on ⅓–1-inch stalks, or petioles, and are divided into 3 parts, each part pinnately lobed, ¾–2¼ inches long, and 1–1½ inches wide.

Flower: The inflorescences are terminal spikes of tightly clustered (umbrella-like) pink to lavender or purple flowers. Each individual flower has bracts that are about as long as the flower itself. The colorful tubular corolla is ¼–½ inch long, with 5 notched lobes that flare out on the end to ⅜ inch across. There are 4 stamens inside the corolla tube and a single 4-lobed pistil. Prairie Verbena blooms April–July.

Fruit: The calyx becomes somewhat more elongate in fruit, enclosing the 4-celled ovary, which separates into four 1-seeded cylindrical nutlets at maturity.

Range: This is a very abundant and widespread wildflower growing in rocky and gravelly soils of barren places, fields, plains, prairies, and roadside ditches in Colorado and Arizona, most of New Mexico into Mexico and from South Dakota to Missouri, Alabama, Oklahoma, and most of Texas.

Remarks: This beautiful matlike plant does not compete well with other plants, which is why one often sees large barren areas covered with just Prairie Verbena—when in full bloom, a spectacular sight indeed. The sweet nectar is most inviting to butterflies and insects.

Verbena bracteata
Prostrate Vervain

Plant: Perennial herb with several rather sprawling square stems growing from a common base to about 12–16 inches long. The leaves are opposite each other, cleft into 3 lobes or segments, each jaggedly toothed. The lateral lobes are narrow, the middle one much larger than the others.

Leaves vary in size from ¾ inch to 2 inches long. Prominent veins line the underside of the leaves, while the upper surface is smoother. Both stems and leaves are coarsely hairy.

Flower: The flowers are on thick terminal spikes. The bractlets are noticeably longer than the calyxes and flowers, which are only ³⁄₁₆ inch long. The tubular corolla is blue-purple, ³⁄₁₆ inch long with 5 lobes, somewhat 2-lipped, and slightly flaring at the end. There are 4 stamens attached to the upper half of the corolla tube. The single pistil has a 2-lobed style. Prostrate Vervain blooms from April to October.

Fruit: The 4-lobed ovary is 4-celled and develops into a fruit that is enclosed by the calyx. At maturity, the fruit breaks apart into 4 seeds.

Range: Roadside ditches, grassy pastures, waste places, and open fields in almost all of the United States and southern Canada.

Remarks: This sprawling plant tends to lie on the ground with only the tips of the flower spikes turned up. One plant can be quite large, but the flowers are so small that they don't show up well, especially since the bracts nearly cover them. Often, on the extreme tip of the floral spike, a small ring or crown of soft blue-purple flowers will encircle the thick spike, thus enabling one to determine that this is indeed another delicate wildflower in bloom.

Verbena officinalis ssp. *halei*
Blue Vervain, Texas Vervain, Slender Vervain

Plant: Perennial herb with 4-angled stems, smooth, tall, slender, and erect. They branch from a woody base and can reach heights of 12–30 inches. The opposite leaves are of different shapes from the bottom to the top of the plant. The lower leaves are deeply and irregularly cleft, rather ovate in shape, 2–3 inches long, and 1–1½

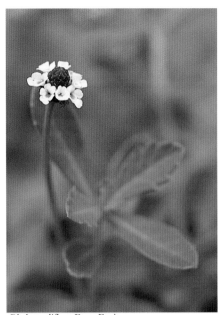

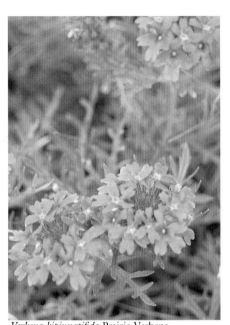

Phyla nodiflora Frog Fruit

Verbena bipinnatifida Prairie Verbena
Opposite: *V. officinalis* ssp. *halei* Blue Vervain

V. bracteata Prostrate Vervain

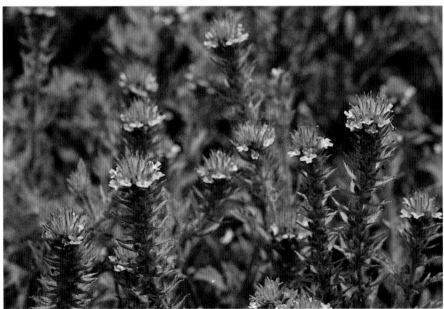

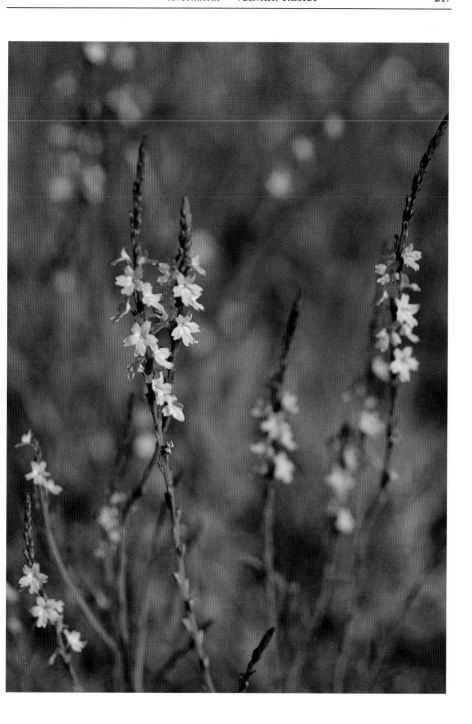

inches wide. The leaves on the middle portion of the stem are 1- or 2-cleft (pinnatifid) and less than 3 inches long. The leaves on the upper stem are less cleft or toothed to almost smooth and ¾–1 inch long.

Flower: The small blue to lavender flowers grow from the bottom toward the top of a tall, slender spike. The long spikes are terminal or growing from the leaf axils. Each individual flower is shaped like a little trumpet, has 5 lobes, is somewhat 2-lipped and about ¼ inch across. The corolla tube is slightly longer than the calyx. There are 4 stamens growing upon the upper half of the corolla tube. A single pistil has a 4-lobed ovary. This delicate plant blooms in April and May.

Fruit: The fruits are four 1-seeded nutlets that separate at maturity. They are enclosed, until they split apart, by the calyx.

Range: Blue Vervain prefers sandy or calcareous soils of roadside ditches, open prairies, fields, pastures, and hillsides. It is widespread and grows from Alabama across Oklahoma and Texas.

Remarks: This graceful wildflower usually forms large stands of plants. The small blue flowers on the slender spikes would not show up well individually; but because there are many, the delicate blue color on the upper portions of the plants looks like a soft blue mist, 18–24 inches from the ground, when viewed from a distance.

All the *Verbenas* have been used for medicines in the past. The leaves and flowers were dried and steeped for teas to be used as sedatives, bitter tonics, and for treating deep bruises. They were also used to induce vomiting, as too much caused nausea.

The name *Verbena* means "sacred plant," which is what Europeans believed *V. officinalis* to be. It was used for its magical powers as well as for its medicinal purposes. The early colonists felt it was important enough to be brought to this country. This European import soon escaped and joined its wild cousins, our native species.

Verbena stricta
Hoary Vervain

Plant: Annual growing to 3 feet or more but on the Western Plains is usually shorter. The stems are stout, coarsely hairy and either unbranched or branched above, forming spikes (sometimes in 3's). The thick-textured leaves are broadly ovate, irregularly incised around the edges, and 1–4 inches long. They are hairy on the upper surfaces and veined prominently on the undersides.

Flower: Many small blue or purple (or bluish-purple) flowers bloom up the spikes, each growing in an axil of a narrow bractlet. The calyx, enveloping the corolla, is 5-angled, 5-ribbed, and 5-toothed. The corolla extends beyond the calyx somewhat, is funnel-shaped, 5-lobed (the lobes being slightly elongate and rounded on the tips), and weakly 2-lipped (the difference between the upper 2 lobes and lower 3 is barely discernible, the upper 2 being slightly longer and a bit more narrow than the lower 3). There are 4 stamens growing on the upper half of the corolla tube. The ovary is 4-celled. Bloom period is from May into September.

Fruit: This flower produces a dry 2-carpeled fruit that splits into 4 brown and wrinkled 1-seeded segments.

Range: Preferring dry soils of pastures, roadsides, hillsides, and disturbed places, this plant grows from Canada, Wyoming, and South Dakota south to Texas and into New Mexico.

Remarks: Hoary Vervain is a fairly prolific spring- and summer-blooming plant. This species is seemingly drought-resistant and can be counted upon to bloom when others may not. The dainty flowers are not easily visible from a distance but are such a nice surprise when one is out walking through the pastures.

ZYGOPHYLLACEAE
Caltrop Family

Distributed worldwide, the Zygophyllaceae are a relatively small family of herbs and shrubs. Only 3 genera are represented on the Western Plains: *Tribulus, Kallstroemia,* and *Peganum.*

The leaves can grow in pairs or singly on the stem and are variously divided into segments. The flowers grow in the axils of the leaves. These plants typically have 4 or 5 petals, which may be white, yellow, or sometimes orange. There are 10–15 stamens. The ovary is superior, which means the petals and sepals grow below it. The style usually persists to form a beak extending from the center of the fruit, which is a winged or lobed capsule that separates at maturity into 5 or 10 units. There are from 1 to many seeds in each locule, or compartment, of the capsule.

The best-known (and least-liked) member of this family is *Tribulus terrestris.* Literally translated, it means "bad ground" and is otherwise commonly known as the Goathead.

Peganum harmala
African Rue

Plant: The succulent stems and leaves of African Rue are fairly smooth and a dark green color. It is a many-branched herbaceous plant that grows from perennial rootstock. The leaves are alternate on the stem, fleshy and irregularly split into threadlike linear segments ¾–2¼ inches long.
Flower: The white flowers (1½ inches across) are solitary, which means they grow singly, not in groups, all over the plant. They have 5 sepals and 5 petals. The sepals are sometimes a bit longer than the petals and are easy to see between the petals. The white petals are oblong-elliptic in shape, ¾ inch long, and about ½ inch wide at the

widest part. African Rue blooms in May and June.
Fruit: Fat capsule, 2-, 3-, or 4-celled with many dark brown wedge-shaped seeds in each compartment. The style remains as the capsule forms and sticks up from the top of the capsule about ½ inch high, drying as the capsule dries.
Range: Preferring disturbed limestone and sandy soils, this plant has been reported in only 6 or 7 counties of the Trans-Pecos area and the Edwards Plateau as well as Garza County in Texas. It also grows in Arizona and New Mexico.
Remarks: African Rue is a native of North Africa and the Asiatic deserts. It was introduced into this country near Deming, New Mexico, and from there has spread to Texas and Arizona.

It is included in poisonous plant publications as being toxic to livestock—cattle, sheep, and probably horses. The seeds are very toxic, the rest of the plant less so.

As a quilter, I enjoyed learning that the seeds of this African native were the source of the dye "Turkey red," used to color fabrics a couple of generations ago. Most reds in antique quilts that have been preserved to this day could be the "Turkey reds" derived from this wildflower.

Tribulus terrestris
Goathead, Puncture Vine, Puncture Weed, Abrojo de Flor Amarilla

Plant: Annual plant producing prostrate, trailing stems that radiate from a taproot and grow 3 feet long or longer. The leaves are opposite on the stem and pinnately divided into many small segments or leaflets (3–7 pairs of leaflets). The leaves are 1–1½ inches long and the leaflets about ¼ inch long.
Flower: The flowers grow singly in the axils, are bright yellow, and have 5 petals and 10 stamens. They are small, only a little

more than ¼ inch across, and bloom from May to September.

Fruit: The ovary is 5-lobed and has 5 locules or compartments. These separate into 5 small nuts at maturity, and each nut has 2 tough, sharp spines up to ¼ inch long.

Range: Goathead is abundant throughout the Western Plains. It also grows from the Atlantic to the Pacific through the southern states. Preferring sandy or gravelly disturbed soil, it will eventually cover overgrazed pastures and can be found on roadsides and in waste places and unkempt yards.

Remarks: This hardy plant was introduced into this country from the Mediterranean region. Although the flower is dainty and attractive, the plant is generally cursed by all who encounter it. For a plant so hated, it certainly has a lot of common names, and they nearly all pertain to its most objectionable feature, the seedpod. When examined closely, each nut resembles the head and horns of a young goat. These "horns" (spines) are most painful when stepped on by bare feet. They have been known to puncture bicycle, car, and even pickup tires as well.

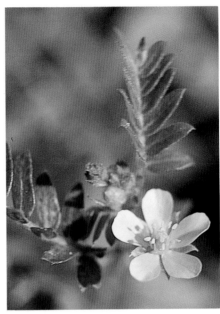

Tribulus terrestris Goathead

Verbena stricta Hoary Vervain

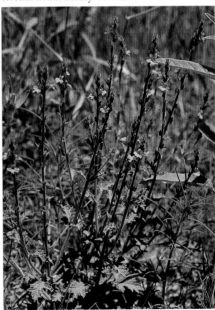

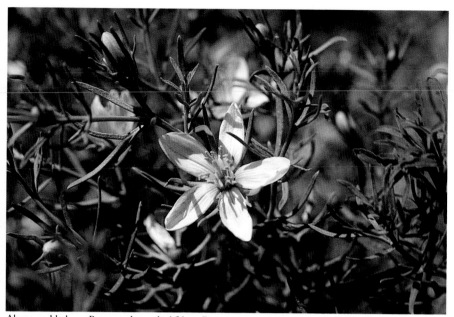

Above and below: *Peganum harmala* African Rue

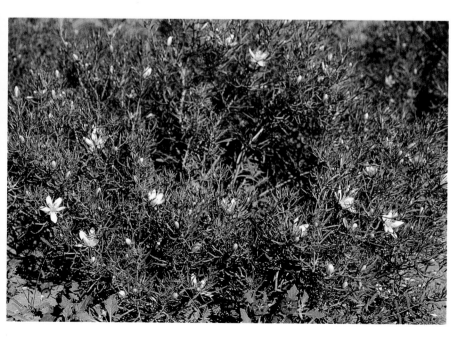

ILLUSTRATED GLOSSARY

Leaf arrangement

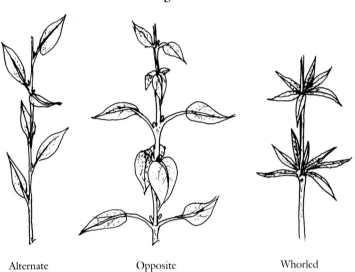

Alternate   Opposite   Whorled

Leaf types

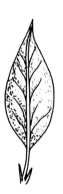
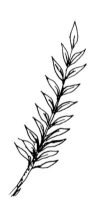
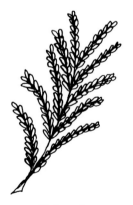

Simple   Pinnately   Bipinnately
                  compound   compound

Leaf margins

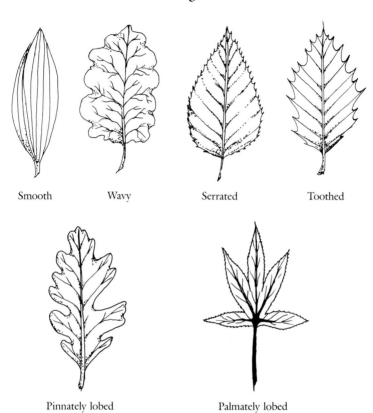

Smooth Wavy Serrated Toothed

Pinnately lobed Palmately lobed

Leaf shapes

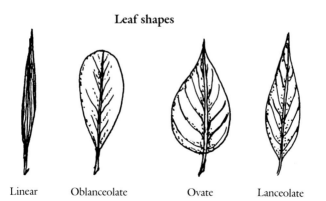

Linear Oblanceolate Ovate Lanceolate

Parts of a flower

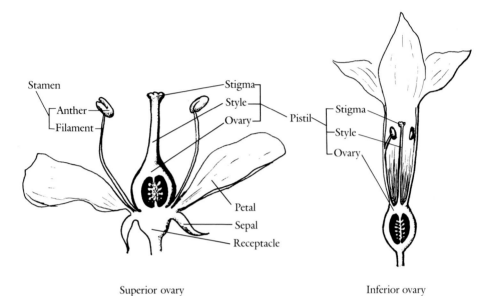

Stamen
⌈Anther
⌊Filament

Stigma⌉
Style ├ Pistil
Ovary⌋

Stigma
Style
Ovary

Petal

Sepal

Receptacle

Superior ovary

Inferior ovary

Types of floral symmetry

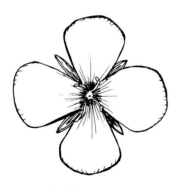

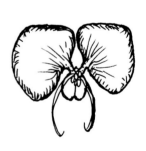

Radial symmetry

Bilateral symmetry

GLOSSARY

Achene. A hard, dry, small 1-seeded fruit that does not split open.

Aff. Abbreviation of *affinis*, Latin term meaning "akin to."

Alkaloid. One of a class of basic nitrogenous organic compounds occurring in plants. Many have medicinal, hallucinogenic, or toxic properties.

Alternate. Leaf arrangement placed singly and at different heights along the stem; not opposite or whorled.

Androecium. The complete set of stamens.

Angiosperm. A plant having its seeds enclosed in an ovary (as opposed to "gymnosperm").

Annual. A plant completing its life cycle during one growing season.

Anther. The male reproductive organ enclosing and containing the pollen grains (the pollen-bearing sac on the tip of a stamen).

Apex. The tip end.

Areole. A spot, either depressed or raised, on the epidermis of a cactus, from which leaves, spines, or glochids grow.

Atropine. A poisonous crystalline alkaloid obtained from belladonna and other solanaceous plants.

Awn. A bristlelike terminal appendage on an organ.

Axil. The upper angle where a leaf or branch joins a stem. A point of attachment other than at the apex.

Basal. Situated at the lower end, or base, of a plant.

Belladonna. A poisonous solanaceous plant (*Atropa belladonna*); also, a poisonous drug derived from this plant.

Berry. A fleshy, pulpy fruit, such as a tomato, with no true stone.

Biennial. A plant that requires two years to complete its life cycle.

Bilateral symmetry. If the flower were cut in half lengthwise, the two halves would be the same.

Bisexual. A flower having both stamens and pistil (both sexes).

Bract. A reduced or modified leaf growing at the base of a flower or a flower cluster.

Bulb. An underground bud, or storage organ, made of layers of fleshy, overlapping, leafy scales (modified leaves). Example: common onion.

Calcareous. Containing calcium carbonate; chalky; pertaining to lime.

Calyx. Collective term for all the sepals of a flower; usually green and enclosing the other parts of the flower when in bud.

Campanulate. Bell-shaped.

Carpel. The ovule-bearing part of a flower, composed of a placental surface and ovules.

Circumscissile. Opening along a circular line. A seed vessel with a top opening as a lid.

Cleft. Cut or lobed about halfway to the middle.

Coma. A tuft of silky hairs at the end of a seed.

Concave. Curved like the interior of a circle or the inside of a spoon.

Convex. Bulging and curved like the outside of a circle.

Corm. An enlarged underground bulblike base of a stem.

Corolla. The inner perianth, or colored petals, of a flower. All the petals collectively.

Corona. A crownlike appendage found at the opening of the corolla tube.

Corymb. A flat-topped or convex flower cluster with the outer flowers opening first.

Cyme. An inflorescence in which the primary axis bears a single terminal flower which opens first; the next flowers are on axes which rise from the axils of bracts that subtend the first flower, and so on.

Deciduous. Shedding its leaves annually.
Dehiscent. Bursting or splitting open when ripe.
Disk flower. The tubular flowers (in Compositae) as opposed to the ray flowers.
Drupe. The single seed, in a fleshy fruit, that is enclosed in a hard, woody covering. Example: a peach or plum seed.

Ellipsoid. A geometric surface whose plane sections are all ellipses or circles. An elliptic solid.
Elliptic (elliptical). Having the form of an ellipse; oval in shape with rounded ends, being broadest in the middle.
Emersed. Risen or standing out of water.
Endosperm. The nutritive matter, in an ovule, surrounding the embryo of a seed.
Entire. Undivided. A continuous margin, not toothed or incised.
Epidermis. The outer layer of cells forming the skin or covering of a plant.
Epipetalous. Being borne or growing upon the petals.
Exude. Emit through pores or small openings; ooze out.

Farinaceous. Seeds containing or yielding starch.
Fibrous. Containing woody fibers.
Filament. The stalklike part of a stamen that supports the anther.
Floret. One of the many and closely clustered small flowers that make up the flower head of a composite flower, such as daisy, aster, gaillardia.
Follicle. A dry 1-celled seed, or fruit, that opens only down one side.

Genus (pl. **genera**). The subdivision of a family consisting of more than one species. The genus designation is the first part of a plant's scientific name.
Glandular. Glandlike or bearing glands.
Globular. Globe-shaped or spherical.

Glochid. A tiny, sharp, hairlike growth (on cactus) that has almost invisible barbs on its surface.
Granulose. Having a covering of tiny granules or grains.
Gymnosperm. A plant, such as a conifer, having its seeds naked or not enclosed in an ovary (as opposed to "angiosperm").

Herb. A flowering plant having an above-ground stem that does not become woody. The term is often used for those aromatic plants valued for their medicinal or culinary properties.
Hood. In botany, a petal or sepal resembling a hood (head and neck covering attached to a cloak).

Inflorescence. The flower cluster on a plant or the arrangement of flowers on the axis.
Inverted. Upside down or reversed in position.
Involucre. A collection of bracts or whorls subtending a flower cluster.

Keel. A longitudinal ridge on a leaf or petal resembling the keel of a boat.

Lanceolate. Shaped like the head of a lance; narrow and tapering toward the apex.
Latex. A milky liquid in some plants that coagulates upon contact with the air.
Linear. Narrow and elongated; resembling a thread.
Lobe. A roundish division of an organ, such as a leaf or petal. Usually cut toward but not through the midrib.
Locule. A small chamber in an ovary, anther, or fruit.

Moniliform. Resembling a string of beads. Certain roots and stems consisting of bead-like swellings alternating with small pinched-in sections.
Monotypic. Having only one type. A single species constituting a genus.

Node. A joint in a stem. That point on a stem where leaves and buds are attached.

Noxious. Harmful to health if eaten.

Oblanceolate. Inversely (or upside down) lanceolate or lance-shaped.
Oblong. Elongated or longer than broad.
Orbicular. Rounded or circular like an orb.
Ovary. The enlarged lower part of a pistil that contains the ovules.
Ovate. Egg-shaped; a leaf with the broader end at the base.
Ovule. That structure in the ovary that becomes the seed.

Palmate. Shaped like an open hand with the fingers extended. A leaf with lobes extended or radiating from a central point.
Panicle. A compound raceme, or a loose flower cluster with the younger flowers at the center.
Pappus. Downy appendage of the achene on certain plants such as dandelions and thistles.
Parasite. An organism that obtains food directly from another living organism. (Parasitic plants have no true leaves nor green pigment.)
Parthenogenetic. Lacking fertile stamens. Developing without fertilization.
Pedicel. The stalk to a single flower in a flower cluster or an inflorescence.
Peduncle. Term used for the stalk of a flower.
Perennial. Having a life cycle lasting more than two years.
Perfect. Having both stamens and pistils (bisexual).
Perianth. The envelope of a flower, calyx or corolla or both. Sepals and petals collectively.
Petal. One of the members, usually colored, of the corolla.
Petaloid. Having the form or appearance of a petal.
Petiole. A slender stalk by which a leaf is attached to the stem.
Phyllary. An individual involucral bract on the head of a member of the Compositae.
Pinna (pl. **pinnae**). One of the first divisions of a pinnately compound leaf.

Pinnate. Having leaflets arranged on each side of a common petiole.
Pinnatifid. Pinnately cleft, with clefts reaching halfway or more to the midrib.
Pistil. The seed-bearing organ of a flower. The female reproductive organ consisting of the stigma, style, and ovary.
Placenta (adj. **placental**). In flowering plants, that part of the ovary that bears the ovules.
Playa lakes. In the Western Plains, any one of thousands of relatively shallow, clay-lined depressions which, following periods of sufficient rainfall, are occupied by intermittent lakes, the contents of which largely evaporate. Sizes range from 30 centimeters to 2 meters (1–6.5 feet) or more deep, and from several meters or yards across to over 16 hectares (40 acres) in area.
Proteolysis (adj. **proteolytic**). The breaking down of proteins into simpler compounds, as in digestion.

Raceme. A simple inflorescence in which the flowers are borne on short pedicels along a common axis or stalk.
Radial symmetry. Petals arranged like rays, radiating from a central point.
Ray flower. One of the marginal florets surrounding the tubular florets in the flower heads of some members of the Compositae.
Receptacle. That portion of a floral axis which bears the organs of a single flower or the florets of a flower head.
Rhizome. A rootlike underground horizontal stem which produces roots below and sends up shoots, or stems, above ground.
Rhombic. Slightly diamond-shaped.
Rosette. A circular cluster of leaves, usually on the ground.
Rotate. Wheel-shaped.

Saline. Salty or saltlike; containing salt.
Scales. Thin, membranous parts of a plant; often used for such structures present on the underground portion of a plant.

Scape. A leafless peduncle, or stalk, rising from the ground. It may have scales or bracts but not leaves.

Scopolamine. A crystalline alkaloid obtained from certain solanaceous plants and sometimes used as a depressant.

Sepal. Each individual part of the calyx of a flower, usually green.

Sessile. Attached by the base without any projecting support; a leaf without a petiole.

Simple. Of one part, not compounded or divided, as a leaf.

Sp. Species (abbreviation).

Spathe. A large bract or pair of bracts enclosing a flower cluster; often colored.

Spatulate. Having a broad rounded end and a narrow base; rounded more or less like a spoon or spatula.

Species. The basic category of biological classification ranking immediately below the genus. The grouping of all those individuals that have the same characteristics and the capacity for interbreeding.

Spine. A sharp-pointed, hard outgrowth on a plant such as a thorn or the visible "stickers" on a cactus.

Spur. A slender, usually hollow projection from some part of a flower, as from the calyx of the larkspur.

Ssp. Subspecies (abbreviation).

Stalk. The stem or main axis of a plant.

Stamen. The pollen-bearing organ of a flower. The male reproductive structure of a flower, consisting of a filament supporting an anther.

Staminode. A sterile or abortive stamen or a part resembling such a stamen.

Stellate. Star-shaped.

Stem. The stalk of a plant which supports the leaves, flowers, and fruit. The axis or axes arising from the root.

Stigma. The part of a pistil that receives the pollen.

Stipule. One of a pair of leaflike appendages at the base of a leaf petiole.

Striations. Marked with stripes, streaks, or furrows.

Style. The narrow extension of the pistil between the ovary and the stigma.

Subtend. Situated closely beneath.

Succulent. Soft, fleshy, and full of juice.

Tannin. Tannic acid obtained from the bark and fruit of certain plants, used in tanning hides and in medicines.

Taproot. Main root descending downward and giving off small lateral roots.

Trifoliate. Having three leaves, leaflike parts, or lobes.

Tuber. A fleshy, rounded, thick outgrowth of an underground stem or shoot (example: potato). It bears many buds, or eyes, from which new plants can grow.

Tubercle. A small, tuberlike swelling or nodule.

Tuberculate. Having many nodules or tubercles.

Tubular. Shaped like a hollow cylinder.

Umbel. A flower cluster, either convex or flat in shape, with pedicels arising from a common point (umbrellalike).

Umbilicus. Depressed in the center. A navel. On cactus plants, the scar left at the tip of the fruit after the floral parts have dried up and dropped.

Unisexual. Of one sex. A flower bearing stamens or pistils but not both.

BIBLIOGRAPHY

Abbott, Carroll. 1982. *How to Know and Grow Texas Wildflowers*. Kerrville, Tex.: Green Horizons Press.

Ajilvsgi, Geyata. 1984. *Wildflowers of Texas*. Bryan, Tex.: Shearer Publishing.

Angier, Bradford. 1978. *Field Guide to Medicinal Wild Plants*. Harrisburg, Pa.: Stackpole Books.

———. 1980. *Feasting Free on Wild Edibles*. Harrisburg, Pa.: Stackpole Books.

Bayberry, Austin John. 1982. *Your Family Herb Guide*. Denver: Distributed by Nutri-Books Corp.

Busch, Phyllis S. 1977. *Wildflowers and the Stories behind Their Names*. New York: Charles Scribner's Sons.

Correll, Donovan Stewart, and Marshall Conring Johnston. 1970. *Manual of the Vascular Plants of Texas*. Renner: Texas Research Foundation.

Dandelion Recipe Book. Vineland, N.J.: City of Vineland, Mayor's Special Events Office, and Cumberland County Board of Freeholders in cooperation with Cumberland County Extension Service, Cumberland County Board of Agriculture, and Vineland Cooperative Produce Auction.

Doane, Nancy Locke. 1980. *Indian Doctor—Nature's Method of Curing and Preventing Disease according to the Indians*. Charlotte, N.C.: Nancy Locke Doane.

Dodge, Natt N. 1963. *100 Desert Wildflowers*. Globe, Ariz.: Southwest Parks and Monuments Association.

Enquist, Marshall. 1987. *Wildflowers of the Texas Hill Country*. Austin: Lone Star Botanical.

Grae, Ida. 1979. *Nature's Colors—Dyes from Plants*. New York: Macmillan Publishing Co.

Hall, Dorothy. 1981. *The Herb Tea Book*. New Canaan, Conn.: Keats Publishing.

Harrington, H. D. 1972. *Western Edible Wild Plants*. Albuquerque: University of New Mexico Press.

Harrington, H. D., and L. W. Durrell. 1957. *How to Identify Plants*. Chicago: Swallow Press.

Hutchins, Charles Robert. 1968. Vascular Flora of Garza County, Texas. M.S. thesis, Texas Tech University.

Johnston, Eliza Griffin. 1972. *Texas Wild Flowers*. Austin: Shoal Creek Publishers.

Johnston, Marshall C. 1990. *The Vascular Plants of Texas: A List, Up-dating the Manual of the Vascular Plants of Texas*. 2d ed. Austin: Marshall C. Johnston.

Lamb, Samuel H. 1975. *Woody Plants of the Southwest*. Santa Fe: Sunstone Press.

Levy, Charles Kingsley, and Richard B. Primack. 1984. *A Field Guide to Poisonous Plants and Mushrooms of North America*. Brattleboro, Vt.: Stephen Greene Press.

Loughmiller, Campbell and Lynn. 1984. *Texas Wildflowers*. Austin: University of Texas Press.

Lust, John. 1974. *The Herb Book*. Simi Valley, Calif: Benedict Lust Publications.

McCoy, Doyle. 1976. *Roadside Flowers of Oklahoma*. Lawton, Ok.: C&J Printing Co.

Martin, Alexander C. 1987. *Weeds*. New York: Golden Press.

Martin, Laura C. 1984. *Wildflower Folklore*. Charlotte, N.C.: Fast & McMillan Publishers.

Martin, William C., and Charles R. Hutchins. 1984. *Spring Wildflowers of New Mexico*. Albuquerque: University of New Mexico Press.

Moore, Michael. 1977. *Los Remedios de la Gente: A Compilation of Traditional New Mexican Herbal Medicines and Their Use*. Compiled and printed by Michael Moore.

————. 1979. *Medicinal Plants of the Mountain West*. Santa Fe: Museum of New Mexico Press.

Niehaus, Theodore F. 1984. *A Field Guide to Southwestern and Texas Wildflowers*. Boston: Houghton Mifflin Co.

Northington, David K., and J. R. Goodin. 1984. *The Botanical World*. St. Louis: Times Mirror/Mosby College Publishing.

Pasture and Range Plants. 1963. Bartlesville, Ok.: Phillips Petroleum Co.

Phillips, John Wesley. 1988. An Annotated Checklist of the Plants of Lake Meredith Recreation Area. Unpublished.

Rechenthin, C. A. 1972. *Native Flowers of Texas*. Temple, Tex.: USDA Soil Conservation Service.

Rickett, Harold William. 1953. *Wildflowers of America*. New York: Crown Publishers.

————. 1969. *Wildflowers of the United States*, vol. 3, *Texas*. New York: McGraw-Hill.

Riotte, Louise. 1983. *Roses Love Garlic*. Pownal, Vt.: Garden Way Publishing.

Rowell, Chester M., Jr. 1972. *A Guide to the Identification of Plants Poisonous to Livestock of the Texas Panhandle and South Plains*. Agricultural Sciences Publication T-9-102. Lubbock: Texas Tech Press.

Shelton, Ferne. 1972. *Colonial Kitchen Herbs*. High Point, N.C.: Hutcraft.

Simpson, Benny J. 1988. *A Field Guide to Texas Trees*. Austin: Texas Monthly Press.

Smith, James Payne, Jr. 1977. *Vascular Plant Families*. Eureka, Calif: Mad River Press.

Stahl, Carmine A. 1977. *Papa Stahl's Wild Stuff Cookbook*. Houston: Grass Roots Enterprises.

Stark, Raymond. 1981. *Guide to Indian Herbs*. Surrey, B.C., Canada: Hancock House Publishers.

Stewart, Anne Marie, and Leon Kronoff. 1975. *Eating from the Wild*. New York: Random House.

Stupke, Arthur. 1965. *Wildflowers in Color*. New York: Harper and Row.

Tatum, Billy Joe. 1976. *Wild Foods Field Guide and Cookbook*. New York: Workman Publishing Co.

Texas Plants Poisonous to Livestock. N.d. College Station: Texas A&M University, Texas Agricultural Experiment Station, and Texas Agricultural Extension Service.

Tierney, Gail D., and Phyllis Hughes. 1983. *Roadside Plants of Northern New Mexico*. Santa Fe: Lightning Tree.

Tull, Delena. 1987. *A Practical Guide to Edible and Useful Plants*. Austin: Texas Monthly Press.

Wills, Mary Motz, and Howard S. Irwin. 1961. *Roadside Flowers of Texas*. Austin: University of Texas Press.

INDEX

Boldface page numbers indicate illustrations.

University of Nebraska Press

Also of Interest:

THE PLATTE
Channels in Time
By Paul A. Johnsgard

Arising in two separate streams high in the Rockies and flowing east across the plains to meet the Missouri near Omaha, Nebraska, the Platte River is a microcosm of the geologic, plant, animal, and human worlds. Way station for the sandhill cranes, home of the Plains Indians, and artery for the great westward migrations of the nineteenth century, the Platte Valley offers a rich diversity of life and history. Focusing on the central role the Platte has played in shaping Nebraska and its heritage, both human and natural, Paul A. Johnsgard presents in this book a "brief and personal portrait of the river as it has existed in the past and still exists today."

ISBN: 978-0-8032-2227-4 (paper)

RECOVERING OUR ANCESTORS' GARDENS
Indigenous Recipes and Guide to Diet and Fitness
By Devon Abbott Mihesuah

Featuring an array of tempting traditional Native recipes and no-nonsense practical advice about health and fitness, *Recovering Our Ancestors' Gardens*, by the acclaimed Choctaw author and scholar Devon Abbott Mihesuah, draws on the rich indigenous heritages of this continent to offer a helpful guide to a healthier life. The first half of the book consists of clear and often-pointed discussions about the generally poor state of indigenous health today and how and why many Natives have become separated from their traditional diets, sports, and other activities. The second half of the book is a collection of indigenous recipes and a one-week diet chart. Savory, natural, and steeped in the Native traditions of this land, these recipes are sure to delight and satisfy.

ISBN: 978-0-8032-3253-2 (cloth)

Order online at www.nebraskapress.unl.edu or call 1-800-755-1105.
Mention the code "BOFOX" to receive a 20% discount.